Winston Cup
1997

© Copyright 1997, UMI Publications, Inc.

Acknowledgments

Another year of NASCAR Winston Cup racing is behind us, and 1997 brought many exciting moments that we will remember for years to come. At the forefront was the spirited three-way battle for the NASCAR Winston Cup championship waged by Jeff Gordon, Dale Jarrett and Mark Martin. Each took their turn at the top of the point ladder during the season, and their championship fight went right down to the final event of the year in Atlanta before Gordon emerged with his second NASCAR Winston Cup. Gordon has to be congratulated not only for his championship run, but also for winning just about everything else in sight this year, including the Busch Clash, The Winston, and finally, for becoming only the second driver in history to win the Winston Million. And let's not forget about two new faces in NASCAR Winston Cup winner's circles in 1997, John Andretti and Jeff Burton, as well as Mike Skinner's fine season to take the NASCAR Winston Cup Rookie-of-the-Year crown. Finally, the Series christened two beautiful new facilities this year in Texas and California, continuing the sport's phenomenal growth by bringing it to more new fans than ever before.

This book would not be possible without the help and guidance of our friends at NASCAR. We would like to express our special thanks and appreciation to Mr. Bill France, Mr. Jim France, Mr. Brian France, Mr. Paul Brooks, Mr. George Pyne, Mr. John Griffin, Mr. Kevin Triplett, Mr. Andy Hall and Mr. Paul Schaefer.

Special thanks also to the members of the NASCAR Winston Cup team at the R.J. Reynolds Tobacco Company for their assistance and support. Mr. T. Wayne Robertson, Mr. Greg Littell, Mr. John Powell, Mr. Nat Walker, Mr. Larry Prillaman, Mr. Curtis Gray, Mr. Steve Tucker, Mr. Chris Powell, Mr. Dennis Dawson, Ms. Sara Ayers and Ms. Mary Reynolds are all deserving of our deep appreciation.

Thanks also to Mr. Bob Kelly, who brought the accounts of the exciting 1997 season to the pages of this book. His knowledge and insight of the sport based on his years of involvement are obvious, and we appreciate his dedication to this effort. Once again, the images included in this book were supplied by some of the best photographers in the business — Mr. David Chobat, Mr. Don Grassman and Mr. Ernest Masche. We thank them for capturing the drama of the season for our enjoyment.

Most of all, we thank you, the fans of NASCAR racing. It is you who make the sport possible, and who are responsible for its continued growth and success. This book is for you, with our gratitude.

Please enjoy.

Publisher
Ivan Mothershead

Associate Publisher
Charlie Keiger

Controller
Lewis Patton

Advertising Manager
Mark Cantey

Managing Editor
Ward Woodbury

Senior Editor
Bob Kelly

Associate Editors
Kathryn Hass
Carolyn Peters

Art Director
Brett Shippy

Layout/Design
Mike McBride
Paul Bond

Administrative Staff
Mary Cartee
Henry Boardman
Carla Greene

© Copyright 1997, UMI Publications, Inc., 1135 North Tryon St., Charlotte NC 28206. All rights reserved under the International and Pan American Copyright Conventions. No part of this publication may be reproduced, stored in a retrieval system or transmitted in any form or by any means, mechanical, electronic, photocopying, recording or otherwise without the prior written permission of the publishers.

NASCAR WINSTON CUP SERIES 1997

Foreword by Bill France

"This year, two venues were added to the schedule — Texas Motor Speedway and California Speedway — both of which played a role in the growth of our sport by allowing new fans to experience the thrill of NASCAR competition."

The 1997 NASCAR Winston Cup season is one that will be remembered for so many significant events expanding our sport.

This year, two venues were added to the schedule — Texas Motor Speedway and California Speedway — both of which played a role in the growth of our sport by allowing new fans to experience the thrill of NASCAR competition. At the same time, Darlington Raceway and Atlanta Motor Speedway completed facelifts during the season, improving those facilities for fans and competitors alike.

It was a year of surprises, with two young drivers making their first trips to victory lane. At Daytona in July, John Andretti celebrated his first career win, which was also a first for three-time NASCAR Winston Cup Champion Cale Yarborough as a car owner. Also breaking into the winner's circle was Jeff Burton, who took his initial career victory at Texas, and followed that with two more wins during the season, establishing himself and his Exide team as bona fide championship contenders for the future.

It was a season in which Ricky Rudd won at The Brickyard in an extremely popular victory for the Virginian and long-time sponsor Tide. And for Darrell Waltrip, the year was a season-long celebration of his 25 years of racing in NASCAR Winston Cup events.

It also was the year of Jeff Gordon and the DuPont Chevrolet, with Gordon finding the key to victory lane in nearly every special event and bonus program throughout the season. He won the Busch Clash, The Winston, and then parlayed victories in the Daytona 500, the Coca-Cola 600 and the Mountain Dew Southern 500 into becoming only the second driver in history to win the Winston Million. All of this took place during a stellar year for the young driver that culminated with his second NASCAR Winston Cup championship.

Looking ahead to 1998, NASCAR will celebrate its 50th anniversary with a year-long celebration which will have several focuses during the season. The most important part of the year for us is the final quarter, which will be dedicated to you, the fan. Without your support in our early, formative years, we would not have lasted, or progressed. And without your ongoing support, our sport would not be the most exciting and fastest-growing of any sport in the world right now. We salute you and your enthusiasm for the competitors, and hope you will continue to support NASCAR Winston Cup racing.

All of the exciting events of the 1997 NASCAR Winston Cup season are included here in these pages for you to enjoy, and I am sure you will be delighted to relive them for years to come.

Bill France
President
National Association for Stock Car Auto Racing

NASCAR WINSTON CUP SERIES 1997

Table of Contents

Preface	6
1997 Champion's Story	12
Daytona 500	18
Goodwrench Service 400	26
Pontiac Excitement 400	32
PRIMESTAR 500	38
TranSouth Financial 400	44
Interstate Batteries 500	50
Food City 500	56
Goody's Headache Powder 500	62
Save Mart Supermarkets 300	68
Winston 500	74
The Winston	80
Coca-Cola 600	86
Miller 500	92
Pocono 500	98
Miller 400	104
California 500 Presented by NAPA	110
Pepsi 400	116
Jiffy Lube 300	122
Pennsylvania 500	128
Brickyard 400	134
The Bud at the Glen	142
DeVilbiss 400	148
Goody's Headache Powder 500	154
Mountain Dew Southern 500	160
Exide NASCAR Select Batteries 400	166
CMT 300	172
MBNA 400	178
Hanes 500	184
UAW-GM Quality 500	190
DieHard 500	196
ACDelco 400	202
Dura-Lube 500 Presented by Kmart	208
NAPA 500	214
Reflections	220
Autographs	223

NASCAR WINSTON CUP SERIES 1997

Preface

The winter months during the brief break between the 1996 finale at Atlanta and the 1997 season-opener in Daytona Beach had been the busiest in recent years as no less than 15 drivers had changed cars when the garage opened for Speedweeks.

The drivers weren't the only ones changing teams, hoping for better results from the previous season. Existing sponsors switched teams, new corporations came into the sport, and three teams changed to Pontiacs during the off-season. Several new teams made plans for competition, and some of the biggest crew chiefs in the sport switched teams. With the addition of these new cars, there was little question that qualifying was going to be a crucial part of every race weekend during the coming season.

Unlike many Silly Seasons of recent years, the changes for 1997 were triggered by the announcement by Kyle Petty and Felix Sabates, last July at the Pepsi 400, that the two would part company at the end of the 1996 season. There was no waiting around until the latter stages of the season. Kyle eventually said he would form his own team, with Pontiacs and the backing of Mattel's Hot Wheels brand of toys, and would begin the season by contracting Petty Enterprises to build the engines.

Terry Labonte wears a look of determination as he prepares to open defense of his 1996 NASCAR Winston Cup championship in Daytona's garage area during Speedweeks '97.

(Above) A common site anytime, but particularly as the season prepares to get underway, Dale Earnhardt grants a television interview before making his bid to capture an unprecedented eighth NASCAR Winston Cup. *(Left)* In one of the most significant personnel moves during the off-season, Larry McReynolds left his post with Robert Yates Racing and changed into the black and white of the vaunted Goodwrench team, hoping to provide the knowledge and leadership that would take him to his first championship.

Sabates went after, and signed, IndyCar driver Robby Gordon to take Kyle's place in the SABCO Racing lineup, and expanded his efforts with two additional teams. Sabates split from Pontiac, so all three teams would campaign the season in Chevrolet Monte Carlos. Coors and Coors Light would continue as the sponsor of Gordon's team. BellSouth joined the circuit, taking over the sponsorship of Joe Nemechek's car after Joe merged his team with Sabates, and Wally Dallenbach also joined the stable, with First Union Bank signing on to sponsor the team for a limited schedule of events. Dallenbach left Bud Moore's team to take the Sabates deal.

The BellSouth situation was a tricky one for Sabates and Nemechek to resolve. The Atlanta-based telecommunications company wanted to join the sport at the NASCAR Winston Cup level, Felix wanted the big sponsorship dollars, and BellSouth wanted to keep Nemechek. Joe's NASCAR Busch Series team had been sponsored for several years by BellSouth Mobility, the company's cellular division, and enjoyed its relationship with the driver. Fortunately, the merger of Joe's team and Sabates' stable worked out for all involved.

When Andy Petree put together all the details to purchase Leo Jackson's team and signed Skoal to stay with the effort, the only missing link in the program was the driver. Petree persuaded Ken Schrader to leave Rick Hendrick's organization and move to the green-and-white car, leaving an opening at Hendrick Motorsports in the Budweiser-sponsored Chevrolet. Hendrick didn't take

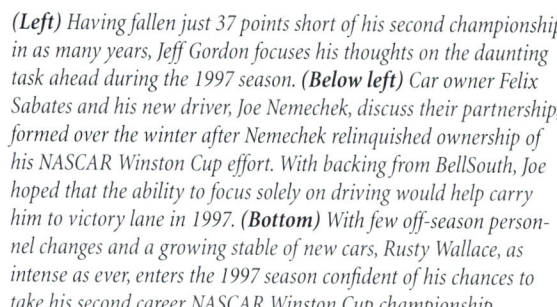

(Left) Having fallen just 37 points short of his second championship in as many years, Jeff Gordon focuses his thoughts on the daunting task ahead during the 1997 season. *(Below left)* Car owner Felix Sabates and his new driver, Joe Nemechek, discuss their partnership, formed over the winter after Nemechek relinquished ownership of his NASCAR Winston Cup effort. With backing from BellSouth, Joe hoped that the ability to focus solely on driving would help carry him to victory lane in 1997. *(Bottom)* With few off-season personnel changes and a growing stable of new cars, Rusty Wallace, as intense as ever, enters the 1997 season confident of his chances to take his second career NASCAR Winston Cup championship.

long to figure out who he and Budweiser wanted in the car — and the phone began ringing at Ricky Craven's home. Craven, considered by many to be one of the future stars of the sport, left his spot at Larry Hedrick's Kodiak team and signed on to drive the red-and-white car.

Hedrick started looking for a replacement for Craven and signed Steve Grissom to drive the Kodiak Chevrolet. Grissom, released at mid-season by the Cartoon Network team owned by Gary Bechtel, was happy to be back behind the wheel. He had spent the second half of 1996 talking with a variety of team owners regarding a driver for 1997, while still collecting his Diamond Ridge paycheck, part of his settlement agreement when he was released.

Robert Pressley, dropped by Petree from the Skoal team, ended up signing on as the driver of the Cartoon Network Chevrolets for the 1997 season. Pressley was released by Petree before the end of the season, and had the chance to work with the

Diamond Ridge team in the final races of 1996, getting a head start for this year. He wasn't the only one in that situation. John Andretti and Jeremy Mayfield were "traded" by respective car owners Michael Kranefuss and Cale Yarborough late in 1996, and the two made their debuts with their new teams at the fall Richmond race.

In another situation that turned out to be a swap, Rick Mast left Richard Jackson's team and cast his lot with Butch Mock and the Remington Fords. Morgan Shepherd was released by Mock, and as the teams prepared for the season-opener at Daytona, Shepherd found himself driving for Jackson. Delco Remy replaced departed sponsor Hooters, and the Jackson team had an entirely new look, with Cruisin' America phone cards also appearing on the car as a major sponsor.

Several other new teams prepared to debut at Daytona. Businessmen Nelson Bowers, Read Morton and Tom Beard put together a team that included Skittles candy and driver Derrike Cope, and joined the Pontiac forces on the track. The Pemberton family of upstate New York celebrated the Christmas holidays with a second son working as a NASCAR Winston Cup crew chief. Ryan, younger brother of Penske South crew chief Robin, was the Skittles team's choice as its new crew chief.

Hormel's Spam brand, left looking for a team to sponsor when Harry Melling's Lake Speed-led team signed on with the University of Nebraska, found a home with ProTech Motorsports and driver Mike Wallace. The new team happily painted Spam's colors on its Chevrolets, and as the teams readied for Daytona, Speed and Melling found the Nebraska program was not going to happen and were left searching for a sponsor.

Two NASCAR Busch Series teams were preparing to make the big move from that series to the NASCAR Winston Cup level. Chad Little and the John Deere folks stepped up their program, bringing the familiar green and yellow colors to NASCAR Winston Cup with a Pontiac team. Driver David Green and NASCAR Busch Series sponsor Caterpillar took the team a step up,

(Top left) Crew chief Tony Glover dons the blue, red and white of the Coors Light team, having made the move to SABCO to work with driver Robby Gordon.
(Above left) Lending his expertise on the Kodak team in Glover's absence is Tim Brewer (left), slated to consult with the team and driver Sterling Marlin in an effort to continue building on the success of two wins and an 8th-place finish in 1996. *(Left)* Gunning to become the 1997 NASCAR Winston Cup Rookie of the Year, Robby Gordon takes his seat in the Coors Chevrolets — changed over from Pontiacs during the winter — for owner Felix Sabates.

After just one win last season and barely missing a top-10 finish in the 1996 standings, Bobby Labonte's Interstate Batteries team made the change from Chevrolets to Pontiacs, hoping to improve their performances on the track and challenge for the 1997 title.

McReynolds had been at the pulse of both engine and chassis development by Ford at the Yates team, and would bring state-of-the-art knowledge with him. Of equal importance to Childress may also have been the fact that if he hired McReynolds, he would weaken the Yates organization, which may have been the biggest obstacle in his path to another championship. It was a brilliant move on paper. If Larry could translate his knowledge from Ford to Chevrolet, there were few garage-watchers who felt Earnhardt would not be at the front of the battle for the championship throughout the 1997 season.

The McReynolds bomb overshadowed the move made by Sabates to hire Tony Glover from the Morgan-McClure team to become crew chief for Robby Gordon and the Coors team. Glover had spent his entire career with Morgan-McClure, and Felix's offer, persuading him to leave Sterling Marlin and the Kodak team, raised the ante for crew chiefs in the sport.

Yet another major change occurred when Paul Andrews packed up his toolbox at Geoff Bodine's shop and moved it to the Kranefuss/Haas effort to work with Mayfield on the Kmart/RC Cola Fords. Andrews had been the crew chief of the "7" car, helping Alan Kulwicki win a championship, and then remained with the team after Bodine bought it from Alan's estate. Tim Brewer, who had worked with Kranefuss/Haas since its beginning, left the team last fall, and as the opening race approached, Brewer was working at Morgan-McClure and wearing the Kodak yellow rather than the red and white colors of Kmart.

hoping CAT would soon be as familiar on the major series as it had become at the Busch level.

Lowe's home improvement stores announced in mid-1996 that it would leave Brett Bodine's team as a sponsor and join forces with Richard Childress with a new team from the Childress stable. Mike Skinner, who won the 1995 NASCAR Craftsman Truck Series championship and finished second to Ron Hornaday in the 1996 truck title chase, was the new driver for the Lowe's effort, and Kevin Hamlin moved from the Jackson/Mast combination to be the crew chief for the team. The move by Lowe's left Bodine searching for a sponsor, and he found what he needed in Close Call, a phone card company.

The addition of Hamlin to the Childress effort was one of the many crew chief moves — but was not the one that shocked the sport. The most surprising move was by Larry McReynolds, who decided to leave Robert Yates and the Texaco Havoline team to join Childress as the new crew chief for Dale Earnhardt's Goodwrench team.

Childress had accomplished several things by hiring McReynolds. Known as one of the best motivators and most dedicated crew chiefs in the sport, Larry brought what Childress felt was needed to his Goodwrench team after the 1996 season. More importantly,

With Steve Hmiel promoted to the general manager's role of Roush Racing, Jimmy Fennig left Bobby Allison Motorsports to join Roush as the new crew chief for Mark Martin and the Valvoline-sponsored Fords.

The changes kept coming. Richard Broome left Ricky Rudd's employment and was hired on as the general manager of the Stavola Brothers' Circuit City team. Rudd then hired Jim Long, who had worked during the 1996 season as crew chief for Speed and Melling, as the new crew chief for the Tide Fords.

While the teams were working their way through all these changes, there was also considerable work being done by track owners in preparation for the coming year. Bruton Smith and Bob Bahre had purchased North Wilkesboro during the 1996 season, and it was clear what was happening there. North Wilkes disappeared from the 1997 NASCAR Winston Cup schedule, and the track's dates were moved. Smith took the spring date to his new Texas Motor Speedway, being

constructed outside Ft. Worth, while Bahre obtained a second race date for his privately-owned New Hampshire International Speedway. The date would be in September, when the New England foliage would be at its peak, encouraging tens of thousands of new fans to spend time in the New England mountains and visit Bahre's splendid track.

While construction continued in Texas and Bahre was preparing to print ticket brochures for his September race, Les Richter was overseeing the final stages of construction of the long-awaited two-mile oval in the Los Angeles area. The new California Speedway was nearing completion, and was preparing to welcome visitors to the first NASCAR Winston Cup race in Southern California since Riverside closed its doors in 1988. The new June date would also be the first time the Los Angeles area fans would see the NASCAR Winston Cup teams and drivers competing on an oval track since 1980, when Ontario Motor Speedway last hosted the Cuppers.

Now, with all the changes among drivers, teams and sponsors finally in place, and after months of anticipation by fans and drivers alike, the 1997 season was ready to debut at Daytona International Speedway.

Dale Jarrett and crew chief Todd Parrott plot their strategy for a run at the '97 championship. In their first year as a start-up effort, they had won four times and finished just 89 points behind Labonte to take third in the final standings. With the schedule set, rosters complete, and new sponsors and teams prepared to hit the race track, the stage is set to begin the 1997 version of the NASCAR Winston Cup Series.

11

NASCAR WINSTON CUP SERIES 1997

NASCAR Winston Cup Champion
Jeff Gordon

To be honest, until I came off the fourth turn on the last lap at Atlanta, knowing I had the car straight enough to run to the checkered flag, I wasn't sure if I would be the NASCAR Winston Cup champion.

I mean, the way the Atlanta weekend had gone, nothing would have been a surprise.

We knew from the weather reports going into the weekend that there was a good chance we would only have a limited amount of practice time on the race track. We also knew that we had a new track to figure out, and that we would need to protect our point lead just a little bit to come out of the weekend with the title.

In the confines of the garage area, crew chief Ray Evernham listens to his driver describe the car's tendencies out on the race track. Ray's understanding, coupled with his ability to translate Jeff's information and incorporate it into the car's setup is a key element in the duo's success.

In the chilly air of the late afternoon, Brooke Gordon joins The Champion after Jeff was awarded his second NASCAR Winston Cup trophy.

What we didn't know was what was going to happen to us during the course of the weekend.

We went to Atlanta with a great car — a car that we honestly felt could challenge for the victory. We went there hoping to win, and without any plans of being ultra conservative in our approach to racing for the title.

Then the rain began to interfere, and Friday's qualifying was rained out and rescheduled for Saturday. We had a brief practice on Saturday morning to scuff tires, and I spun out on pit road and hit Bobby Hamilton's car, which was parked and waiting to enter the track. It was embarrassing, for sure, but even more, it damaged both Bobby's and my cars so much that our crews had to pull the backups off the trailers. My mistake cost both crews extra work at a time when neither needed to spend time getting a backup car ready for qualifying.

Then we decided to put the qualifying engine from my damaged car into the backup, and when we did, we over-filled the oil tank. During my lap around the track, some of the excess oil came out, and I got into it and didn't get a good qualifying lap. I ended up starting 37th — the worst I had started all year — so my mistake had led to an even more difficult situation for my team.

We had a meeting Sunday morning, and the decision was made not to take any extra chances or do anything stupid. We had fought all season for the opportunity to win the championship, and there was no reason to throw it out the window by trying to go out and win the race. We didn't need a home run in the bottom of the ninth. We needed just to do what we had to do — be solid and workmanlike, and not put ourselves in a position to lose the championship.

With that in mind, our goal was to get ourselves up to 15th place, where we could win the championship no matter what Mark and Dale did, and then, if the opportunity presented itself, to go further forward as the race progressed.

As it turned out, we did what we had to do. The car didn't really handle well, and the new surface was eating tires pretty regularly. In the end, we had to hold on to what we had and nurse the car through the final laps of the race to finish 17th. With Bobby Labonte winning the race and leading the most laps, Dale and Mark couldn't capitalize on those opportunities, and we ended up winning the championship by 14 points over Dale.

The way we won it wasn't what we had envisioned when we started out the Atlanta weekend. But the reality is that we have become the champions for the second time in three seasons, and we made it three consecutive titles for Hendrick Motorsports. That is what makes it very pleasing to all of us on the team, no matter what the point spread was, or what the final finishing position was. We had accomplished our goal.

It has been an incredible year for us. It all began at Daytona, where we had plenty of opportunity for distraction with all the problems that our car owner, Rick Hendrick, was having, and knowing that there was a good possibility he was not going to be coming to many, if any, of the races this season while he fought through his battle with leukemia. I have said over and over that Rick has been so important to all of us — not just as a car owner, but as a friend — that we all took the news of his problems in a very hard way.

But Rick came to the shop and told us all what was happening with him. The most unbelievable thing to us was that he turned it all around. Instead of us feeling sorry for him, he made us understand that he believed there was some other reason for his having the illness, and perhaps it was to help raise awareness and help find ways to assist others with the same type of problem.

His attitude and the way he talked with us about it became a motivational force rather than a distraction, and when we went to Daytona, we wanted more than anything to run well. Not just the DuPont team, but all three of the teams. To go down there, win the Busch Clash and then also win the Daytona 500 was simply an outstanding achievement for my team. To have the other teams — Terry Labonte's and Ricky Craven's — come home second and third for a Hendrick sweep was almost unbelievable.

It started our season off in a way we never have started before. It seemed that in the past we had a slow start and then had to gather things up in the middle of the season. This year, man, we came out of the box firing, and we backed up the Daytona win with a victory at Rockingham and then a fourth place at Richmond.

If there was a tone for the season, it was set early in the year. Every time we had a problem, it seemed, we popped right back with a strong finish the next weekend. At Atlanta we blew up, the only motor problem we had all season, but came back with a third at Darlington. We went to Texas and had a good car and a chance to win the race, but then were involved in a wreck not of our making. The next race, we bounced back to win at Bristol. We won at Martinsville, finished second at Sears Point and were fifth in the spring Talladega race. Then we had a simply outstanding weekend at Charlotte, winning The Winston, and backing that up the following weekend with a win in the Coca-Cola 600.

After we finished 26th at Dover, we came right back and won at Pocono, taking back the point lead we had lost after Atlanta. For the rest of the season, we were either in the lead or right in the hunt, threatening, where we wanted to be.

We won the inaugural race at California, another big coup for our team, in a fuel-mileage victory using some great pit strategy, but there's no question that the first race at New Hampshire sticks out in my mind as my biggest disappointment of the season.

We just had a bad weekend at that event. We didn't qualify well, and when we started the race, we just couldn't get anywhere trying to move up in the field. We came in and changed tires, and then had a flat right rear and went a lap down. No matter what we did, it didn't seem like we could make any headway. The caution came out when we didn't need it to, and when we needed a long green, we didn't get that, either. It was just a bad weekend.

But once again, we bounced right back from that, finishing second at Pocono and fourth at The Brickyard. Then we scored the first victory of my career at a road-racing track when we won at The Glen.

(Above) Jeff and Ray show off their check for the champion's share of Winston's point fund after they captured the Cup at Atlanta.
(Right) Taking yet another 7-figure check off R.J. Reynolds' hands, Jeff and Brooke celebrate at Darlington following Jeff's win in the Mountain Dew Southern 500 that brought him the Winston Million.

At Bristol, we were involved in an accident and finished 35th — and then we went to Darlington. We had the chance to win the Winston Million there, something that was very special to all of us if we could do it, which we did. It was simply one of the greatest days of my life on a race track, being able to complete the hat-trick that makes up the Winston Million, and becoming only the second driver in the history

Jeff and Brooke Gordon are joined by Ray Evernham and his wife, Mary, in victory lane after their overwhelming victory in The Winston. One week later, Jeff would win from the pole in the Coca-Cola 600, capturing the second leg of the Winston Million and capping off a dominating week at Charlotte.

of the award to win it. That it came with my third consecutive Mountain Dew Southern 500 victory made it even more important to me and the team.

That put us in the point lead going into the final races of the season.

I think some of the people in the garage expected us to lose a little focus after we won at Darlington and got the Winston Million, but it didn't change us at all. We were still thinking championship. After finishing third at Richmond, we went back to New Hampshire with a vengeance. We were determined not to have the same type of weekend there that we had had the first time, and we came away with our 10th victory of the season.

At every event following that win at New Hampshire, we went to the track with plans to do the best we could and try to win the race. We didn't accomplish that in the final seven races of the season, and our problems at Talladega and Phoenix helped shrink the gap we had built in the point standings. Dale and Mark aren't the kind of drivers who roll over and play dead when they are behind in the points. We knew they would fight back, and we knew that if we were going to win the NASCAR Winston Cup, we would have to find ways to beat them.

In the end, we had just enough to make sure that we claimed the title.

As I said before, we had never started off a season quite the way we did this year. It seems like when we have been a contender for the championship — even in '95 — we haven't been able to keep the consistency and win as many races as we have this year. It is an awesome thing, and a tribute to the team and the way they work together all year to find, and then keep, that kind of consistency and win as many races as we have. We never thought or dreamed that we would start the season the way we did, and looking back, I think that had a lot to do with our entire season.

We gained some confidence early in the season and got some momentum, and it carried us through the entire year. It helped us bounce back when we had a bad race or two, and it stayed with us all season. We knew we were good. We knew we had good motors, good cars, good people, and all of the ingredients it took to win the championship. But we also knew that a lot of other teams in the garage area have exactly the same things.

They have good motors, drivers, people, cars, motivation. It's all equal among the top teams in NASCAR Winston Cup racing today. The difference is in what you do with all those ingredients, and I believe there is no better crew chief in the sport right now than the one I have.

Ray doesn't get flustered. He keeps everyone focused on the goal at hand. During all the problems we had on Saturday at Atlanta, he never fussed at anyone or blamed anyone for anything. He just kept us all pointed in the right direction, and then did it again Sunday morning when the decision was made to simply win the championship and not be foolish trying to be heroes.

That's what makes the difference in things — at least for our race team. And Sunday, watching the crew work and seeing the over-the-wall guys and the way they were focused on the goal, everyone knew that we were all on the same wavelength. We were all in the game, everyone's head was in the right place, and after the first couple of pit stops, I knew that we were going to be all right on pit road. Then it was up to me to do my job on the race track with what I had at hand.

And when it was all over, we had all done what we were supposed to do.

One of the things that I will enjoy most about going to New York and the NASCAR Winston Cup Awards Banquet is something I'd like to share with you. Yes, we'll be having a great time, and doing lots of cool things with the media and others. Yes, we'll sit at the head table in the Grand Ballroom and have the chance to accept the championship and the trophy and all of that.

But one of the things I am looking forward to the most is getting the gold car from Goodyear. That is one of the coolest trophies in the sport — and when I won the championship in 1995, I asked Rick if I could have that gold car. He told me I could, and it occupies a very special place in my house.

Last year, when Terry won the title, he also asked Rick if he could have his, because when he won the championship in 1984, they didn't give the car as a special award. Rick told Terry that he could keep that gold car, too.

This year, when we were all talking at the beginning of the season about our goals and all, Rick said, "Win us another one, and I want it."

I told him then, that we would win a gold car for him this year, and that was a goal of mine right from the beginning of the season. It made winning the championship extra special for me — and it will be great to give Rick the gold car from Goodyear.

I hope the fans enjoy my second championship as much as I am going to. When I won the first one, I didn't know what to expect — and we weren't really expected to be the ones to win it that year.

This one is different, and I guess that is part of the reason I pulled up on the start/finish line after my victory lap at Atlanta and got out of the car. I wanted the fans to share it with me — the excitement I felt about finally winning the championship. I was pumped up, and I wanted to show the fans my emotions and let them share what winning a championship means to a driver.

When I got out of the car and jumped up and down on the roof, they got excited too. That made me feel really good. It was just a way of sharing with them, and I hope that they enjoyed it as much as I did.

I am really looking forward to next year and to all of the things that come with representing the sport as its champion. This was an incredible season for me, for my family, and for our team. In some ways, I guess it was really like an entire career all rolled into one single season.

To have accomplished all the things that we did — winning the Daytona 500, the Winston Million, The Winston, and then to win the NASCAR Winston Cup along with 10 races — is something that will be difficult to top, even for our team!

But we'll go to Daytona in February and start all over again.

I hope you have enjoyed the 1997 season, and will continue to pull for your favorite driver or team, no matter who it is. It is you, the fan, who continues to help our sport grow with your enthusiasm and support, and I would like to take this chance to thank you for it, no matter who you pull for.

I hope to be a good champion and represent your sport well. And I hope to see you along the circuit next season and have the chance to say hello.

JEFF GORDON
1997 NASCAR Winston Cup Champion

(Above) The Rainbow Warriors proclaim their 10th victory of the season after their win at New Hampshire in September. With the win, the team had reached double figures for the second consecutive season, making Jeff the first driver to accomplish that feat since Darrell Waltrip did it in 1981-82. (Left) After acknowledging the crowd at Atlanta, Jeff turns toward pit road and salutes his team for their season of outstanding preparation and performance that led to the NASCAR Winston Cup championship.

NASCAR WINSTON CUP SERIES 1997

Daytona 500

(Daytona International Speedway • February 16, 1997)

Of all the team, driver and sponsor changes, the new paint schemes and the new team suits that were unveiled the first day of practice at Daytona, perhaps the most eye-catching of all was the chrome Chevrolet Monte Carlo carrying orange lettering that read "Parts America."

He had been teased about silver helmets and silver driving shoes in the past. Now Darrell Waltrip planned his own "one-upsmanship" by taking a silver car through technical inspection. It glittered in the sunlight, blinding those without sunglasses. It was, Darrell proudly pointed out, the painstaking work of his dedicated crew, which had precisely cut and fitted silver vinyl pieces that were heated and stretched with hand-held hair dryers, and applied to the sheet metal of the Chevrolet.

The purpose of the car color was to begin the celebration of Waltrip's silver anniversary season in NASCAR Winston Cup competition. Darrell went on to explain that his car colors would change throughout the year. At times, the Chevrolets would carry the different paint schemes that had been on his cars through his quarter-century of competing at the highest level of stock car racing. Green, red and white coloring would mark the time he drove for Mountain Dew in 1981-82, while yellow and white would denote Pepsi and Darrell's year as

(Right) Ernie Irvan (28) and Mark Martin (6) hold the inside draft next to Bill Elliott (94) through Daytona's tri-oval. The three Ford drivers swapped the lead throughout the middle portion of the race, before Elliott established himself as the best of the Fords, finishing fourth behind the Hendrick Chevrolets.

(Below) Taking the checkered flag under caution, Jeff Gordon (24), Terry Labonte (5) and Ricky Craven cross the finish line in formation, completing a 1-2-3 sweep of the Daytona 500 for Hendrick Motorsports.

18

the Pepsi Challenger in 1983. Red and white would remind fans of his years as a Budweiser driver from 1984-86, and the orange-and-yellow bull's-eye would bring memories of the 1987-90 seasons when he drove for the Tide team.

For the Daytona 500, however, the chrome car would kick-off Darrell's celebration of 25 years as one of the most competitive and winning drivers in the history of the sport. Darrell was proud of the handiwork of his crew — and the record he had compiled during the previous 24 seasons.

During his stint behind the wheel, he had driven for some of the most famous car owners in the sport, had brought DiGard into its heyday, had won three championships with Junior Johnson, and had helped formulate Hendrick Motorsports into the powerful organization it is today. He had claimed 84 victories, had been nearly unbeatable on the short tracks in Johnson's cars, and had piled up more than $15 million in prize money. He had established himself as a modern-day legend. In what many felt was the twilight of his career, Waltrip still held that he could race with the best, and given the right circumstances, could even win again.

For others in the Daytona garage area, there were considerably more questions than whether Darrell could return to victory lane for the first time since 1992.

For many, the focus was on Dale Earnhardt, who was trying once again to win the prize that had eluded him during his career. Dale's Goodwrench Chevrolet proved to be one of the fastest cars on the track during practice sessions, and it appeared that the addition of Larry McReynolds as the team's new crew chief was paying immediate dividends. How the Richard Childress stable would do during the course of Speedweeks, however, was questionable as Lowe's, Mike Skinner and crew chief Kevin Hamlin were added to the Childress effort during the winter months.

(Left) Veterans Darrell Waltrip and Ricky Rudd discuss the finer points of racing at Daytona before the start of the race. The 1997 season-opener would mark the beginning of Rudd's 23rd season in the NASCAR Winston Cup Series. (Below) Rookie Mike Skinner (31), with Steve Grissom on his right, leads the Daytona 500 field to the green flag to start the 1997 NASCAR Winston Cup season.

(Above) Darrell Waltrip, who leads Morgan Shepherd in the Precision Racing Pontiac, unveiled a special-edition "chrome" Monte Carlo at Daytona to commemorate his silver anniversary season in stock car racing's top division. *(Right)* Dale Jarrett (left), Terry Labonte (middle) and Dale Earnhardt (right) stroll into the NASCAR garage area early in the week. All had to be considered preseason favorites to win the 1997 NASCAR Winston Cup championship.

With McReynolds gone from the Robert Yates team, Yates had named Ernie Irvan's longtime friend Marc Reno as the crew chief for the Havoline Ford. Would the team come out of the box the way Dale Jarrett had with crew chief Todd Parrott last year, and win the season-opener?

The same questions were being asked of the "4" and "40" teams. Tony Glover had left the Morgan-McClure effort to become the crew chief for Robby Gordon and Felix Sabates' Coors Chevrolet, and Tim Brewer had signed on as the head wrench of the Kodak team to work with Daytona expert Sterling Marlin.

Another major question had to be answered by the Valvoline Ford team owned by Jack Roush. Driver Mark Martin had not been to the winner's circle since the fall race at Charlotte in 1995, and Jimmy Fennig was his new crew chief, moving from Bobby Allison Motorsports. Steve Hmiel was still a vital part of the team, but Fennig was now the day-to-day man. Would the change bring Fennig his first NASCAR Winston Cup victory?

There were also new teams to be introduced. Kyle Petty, Derrike Cope, Chad Little, David Green, Mike Wallace and Wally Dallenbach were all with new efforts, and Joe Nemechek, among others, was also in a new seat working with a new team.

Ricky Craven was now in the Hendrick Motorsports Budweiser car, and Ken Schrader was paired with Andy Petree in the Skoal Chevrolet. Robert Pressley, Jeremy Mayfield and John Andretti were all with teams they had driven a few races for last year, and no one really knew how those so-called extended test sessions would reflect the team's performance over a full season.

One thing, however, was very clear. There would be some high-dollar teams headed home after qualifying at races this season, with the number of quality efforts far exceeding the slots available on the starting grid at each event.

Daytona's field was once again one of the largest of the season, and 51 cars took laps during the first qualifying session. Teams faced the problem of either posting a lap fast enough to safely make the Daytona 500 field, or being forced to race their way into the lineup during the Gatorade Twin 125s on Thursday.

Only the front row was locked in after Busch Pole qualifying, and when the time sheets were posted, two unlikely candidates stood the garage area on its ear. Mike Skinner, rolling out 16th on the line, drove around debris on the track, withstood three rain delays and late-session efforts by Dale Jarrett and Rusty Wallace, and handed sponsor Lowe's its first Daytona 500 pole in the new team's first outing. It was a shocker that no one in the garage area believed at first. Skinner had blistered the field with a lap at over 189.8 mph to claim the pole.

Right beside him was Steve Grissom, who was making his first appearance behind the wheel of Larry Hedrick's Kodiak Chevrolet. In his first NASCAR Winston Cup race since being released by the Diamond Ridge team last season, Steve claimed the outside of the front row with a lap at more than 189.3 mph. Jarrett and Wallace had the third- and fourth-fastest laps, but only the top two positions were locked into the field on the first day.

The next day, the Busch Clash, a 20-lap dash for cash, was held. The Busch Clash matches the pole winners from the previous season, and the 14-car field, including Busch Pole "wild card" winner Rusty Wallace, rolled off the line in search of the winner's share of the purse.

The event is split into two 10-lap segments, and for the start of the second segment the field is inverted, based on finishing positions in the first segment.

With restrictor-plate racing making it difficult to pass in a short race, clearly, the position to be in for the start of the second half of the race was at the front, and that meant finishing at the back in the first segment. Bobby Labonte, who drew the fifth starting position, immediately fell back through the field at the start of the first segment, as did Earnhardt. Jeff Gordon was already there, having drawn the 13th starting spot.

Terry Labonte, the defending NASCAR Winston Cup champion, had drawn the pole position for the event, and he led all 10 laps of the first segment, earning an automatic $30,000 paycheck for finishing the first half at the front. Labonte, however, went to the back of the pack for the second portion of the race, and stayed there, finishing 11th at the conclusion of the second 10 laps.

Gordon's strategy of hanging back for the first half worked. As Bobby Labonte again plummeted toward the back of the field, Gordon was riding high at the front, and he withstood a charge from Rusty Wallace to claim the victory. Wallace had fought his way to third place in the event's first segment. After starting 12th in the field for the second half, he absolutely rocketed his way to the front and missed the Busch Clash victory by just over a car-length.

Thursday's Gatorade Twin 125s are one of the highlights of

Jeff Burton (99) and Jeremy Mayfield (37) make a Skittles sandwich out of Derrike Cope — a daring move on Daytona's 31-degree banks. Mayfield got his season off to an impressive start with a sixth-place finish in the Daytona 500.

(Above) Jeff Gordon's Rainbow Warriors fall to work during an unexpected stop under green midway through the race. Their superb two-tire change allowed Gordon to remain on the lead lap. *(Right)* Geoff Bodine's QVC Ford shows the aftermath of a tangle with Hut Stricklin, Derrike Cope and Jimmy Spencer along the backstretch on lap 48. Bodine was able to return to the action, but finished a disappointing 34th.

Speedweeks at Daytona. The tension in the garage area is as palpable as it is Sunday morning prior to the Daytona 500. Teams who qualified poorly are faced with the reality of having to finish in the top 15 in their Gatorade Twin or getting into the field based on their qualifying time in one of the final 10 starting positions. A lucky few might get to use provisionals, but for some teams, this is their opportunity to either make the race or load up and go home.

In the first Gatorade Twin, Busch Pole winner Skinner was at the point, but few expected him to last there long. He was the first to admit that he needed "seat time" in the Lowe's Chevrolet, and he wanted to bring the car home intact to avoid going to the backup car for the main event on Sunday. On his right was Dale Jarrett, and the second-generation driver was ready to show what was under the hood of his Quality Care/Ford Credit Ford from the Yates shop. Dale didn't take long to display the car's power.

He streaked to the point by the end of the first lap, hung behind teammate Ernie Irvan when Irvan moved to the front with nine laps left, and with just four laps remaining, swept the red-white-and-blue Thunderbird into the lead for the final time. Irvan began to struggle with overheated tires, and Skinner moved to second on the final lap. He was more than a car-length behind Jarrett, but for the rookie, he had accomplished his goal. The blue-and-yellow Lowe's Monte Carlo had made it back without a scratch.

Grissom and Wallace were on the front row for the second Gatorade Twin, and Earnhardt was in fifth place for the start of the 50-lap event.

No one would bet against the black Chevrolet, and Dale showed why as he rolled to a convincing eighth consecutive Twin 125 victory at The Beach. In all, it was his 10th trophy from the Twins, and when he arrived in the press box after his victory over Gordon, Dale had a question for the media. "So," he said with a chuckle. "Did you expect someone else?"

His strategy of moving to the front and letting the rest of the pack chase him worked perfectly. He led the final 30 laps of the race, and in the end, no one had anything for the Goodwrench Chevrolet and the seven-time champion.

The results of the Gatorade Twins led to some serious bidding and check writing in the garage area following the race. Joe Nemechek failed to make the event, and car owner Felix Sabates bought Phil Barkdoll's spot and put the BellSouth colors on Phil's Chevrolet. Rick Mast, in his first outing for Butch Mock's team, also failed to make the field, and Mock worked a deal with TriStar Motorsports to put Remington's logo on the Ford driven by Loy Allen.

Ricky Craven, Ted Musgrave, Bobby Hamilton and Morgan Shepherd all got in using provisionals based on car owner points from the final standings of 1996. Mike Wallace, whose ProTech team had undergone an ownership switch before the start of Speedweeks, was unable to get the Spam colors into the field. Billy Standridge, Gary Bradberry, Chad Little, David Green and Norm Benning all went home, as well, but the biggest news was the fact that Bud Moore's Ford team, sponsorless at the event, failed to race its way into the field in the second Twin 125. Larry Pearson came up two positions short, and it marked the first time that Bud's Fords had failed to qualify for a Daytona 500 since 1973.

Dale Earnhardt's Goodwrench Chevrolet (above) and Dale Jarrett's Quality Care Ford (left) show the results of their altercation on the backstretch that also included Ernie Irvan with just 11 laps remaining in the event. Jarrett remained on the lead lap, while Earnhardt, although running at the end, lost five laps during repairs.

During the first half of the Daytona 500, it appeared that the strongest cars on the track belonged to Earnhardt, Jarrett, Irvan, Gordon, Mark Martin and Bill Elliott, while Craven and Marlin were battling among the leaders. Gordon had moved to the front of the field on lap 57, and looked like he would be a contender, but on lap 111, the DuPont Chevrolet swerved near the second turn wall, and Gordon immediately headed for pit road. He had a slow leak in a tire, but made it to his crew without incident. Crew chief Ray Evernham directed a two-tire change, and Gordon returned to the track without being lapped, although the race leaders were breathing on his rear bumper. Had he taken four tires, he would have lost a lap.

Some 11 laps later, Greg Sacks and Jeff Burton tangled, bringing out a caution flag, and

Race winner Jeff Gordon is joined in victory lane by his Hendrick Motorsports teammates Terry Labonte (left) and Ricky Craven (right) to celebrate their sweep in the 1997 season-opener.

Gordon was saved from being lapped. He made up his deficit under the yellow, but the battle was just beginning. He was locked in 24th place, and for the next 40 laps, he tried to work his way to the front — without much success.

Another caution helped Gordon move to ninth place for the restart, and seven laps later, he had rocketed to third place with just 22 laps left in the race.

With 11 laps left and Bill Elliott trying to win his first race since the 1994 Mountain Dew Southern 500 at Darlington, Gordon made his move to get past Earnhardt. Dale's Chevrolet clipped the wall, ricocheting into Gordon, and was drilled by Jarrett's Ford. Earnhardt slid before rolling into the air and landing on Irvan's Ford. The black Chevrolet came to rest on its wheels, but three hot-running contenders were eliminated from the race.

Earnhardt drove his car to pit road, and returned to the race, scrambling to a 31st-place finish.

That left the battle for the victory to Gordon and Elliott, and Bill knew he did not have the horses under the hood of his Ford to hold off the DuPont Chevrolet. He was right. With Terry Labonte and Craven lined up behind Gordon, the Hendrick team would certainly work together during the closing laps. Bill knew he was a dead duck.

With five laps left in the race, Gordon made a daring move, driving all the way down onto the apron of the track in the first turn and grabbing the lead for what would be the final lead change of the race. Labonte and Craven rocketed around the high side of Elliott at the same time, and the three Hendrick cars emerged in 1-2-3 order ahead of the McDonald's Ford.

As the three teammates crossed the line at the conclusion of the lap, an 11-car accident ensued behind them, bringing out the final caution of the event and ultimately determining the finishing positions. The Hendrick cars continued around behind the pace car for the final four laps, forming up for a photo finish at the conclusion of the event.

It was spectacular stuff, and it brought a smile to the face of team owner Rick Hendrick, who was home in Charlotte preparing for chemotherapy treatments for his recently diagnosed leukemia. Gordon was handed a cellular phone as he drove into victory lane, and his first words after he shut off the motor in the Chevrolet were to the car owner who had given him his chance in NASCAR Winston Cup competition. There were plenty of tears to go with the victory celebration.

Elliott was fourth behind Craven, and Marlin took fifth place. Mayfield had a rock solid run to sixth place with the Kmart/RC Cola Ford, while Martin was satisfied with his performance to take his Ford to seventh place. Ward Burton and Ricky Rudd were eighth and ninth.

What about the chrome car? Well, Waltrip worked his way from his 22nd starting position, and celebrated the first race of his silver anniversary celebration with a strong 10th-place finish.

Daytona 500

Fin. Pos.	Start Pos.	Car #	Driver	Team
1	6	24	Jeff Gordon	DuPont Refinishes Chevrolet
2	18	5	Terry Labonte	Kellogg's Corn Flakes Chevrolet
3	40	25	Ricky Craven	Budweiser Chevrolet
4	8	94	Bill Elliott	McDonald's Ford
5	9	4	Sterling Marlin	Kodak Film Chevrolet
6	21	37	Jeremy Mayfield	Kmart/RC Cola Ford
7	11	6	Mark Martin	Valvoline Ford
8	17	22	Ward Burton	MBNA America Pontiac
9	13	10	Ricky Rudd	Tide Ford
10	22	17	Darrell Waltrip	Parts America Chevrolet
11	23	99	Jeff Burton	Exide Batteries Ford
12	1	31	Mike Skinner	Lowe's Chevrolet
13	41	16	Ted Musgrave	Family Channel/PRIMESTAR Ford
14	30	44	Kyle Petty	Hot Wheels Pontiac
15	39	43	Bobby Hamilton	STP Pontiac
16	20	40	Robby Gordon	Coors Light Chevrolet
17	24	71	Dave Marcis	Realtree Camouflage Chevrolet
18	37	11	Brett Bodine	Close Call Phone Card Ford
19	28	8	Hut Stricklin	Circuit City Ford
20	5	28	Ernie Irvan	Texaco Havoline Ford
21	15	18	Bobby Labonte	Interstate Batteries Pontiac
22	36	81	Kenny Wallace	Square D Ford
23	3	88	Dale Jarrett	Quality Care/Ford Credit Ford
24	35	9	Lake Speed	Melling Engine Parts Ford
25	32	98	John Andretti	RCA Ford
26	33	19	Loy Allen	Remington/Child Support Ford
27	38	73	Joe Nemechek	BellSouth Chevrolet
28	16	30	Johnny Benson	Pennzoil Pontiac
29	42	1	Morgan Shepherd	Delco Remy America Pontiac
30	27	90	Dick Trickle	Heilig-Meyers Ford
31	4	3	Dale Earnhardt	GM Goodwrench Service Chevrolet
32	12	21	Michael Waltrip	CITGO Ford
33	10	33	Ken Schrader	Skoal Bandit Chevrolet
34	25	7	Geoff Bodine	QVC Ford
35	7	23	Jimmy Spencer	Camel Cigarettes Ford
36	29	36	Derrike Cope	Skittles Pontiac
37	34	20	Greg Sacks	Hardee's Ford
38	31	77	Bobby Hillin	Jasper Engines/Federal-Mogul Ford
39	19	29	Robert Pressley	Cartoon Network Chevrolet
40	2	41	Steve Grissom	Kodiak Chevrolet
41	14	2	Rusty Wallace	Miller Lite Ford
42	26	46	Wally Dallenbach	First Union Chevrolet

NASCAR WINSTON CUP SERIES 1997

Goodwrench Service 400

(North Carolina Motor Speedway • February 23, 1997)

Five days after the victory lane celebrations at Daytona, with the huge crowd standing and applauding Jeff Gordon for his gutsy pass of Bill Elliott in the closing laps to clinch his first Daytona 500 victory, the NASCAR Winston Cup teams were filing into the garage area at North Carolina Motor Speedway.

The months of testing and preparation for the season lid-lifter were a memory, and the hype and hoopla that goes with the first race of the season — the sport's equivalent of the Super Bowl — had been filed away.

Now it was time to face The Rock, and despite all the long hours spent preparing for Daytona, the Goodwrench Service 400 paid exactly the same number of points toward the year-end title as the 500-miler the previous weekend.

It would be the same for the rest of the season — a race to be held, points to be won — and at the end of the year, the key to the championship could come at any track on the tour.

(Left) The Gibbs Racing crew rolls their mount to the starting grid for the Goodwrench Service 400. Driver Bobby Labonte and the Interstate team made the switch to Pontiacs during the winter, but showed no ill-effects by taking the outside pole for the season's second event.

(Right) Jeff Gordon collects his thoughts prior to the start of the race. He would go on to win the event, making him two for two on the season and solidly in control of the early-season point chase.

With the capacity crowd on their feet for the start of the race, pole-winner Mark Martin (6), fresh off his NSACAR Busch Series win on Saturday, leads the field into the first turn after taking the green flag.

With 47 cars on hand and with a maximum of 43 starting positions (if a previous champion were to use a champion's provisional to make the field), the practice sessions were critical as teams tried to find the right combinations for fast laps on the 1.017-mile oval. As the cars left the garage to make their laps, one team was glaringly absent.

For the first time since 1976, Bud Moore's team was not in the garage area to attempt to qualify for a race. Lack of sponsorship had forced Moore to make the difficult decision to remain home in Spartanburg, S.C., and the "15" Fords, among the most familiar cars to any fan for decades, were parked in the shop. Following the failure of his team to make the field at Daytona, Moore said he would not put the team back on the track until a sponsor was found. He is truly one of the pioneers in the sport, and had been involved since the very beginnings of NASCAR. His team has nurtured some of the biggest stars in the sport over the last four decades, and he is the fourth-winningest car owner in history. But Moore needed dollars to compete, and without them, he would remain in Spartanburg.

Gordon was fast during the practice sessions at The Rock, and many expected him to shatter the track record he set while qualifying for this race two years ago. But when Jeff made his laps during the first qualifying session, he fell short of the mark set earlier in the day by Bobby Labonte. The Interstate Batteries Pontiac driver was third out on the track during qualifying, and driver after driver failed to dislodge the green-and-black Grand Prix from the top of the scoring pylon.

Labonte was not high-fiving with his crew yet. He knew that Mark Martin had yet to run, and the Valvoline Ford had been one of the

Dale Earnhardt ducks to the inside of Ricky Rudd (10) and Lake Speed (9) along Rockingham's frontstretch, as he works his way through the field from his 27th-place starting position.

fastest during practice sessions, as well. Less than an hour earlier, Mark had streaked his Winn-Dixie Ford to the pole for the NASCAR Busch Series race on Saturday, and Bobby was concerned that Martin would have the goods to sweep the poles for both events.

He was right.

Martin simply blistered the field with his run, chalking up a lap that was more than a mile per hour faster than Bobby's, and grabbed his 33rd career NASCAR Winston Cup pole in the process. Labonte had to settle for second place on the grid.

He had led the most laps at Daytona, and this performance proved that Martin and new crew chief Jimmy Fennig were on the same wavelength early in the season. There was reason for it. Fennig had worked with Martin during the early days of Mark's career on the ASA tour, and the two had combined for the 1986 championship on that circuit. They parted company at the end of that season, and Martin moved to a NASCAR Busch Series ride while Fennig signed on as the crew chief for Bobby Allison. They had not worked together since then — until now. Mark said after his pole runs that Fennig brought some fresh ideas to the team. Clearly, those ideas were working.

Dale Jarrett dives into turn one after putting Robert Pressley (29), Kenny Wallace (81) and Derrike Cope (36) a lap down. Jarrett dominated most of the event, but couldn't hold off Gordon in the final 50 laps and was forced to settle for second place.

The twin poles brought a smile to Martin's face, and after the way he had run at Daytona, he said there was plenty of reason to grin. "That was an awful lot of bottled up frustration unleashed here today," Martin said. "It came from two Winston Cup tests and two Busch tests and Busch qualifying and a Busch race and the Busch Clash and the Gatorade 125 and the Daytona 500. That's a lot of whippings I took fourth row from Ricky Craven. Brett Bodine and Ricky Rudd completed the top 10, ahead of Ward Burton and Mike Skinner.

Missing from the top 25 qualifiers during the first round were the likes of Dale Earnhardt, Darrell Waltrip, Bill Elliott, Sterling Marlin, Ernie Irvan, Michael Waltrip and Jimmy Spencer. Only eight drivers chose to run in the second session, and none of them recorded a time

Jarrett blasts out of his pit after another fine stop by the Quality Care crew, as Gordon's DuPont team finishes their stop for four tires and fuel. Rudd's Tide team and Labonte's Kellogg's crew aren't far behind, and turned their drivers out in hot pursuit of the leaders.

down there, and let me tell you, it's real frustrating when you go out there and you put your foot on the floor and your lap time is one second slower than anybody else who does the same thing."

Dale Jarrett put his Quality Care/Ford Credit Ford right behind Martin's Valvoline Thunderbird for the start of the Goodwrench Service 400, and Jeff Gordon was on his right. Geoff Bodine had a solid qualifying effort and slapped the QVC Ford on the inside of the third row, with Ken Schrader and the Skoal Bandit in sixth. Steve Grissom continued to qualify strongly and took the inside of the

John Andretti (98) and Jeremy Mayfield (37) engage in a fierce battle for position at the entrance to the first turn. Mayfield emerged the better of the two at the end of the day with a 16th-place finish. Andretti came home 34th.

faster than they ran in the first one. Elliott chose to use a champion's provisional, allowing another car to get into the field, and other drivers who used provisionals were Michael Waltrip, Spencer, Robby Gordon and Loy Allen. Gordon was able to use a provisional because he was running with a newly created team fielded by Felix Sabates. When Felix had changed the car number from "42" to "40," he had arranged to use the owner points piled up by Kyle Petty in 1996 in the Coors Light "42" car. His prudent thinking allowed Gordon to make the field at The Rock. Failing to qualify for the event were Chad Little, Billy Standridge, Mike Wallace and Gary Bradberry.

After winning Saturday's NASCAR Busch Series race, it appeared that Martin was ready to claim all the hardware at The Rock when he rolled off to lead the race for the first dozen laps on Sunday afternoon. But right on his bumper was the

30

Wallace, Terry Labonte and Geoff Bodine were sixth, seventh and eighth, respectively. Ernie Irvan was ninth, ahead of Morgan Shepherd. Earnhardt finished 11th.

Gordon's surprising victory sent reporters digging through the record books. His wins in the opening two races of the season marked the first time a driver had accomplished that feat since David Pearson won at both Riverside and Daytona in 1976.

Ricky Craven has a discussion with a team member prior to his second outing in the Budweiser Chevrolet. Craven followed up his impressive third at Daytona with a fifth at Rockingham and moved to second place in the point standings.

red-white-and-blue Thunderbird driven by Jarrett, and on the 13th lap, Dale flashed past to take over the point. From then on, Jarrett proceeded to dominate the race.

He led 323 laps, and his crew had one of the easiest days in the brief history of the team. There were no major changes to the chassis — in fact, the team added just a half-turn of wedge at one point, and then took it out at the end. A minor air pressure change in the tires was the only other adjustment, and all the Quality Care crew had to do during pit stops was hammer on new tires and fill the tank. Jarrett appeared headed for his first victory of the season.

During the final caution flag of the race, however, Ray Evernham and the Rainbow Warriors made the final adjustments to the chassis they had been working on all afternoon. Jeff Gordon put the bit in his teeth, found a slightly higher groove to his liking, and began chopping at Jarrett's lead. He picked up a tenth of a second here and two-tenths there, and began closing the gap on the Ford. Gordon pulled up onto Jarrett's rear bumper, and then, with just over 40 laps remaining, Gordon found the opening he wanted and swept past the Ford.

He began stretching the lead, and by the conclusion of the race, had built a 2.43-second margin over the Ford. There was nothing Jarrett could do to hold off the charging Gordon, who rolled to his fifth victory in his last nine NASCAR Winston Cup starts. Behind them, Jeff Burton came home third, ahead of Ricky Rudd and Ricky Craven, who was working with new crew chief Andy Graves for the first time.

Goodwrench Service 400

Fin. Pos.	Start Pos.	Car #	Driver	Team
1	4	24	Jeff Gordon	DuPont Refinishes Chevrolet
2	3	88	Dale Jarrett	Quality Care/Ford Credit Ford
3	17	99	Jeff Burton	Exide Batteries Ford
4	10	10	Ricky Rudd	Tide Ford
5	8	25	Ricky Craven	Budweiser Chevrolet
6	23	2	Rusty Wallace	Miller Lite Ford
7	15	5	Terry Labonte	Kellogg's Corn Flakes Chevrolet
8	5	7	Geoff Bodine	QVC Ford
9	32	28	Ernie Irvan	Texaco Havoline Ford
10	16	1	Morgan Shepherd	Delco Remy Pontiac
11	27	3	Dale Earnhardt	GM Goodwrench Service Chevrolet
12	28	16	Ted Musgrave	Family Channel/PRIMESTAR Ford
13	1	6	Mark Martin	Valvoline Ford
14	2	18	Bobby Labonte	Interstate Batteries Pontiac
15	22	9	Lake Speed	Melling Engine Parts Ford
16	24	37	Jeremy Mayfield	Kmart/RC Cola Ford
17	9	11	Brett Bodine	Close Call Phone Card Ford
18	6	33	Ken Schrader	Skoal Bandit Chevrolet
19	37	90	Dick Trickle	Heilig-Meyers Ford
20	35	4	Sterling Marlin	Kodak Film Chevrolet
21	38	75	Rick Mast	Remington Arms Ford
22	43	94	Bill Elliott	McDonald's Ford
23	11	22	Ward Burton	MBNA America Pontiac
24	7	41	Steve Grissom	Kodiak Chevrolet
25	12	31	Mike Skinner	Lowe's Chevrolet
26	39	21	Michael Waltrip	CITGO Ford
27	21	30	Johnny Benson	Pennzoil Pontiac
28	19	43	Bobby Hamilton	STP Pontiac
29	20	44	Kyle Petty	Hot Wheels Pontiac
30	34	71	Dave Marcis	Realtree Camouflage Chevrolet
31	26	36	Derrike Cope	Skittles Pontiac
32	30	17	Darrell Waltrip	Parts America Chevrolet
33	41	40	Robby Gordon	Coors Light Chevrolet
34	25	98	John Andretti	RCA Ford
35	33	42	Joe Nemechek	BellSouth Chevrolet
36	29	8	Hut Stricklin	Circuit City Ford
37	18	29	Robert Pressley	Cartoon Network Chevrolet
38	14	96	David Green	Caterpillar Chevrolet
39	36	20	Greg Sacks	Hardee's Ford
40	40	23	Jimmy Spencer	Camel Cigarettes Ford
41	13	81	Kenny Wallace	Square D Ford
42	31	77	Bobby Hillin	Jasper Engines/Federal-Mogul Ford
43	42	19	Loy Allen	Child Support Recovery Ford

NASCAR WINSTON CUP SERIES 1997

Pontiac Excitement 400

(Richmond International Raceway • March 2, 1997)

With a pair of come-from-behind victories in the first two races of the season already in the books, Jeff Gordon and his Rainbow Warriors arrived in Virginia's capital city ready to try for the hat trick.

The Daytona and Rockingham victories pushed the DuPont Chevrolet driver into an early 40-point lead over Hendrick Motorsports teammate Ricky Craven. Yes, that's right. Ricky Craven, Ken Schrader's replacement in the Budweiser Chevrolet.

The New Englander has been considered one of the future stars in the sport, but Ricky was letting nothing get in his way as he helped the Budweiser team return to the front of the pack. He had taken a backup car to third at Daytona, and came home a solid fifth at Rockingham, stealing the limelight from the defending NASCAR Winston Cup champion, Terry Labonte, who was in third place after two races, just four points behind the driver of the red-and-white Chevrolet.

(Right) Rusty Wallace sits in his "office" contemplating the start of the Pontiac Excitement 400. After a rough start to the season, Wallace was determined to right his team with a win at Richmond.

(Below) Geoff Bodine (7) and Dale Jarrett flash toward the start/finish line at Richmond in their duel for position during the closing laps. Bodine was finally able to squeeze past to take second at the finish, shuffling Jarrett to third place.

32

The Penske South crew outfits the Miller Ford with fresh rubber after a cut tire and subsequent spin forced Rusty onto pit road for an unexpected early-race pit stop. Rusty returned to the action in 40th place, and began a stirring charge through the field.

Jeff Burton was a surprise near the top of the point ladder, and was in fourth place, 60 points behind Gordon. Ricky Rudd was two points behind Jeff in fifth place, and Mark Martin, Dale Jarrett and Jeremy Mayfield (another surprise in the top 10) were in sixth, seventh and eighth place, respectively. Sterling Marlin and Bill Elliott occupied the final positions in the top 10 after just two races.

Where were the pre-season favorites for the championship? Where were the likes of Ernie Irvan, Dale Earnhardt and Rusty Wallace?

Irvan was the best situated of the group, in 11th place, only 11 points behind Elliott, while Earnhardt and Wallace were mired deep in the standings. Dale was 19th, trying to pull himself from the morass created by his 31st-place finish in the Daytona 500, and Wallace was stuck in 24th place, already 170 points behind Gordon. It was a bitter beginning for Wallace, who had confidently predicted before the start of the year that "this was his season for the taking." So far, it had been a nightmare, other than his second-place finish in the Busch Clash, which paid money, but not points.

Facing their third race in as many weekends, some teams were already making changes within their cast of characters. The trigger had come the previous week, when Andy Graves replaced Phil Hammer as Craven's crew chief, and by the time the teams arrived at Richmond, Philippe Lopez had turned in his Circuit City uniform at the Stavola Brothers team, and had been replaced by Richard Broome as Hut Stricklin's crew chief. TriStar Racing, which had opened the season with two less than pleasing finishes, had accepted the resignation of Loy Allen and signed Gary Bradberry to drive the Child Support Recovery Thunderbirds.

The teams had no real chance to see what difference the changes would make for Busch Pole qualifying, which was rained out. With the field expanded to a maximum of 43 cars, and

OFFICIAL FUEL
NASCAR
76
Miller
RACING
Lite
BOSCH
Rusty Wallace
PPG
Mazak
MATCO TOOLS
BOSS
Mobil
Winston Cup
BUSCH
True Value
Gatorade
Western Auto
FRAM
MOOG
plasti-kote
SIMPSON
RCA
Edelbrock
CLEVITE
EAGLE
Ford

with both Friday and Saturday's sessions washed out, the first 33 positions in the starting lineup were determined by 1996 car owner points.

Had the current owner points been used, Gordon would have started from the inside of the front row, but for the first four races of the new season, the points from the previous year were used to determine provisionals. That meant Terry Labonte would start his Kellogg's Chevrolet from the pole, with Gordon alongside him on the front row, and "The

(Above) Dale Jarrett tucks the nose of his Quality Care Thunderbird under Rusty Wallace's Miller Ford in their fight for the lead. The two drivers battled at the point on several occasions during the race, before Rusty slipped past Dale for good on a restart with just two laps remaining in the race. (Left) With Darrell Waltrip (17) in tow, Rusty Wallace takes to the outside of his old nemesis, Dale Earnhardt (3), who eventually fell three laps off Rusty's pace and finished 25th.

Dales," Jarrett and Earnhardt, would be right behind the two Hendrick drivers.

Mark Martin and Ricky Rudd made up the third row, followed by Wallace and Marlin. Bobby Hamilton and Irvan completed the top 10.

The problem for some teams — particularly the newest members of the NASCAR Winston Cup family — came at the bottom end of the field. Positions 34-43 were determined by entry form postmarks, and when the pile was sorted through, Mike Wallace, Greg Sacks and Billy Standridge had missed the race. The three drivers had sat patiently through the driving and misting rain for two days, never turning a lap in their cars.

On the other hand, the postmarks were kind to Kyle Petty, David Green, Mike Skinner and Derrike Cope, while Bradberry and Chad Little sat sweating, waiting to see if their teams had made the cut. They did, barely. Little gained the 42nd starting position, while Bradberry's debut with the TriStar team would come from the final position in the field.

The irony of the situation was that if Bud Moore had entered and arrived at the track with his Ford team, he would have made the field without having to turn a qualifying lap. His owner's points from 1996 would have put his Thunderbird into the field, but the team remained in Spartanburg, S.C., still searching for corporate sponsorship that would return the team to competition.

The weather cleared enough Saturday afternoon for the NASCAR Busch Series event — but it took a while for it to happen. The Hardee's Fried Chicken Challenge 250 finally started 56 minutes late, and for the thousands who braved the weather to watch, the closing laps were worth the wait. Jason Keller and Jeff Burton, racing for the victory, collided exiting the fourth turn headed for the white flag and both drivers spun into the inside of the frontstretch. That collision opened the door for Mark Martin to win his second straight NASCAR Busch Series race and the 28th of his career.

After Saturday's late-race fireworks, the Richmond faithful had plenty of reason to turn out in enormous numbers for the 400-lapper on Paul Sawyer's three-quarter-mile track. They expected action in every corner of the track — and they got it in the form of a Miller Lite Ford that was forced to fight all the way from the very back of the pack.

Rusty Wallace spun in the early going when he cut a tire on the sixth lap and fell to 40th in the field. After a pit stop, it took him the first 100 laps of the race to work his way back to the top 10. Once there, he ripped and snorted his way to the front, and took the lead on lap 159.

36

But Jarrett, after commanding most of the Rockingham event, had other ideas, and he moved back to lead the field. After the race ran through nearly 300 laps of green-flag racing, only Wallace, Jarrett and Geoff Bodine remained on the lead lap to challenge for the victory. When the third and final yellow of the event waved with just seven laps remaining, the three leaders staged a frantic run for the yellow flag, thinking that Irvan's wreck had essentially ended the race. Jarrett won the dash by a fender, with Wallace barely ahead of Bodine. The cleanup, however, was speedy, and the field got the "one-to-go" signal, and rumbled under the green flag with three laps remaining in the event.

Wallace managed to get the momentum he needed and rocketed past Jarrett on the inside as the field flashed under the flagstand to take the green. The move caught Jarrett by surprise and by the time he had reacted, Rusty was gone. Try as they did, neither Jarrett nor Bodine could catch the Miller Lite Ford, although Bodine managed to squeak past Jarrett for second place, nearly a half-second behind Wallace. Gordon, a lap behind, finished fourth, ahead of Hamilton, Rudd and Terry Labonte. Bobby Labonte, Johnny Benson and Kyle Petty claimed the final positions in the top 10.

A triumphant Wallace emerges from his car in victory lane after a well-earned — and much-needed — win. His sixth career victory at Richmond tied him with Darrell Waltrip for the lead among active drivers at the Virginia short track.

Wallace was jubilant in victory lane. He had fought all the way through the field and had managed to pull off a pass for victory in the final laps. It was his first win of the season and the 47th of his career.

Or was it?

During the post-race inspection, the compression ratio in Rusty's hot engine was found to be larger than the allowable 14:1, and NASCAR officials impounded the motor. The results of the race were determined to be unofficial pending notification from NASCAR, which came the following day. After the engine cooled, the compression ratio was found to fit the guidelines, NASCAR officials said, making the results of the Pontiac Excitement 400 official. The victory was Wallace's to savor.

Pontiac Excitement 400

Fin. Pos.	Start Pos.	Car #	Driver	Team
1	7	2	Rusty Wallace	Miller Lite Ford
2	18	7	Geoff Bodine	QVC Ford
3	3	88	Dale Jarrett	Quality Care/Ford Credit Ford
4	2	24	Jeff Gordon	DuPont Refinishes Chevrolet
5	9	43	Bobby Hamilton	STP Pontiac
6	6	10	Ricky Rudd	Tide Ford
7	1	5	Terry Labonte	Kellogg's Corn Flakes Chevrolet
8	11	18	Bobby Labonte	Interstate Batteries Pontiac
9	23	30	Johnny Benson	Pennzoil Pontiac
10	37	44	Kyle Petty	Hot Wheels Pontiac
11	21	41	Steve Grissom	Kodiak Chevrolet
12	26	9	Lake Speed	Melling Engine Parts Ford
13	5	6	Mark Martin	Valvoline Ford
14	12	25	Ricky Craven	Budweiser Chevrolet
15	17	94	Bill Elliott	McDonald's Ford
16	30	17	Darrell Waltrip	Parts America Chevrolet
17	33	37	Jeremy Mayfield	Kmart/RC Cola Ford
18	20	75	Rick Mast	Remington Arms Ford
19	8	4	Sterling Marlin	Kodak Film Chevrolet
20	16	16	Ted Musgrave	Family Channel/PRIMESTAR Ford
21	39	29	Robert Pressley	Cartoon Network Chevrolet
22	15	23	Jimmy Spencer	Camel Cigarettes Ford
23	27	11	Brett Bodine	Close Call Phone Card Ford
24	31	22	Ward Burton	MBNA America Pontiac
25	4	3	Dale Earnhardt	GM Goodwrench Service Chevrolet
26	36	31	Mike Skinner	Lowe's Chevrolet
27	14	21	Michael Waltrip	CITGO Ford
28	24	40	Robby Gordon	Coors Light Chevrolet
29	40	90	Dick Trickle	Heilig-Meyers Ford
30	38	36	Derrike Cope	Skittles Pontiac
31	22	98	John Andretti	RCA Ford
32	25	8	Hut Stricklin	Circuit City Ford
33	41	96	David Green	Caterpillar Chevrolet
34	42	97	Chad Little	John Deere Pontiac
35	28	33	Ken Schrader	Skoal Bandit Chevrolet
36	10	28	Ernie Irvan	Texaco Havoline Ford
37	34	71	Dave Marcis	Realtree Camouflage Chevrolet
38	43	19	Gary Bradberry	Child Support Recovery Ford
39	32	42	Joe Nemechek	BellSouth Chevrolet
40	29	81	Kenny Wallace	Square D Ford
41	35	77	Bobby Hillin	Jasper Engines/Federal-Mogul Ford
42	13	99	Jeff Burton	Exide Batteries Ford
43	19	1	Morgan Shepherd	Delco Remy Pontiac

NASCAR WINSTON CUP SERIES 1997

PRIMESTAR 500

(Atlanta Motor Speedway • March 9, 1997)

Everyone in the garage area agreed that it was just a matter of time before all the chips fell into place and Dale Jarrett rolled into the 1997 winner's circle. He had been second twice in NASCAR Busch Series events this year, and had finished second at Rockingham and third at Richmond after showing that his Quality Care/Ford Credit Thunderbird was the class of the field in each event.

The second generation driver had dominated both those events, seemingly at will, but Jeff Gordon had found a way in the closing laps to win at Rockingham. Richmond had been a lesson that Jarrett firmly said would not be forgotten, and any hopes Rusty Wallace had of lagging back, getting a running start and zapping the leader at the line on the restart were now gone. Jarrett noted that he had been raised in the "fool me once, shame on you; fool me twice, shame on me" line of thinking, and once had been more than enough for him.

(Left) Dale Jarrett displays the winner's trophy with some help from his dad, former two-time NASCAR Champion Ned Jarrett, also a former winner at Atlanta. After dominating the previous two races, Jarrett finally posted his first win of the season, and jumped to the top of the point standings.

(Right) Robby Gordon (40) smokes off pit road during an early-race caution. Gordon led most of the early laps, before Jarrett assumed the lead on lap 51.

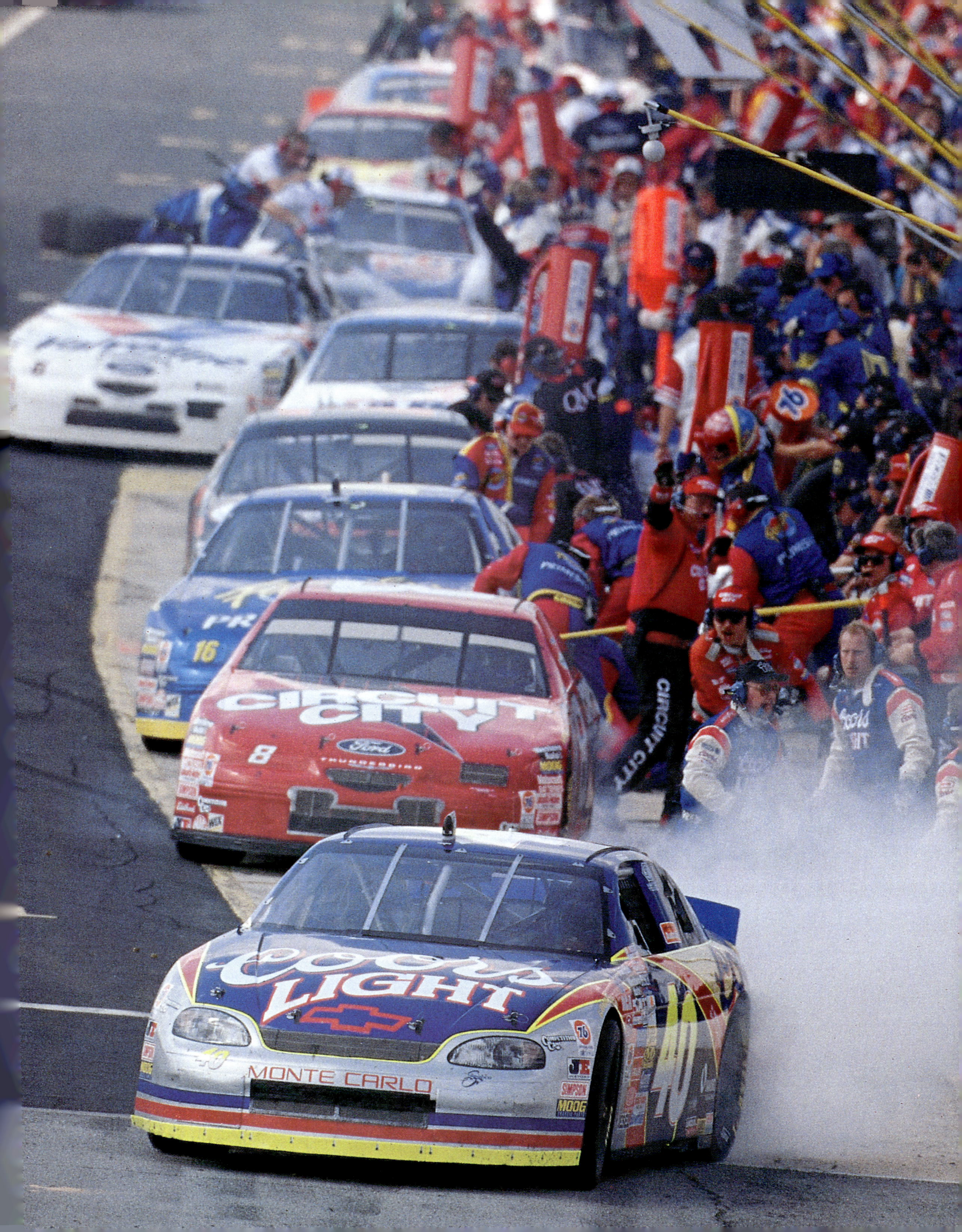
Coors
LIGHT
MONTE CARLO
40
CIRCUIT CITY
Ford
8
16

(Above) The starting field lines up for a historic photo on Atlanta Motor Speedway's start/finish line. THE PRIMESTAR 500 would be the last time the track would be used in its current configuration, with remodeling scheduled to begin immediately after the event. *(Below)* Robby Gordon displays the pole-winner's award after winning his first career NASCAR Winston Cup pole position with a blistering lap around the 1.522-mile oval, setting a track record at 186.507 miles per hour.

The PRIMESTAR 500 weekend marked the end of an era at Atlanta Motor Speedway. During the summer months, the long-awaited "flip-flop" of the track would occur, with the current frontstretch becoming the backstretch. Speedway president Ed Clark had his hands full. A new pit and garage area were ready to be built, and new grandstands, corporate hospitality suites, a press box, a media center, a Goodyear tire center and numerous other support buildings were all on the blueprints for construction between the drop of the checkered flag in March and the November season finale. Atlanta Motor Speedway employees would have little time to swing a golf club this summer.

The track had originally opened for business with a pair of races in 1960, and for the majority of the last four decades, had been one of the fastest on the circuit. The half-mile corners and quarter-mile straights sent cars whistling around the track, and the sustained speeds make the average laps among the fastest on the tour. The new track, similar in shape and appearance to Charlotte Motor Speedway, would mean a slight decrease in those speeds, but Atlanta would still be a handful for drivers and teams.

Jeff Gordon's fourth place at Richmond, and the finishes of his nearest competitors, had allowed the 1995 NASCAR Winston Cup champion to extend his lead to 63 points over teammate Terry Labonte. The strong finishes in the last two races by Jarrett had pulled the Ford driver into third place on the point ladder entering Atlanta. Ricky Rudd had moved to fourth place, and Ricky Craven had fallen to fifth following Richmond. Mark Martin and Bill Elliott continued to move toward the top five, and Geoff Bodine's superb second place at Richmond had helped

Robby Gordon and Mark Martin (6) pace the field from the front row as 42 cars rumble toward the green flag to start the race.

him move to eighth place in the standings, ahead of Jeremy Mayfield and a surging Rusty Wallace.

Dale Earnhardt, struggling early in the season after his late-race Daytona 500 accident, was 25th in the standings and hoped his luck would turn at Atlanta.

In the days between Richmond and Atlanta, NASCAR officials announced that Chad Little and Robby Gordon had been fined $10,000 and $5,000, respectively, for their late-race actions at Richmond. The two drivers had collided in the third turn on the final lap, and Little's John Deere Pontiac smacked the wall. On the "cool down" lap, Little whacked Gordon's Coors Chevrolet, and Robby drilled him in return. The altercation was costly for both drivers, who disagreed on what happened but agreed to put it behind them.

The famed road course at Watkins Glen, after years of working within a joint management program with International Speedway Corporation and Corning, Inc., became the sole property of ISC when the speedway management company exercised its option to purchase the property. The management would remain intact, and The Glen joined Daytona, Talladega, Darlington, MRN Radio, Daytona USA and 12 percent of Penske Motorsports, Inc., as part of the ISC portfolio.

Philippe Lopez, who left the Stavola Brothers team prior to the Richmond race, found himself working for Dale and Teresa Earnhardt, leading the development of the Earnhardts' new NASCAR Winston Cup team that is expected to campaign the entire circuit in 1998.

With all of this happening within a matter of days and with 49 cars on hand attempting to qualify for the race, it was easy to overlook the fact that a rookie driver was among the fastest on the track during the practice sessions at Atlanta. The same thing had happened last spring when Johnny

41

Benson surprised everyone in the garage area by claiming the Atlanta pole in his Pennzoil Pontiac. This year, Gordon won the pole.

Not that Gordon. The other one.

Under sunny skies, Robby Gordon drove his way to the first NASCAR Winston Cup pole of his career, and the first for SABCO Racing since 1990.

On Gordon's right for the start of the race was Mark Martin, with Darrell Waltrip and Dick Trickle sending another shock wave through the garage by claiming the second row of the grid. Hut Stricklin and Lake Speed continued the surprises by notching laps good for fifth and sixth place, and Ted Musgrave and Geoff Bodine nailed down the fourth row starting slots. Jarrett and Kenny Wallace completed the top 10 after the first round of qualifying, and Billy Standridge and Jimmy Spencer barely missed the mark and had to settle for the sixth row.

The rest of the hotshoes — Jeff Gordon, Terry Labonte, Rusty Wallace, Dale Earnhardt and Ricky Rudd — were farther back in the field. In the case of Earnhardt, way farther back. The GM Goodwrench Chevrolet driver's speed in the first

*(Above) Dale Jarrett (88) leads a pack of Fords consisting of Hut Stricklin, Ernie Irvan, Jeff Burton, Mark Martin and Dick Trickle, all bearing down on race-leader Robby Gordon in the early stages of the event. (**Left**) Jeff Burton (99) tries to gain position on the inside of Terry Labonte (5) as they flash down the frontstretch. Burton would post his second top-five finish of the young season. (**Below Left**) The DuPont crew pushes their Monte Carlo to the garage after the engine let go just 59 laps into the race. The resulting last-place finish dropped Gordon from first to fourth in the point standings.*

session was only good enough for 43rd place. He improved enough on the second day to claim the second-round bonus from Busch Beer and would start 26th on the grid. Steve Grissom, who had claimed the outside pole at Daytona, needed a provisional to make the Atlanta field, as did last year's pole-sitter Johnny Benson. Brett Bodine and Joe Nemechek also used provisionals, sending Robert Pressley, Derrike Cope, Bobby Hillin, Wally Dallenbach, Ed Berrier, Dave Marcis and Mike Miller home.

The final race on the old configuration of Atlanta Motor Speedway took the green flag Sunday afternoon, and the pole-sitter surprised many in attendance by leading 40 of the first 50 laps of the race. Most had expected the rookie to fade quickly, but Robby had plenty of car —

(Top) What's left of Steve Grissom's Kodiak Chevrolet arrives in the garage area after a spectacular crash that included Jimmy Spencer and Kenny Wallace. Grissom was unhurt in the incident, but the red flag was thrown while repairs were made to the wall. *(Above)* During the red-flag delay, the Tide crew takes the opportunity to relax and enjoy some ice cream.

and race savvy. On the 51st lap, Jarrett found a lane and moved past the Coors Monte Carlo, and while he moved to a comfortable lead, the attention of the crowd shifted to Jeff Gordon's DuPont Chevrolet, which peeled off and headed for the garage after just 59 laps. An uncharacteristic engine failure put the point leader last in the race results, and Jarrett's radio came alive in his ear. Crew chief Todd Parrott reported the Gordon incident, and reminded his driver that this was a golden opportunity to strike.

Dale heeded the advice. He put on another overpowering show during the remainder of the race, leading 253 of the 328 laps. For the third straight race, his was the dominant car in the field, but staying up front wasn't as easy as it looked. On lap 191, the coil in the primary ignition system failed, and Jarrett started flicking switches on the backup ignition system. The car refired, damaging a header pipe when it did, but the Robert Yates engine took the beating. Later in the race, Jarrett and the other drivers had to sit and wait for a 52-minute red flag brought out by Steve Grissom's accident, which damaged the inside of the second turn wall. After the restart, Jarrett had to fight off determined charges by teammate Ernie Irvan and Morgan Shepherd, but when the event was completed, the Quality Care/Ford Credit Ford was in victory lane for the first time this season.

Bobby Labonte finished fourth and Jeff Burton was fifth, ahead of Mark Martin and Michael Waltrip, who had his best run of the season with the Wood Brothers' CITGO Ford. Earnhardt fought his way to a solid eighth place, and he was beginning to feel the team was making headway. Now, if he could just find the key to qualifying. Terry Labonte and Bobby Hamilton claimed the ninth and 10th spots, and Johnny Benson was 11th, the final car on the lead lap.

Jarrett was proud of his accomplishment — he finally had won at the same place where his father, Ned, had won the 1964 running of the Dixie 400 in a Ford owned by Bondy Long.

PRIMESTAR 500

Fin. Pos.	Start Pos.	Car #	Driver	Team
1	9	88	Dale Jarrett	Quality Care/Ford Credit Ford
2	17	28	Ernie Irvan	Texaco Havoline Ford
3	21	1	Morgan Shepherd	Delco Remy America Pontiac
4	29	18	Bobby Labonte	Interstate Batteries Pontiac
5	27	99	Jeff Burton	Exide Batteries Ford
6	2	6	Mark Martin	Valvoline Ford
7	31	21	Michael Waltrip	CITGO Ford
8	26	3	Dale Earnhardt	GM Goodwrench Service Chevrolet
9	22	5	Terry Labonte	Kellogg's Corn Flakes Chevrolet
10	18	43	Bobby Hamilton	STP Pontiac
11	40	30	Johnny Benson	Pennzoil Pontiac
12	36	22	Ward Burton	MBNA America Pontiac
13	30	44	Kyle Petty	Hot Wheels Pontiac
14	1	40	Robby Gordon	Coors Light Chevrolet
15	33	98	John Andretti	RCA Ford
16	3	17	Darrell Waltrip	Parts America Chevrolet
17	16	75	Rick Mast	Remington Arms Ford
18	41	11	Brett Bodine	Close Call Phone Card Ford
19	32	97	Chad Little	John Deere Pontiac
20	8	7	Geoff Bodine	QVC Ford
21	24	31	Mike Skinner	Lowe's Chevrolet
22	6	9	Lake Speed	Melling Engine Parts Ford
23	20	4	Sterling Marlin	Kodak Film Chevrolet
24	19	96	David Green	Caterpillar Chevrolet
25	35	33	Ken Schrader	Skoal Bandit Chevrolet
26	37	91	Mike Wallace	Spam Chevrolet
27	28	20	Greg Sacks	Hardee's Ford
28	4	90	Dick Trickle	Heilig-Meyers/Simmons Ford
29	10	81	Kenny Wallace	Square D Ford
30	25	10	Ricky Rudd	Tide Ford
31	38	2	Rusty Wallace	Miller Lite Ford
32	12	23	Jimmy Spencer	Camel Cigarettes Ford
33	39	41	Steve Grissom	Kodiak Chevrolet
34	7	16	Ted Musgrave	Family Channel/PRIMESTAR Ford
35	13	25	Ricky Craven	Budweiser Chevrolet
36	11	78	Billy Standridge	Diamond Rio/Hanes Ford
37	14	37	Jeremy Mayfield	Kmart/RC Cola Ford
38	15	94	Bill Elliott	McDonald's Ford
39	42	42	Joe Nemechek	BellSouth Chevrolet
40	34	19	Gary Bradberry	Child Support Recovery Ford
41	5	8	Hut Stricklin	Circuit City Ford
42	23	24	Jeff Gordon	DuPont Refinishes Chevrolet

NASCAR WINSTON CUP SERIES 1997

TranSouth Financial 400

(Darlington Raceway • March 23, 1997)

For the second time in as many races, competitors rolled into the parking areas in the infield of a track knowing that this would be the final time they would compete on a pioneer superspeedway in its current configuration.

At Atlanta in the last race, Dale Jarrett finally took his red-white-and-blue Ford to victory lane for the first time this season. The victory, coupled with the engine failure in Jeff Gordon's DuPont Chevrolet that left the 1995 champion in the garage area and in last place in the race results, combined to push Jarrett to the top of the NASCAR Winston Cup point ladder. Gordon fell like a rock in a well, ending up fourth in the standings after the Atlanta race.

Jarrett's lead was 29 markers over Terry Labonte as the crew members began working on their mounts prior to the first practice session. Mark Martin's sixth place at Atlanta had helped pull him into third place, two points ahead of Gordon and 70 behind Jarrett.

Bobby Labonte had grabbed fifth place in points, ahead of Ricky Rudd and Ricky Craven, with Jeff Burton, Bobby Hamilton and Geoff Bodine completing the top 10.

(Right) Currently the hottest crew chief/driver combination on the circuit, Todd Parrott and Dale Jarrett, review their notes going into the TranSouth 400. The team had dominated the previous three events and was fresh off a win at Atlanta.

(Below) Dale Jarrett takes the checkered flag ahead of Ted Musgrave (16) to score his second straight victory. Jarrett, who started from the pole, also led the most laps for the fourth consecutive race.

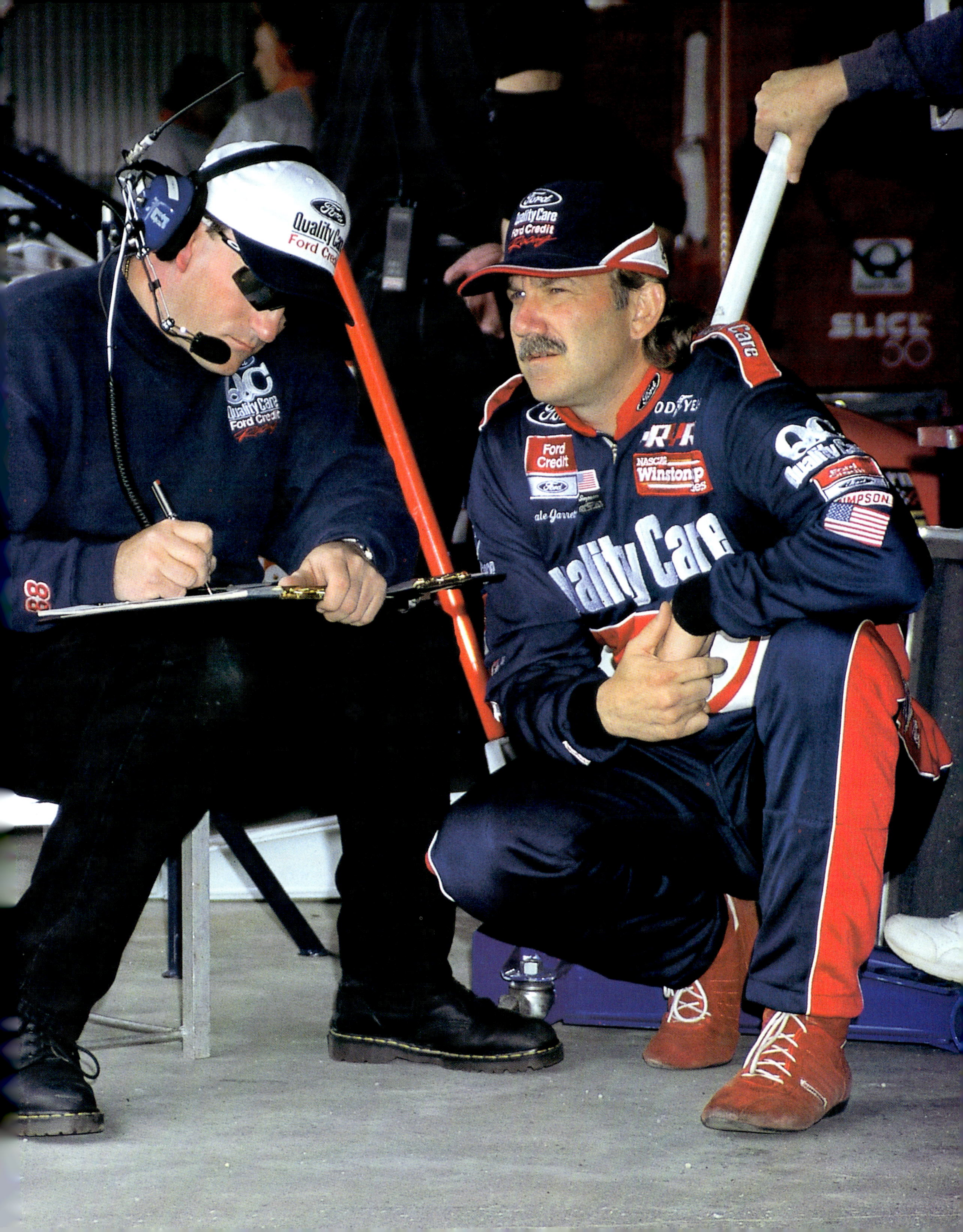
Quality Care
Ford Credit
Ford Credit
SLICK 50

Leonard Wood guides a fresh motor into place in the engine bay of the CITGO Ford.

The coming changes for Darlington, the original superspeedway that boasts a tradition like no other track on the circuit, were similar to those at Atlanta. The track was built next to a main road, and there was little parking available for the fans sitting in the frontstretch grandstands. The majority of parking was available behind the backstretch grandstands, and work was ongoing to "flip-flop" the track in time for the Mountain Dew Southern 500 during Labor Day weekend. This race marked the last time the teams would use the current garage area and the final time the media would use the tiny, cramped infield media center. Both would be state-of-the-art facilities in September.

*(**Left**) The side of Kenny Wallace's Square D Ford clearly illustrates what's known as a "Darlington stripe." (**Below**) Dale Jarrett leads the field through turn two on a restart after one of the race's 10 caution periods, as Greg Sacks (20) tries to regain a lap on the inside.*

Dale Jarrett, Ricky Craven, Bobby Labonte, Geoff Bodine and Mark Martin line up on pit road in the same order in which they qualified. Jarrett gets the jump out of the pits to take the lead, a position he would not relinquish for the remainder of the race.

As far as Jeff Gordon was concerned, the track's management could leave the egg-shaped oval just the way it was. He strolled into the garage area as the winner of the last three NASCAR Winston Cup events at the track, including back-to-back Mountain Dew Southern 500s. Leave Darlington alone, he said with his smile. The track had been good to him.

But in the history of the oval, no driver has put his name in the record books at Darlington as many times as Dale Earnhardt has. He has won nine NASCAR Winston Cup events at Darlington — and in that category, trails only David Pearson, who posted 10 NASCAR Winston Cup victories there in his legendary career. But Earnhardt had also toted home the trophies from three NASCAR Busch Series victories at the track, making it an even dozen pieces of hardware in his trophy room from the speedway.

The seven-time NASCAR Winston Cup champion came to the track hoping it would be the site of his return to the front of the pack. He had struggled throughout the first four races and, although he had a gut-wrenching desire to win, there were many theories circulating about why the black Chevrolet was not dominating the way it had in the past. They ranged from crew chief Larry McReynolds' lack of career work with Chevrolets to the changes within the GM Goodwrench team to an aerodynamic edge many claimed the Ford teams had developed over the Monte Carlos. Earnhardt's desire to win was never doubted.

What had been forgotten in the span of four races was the outstanding run Dale had posted until the closing laps of the Daytona 500. He had been in a position to challenge for victory in the event he

Robert Pressley loops the Cartoon Network Monte Carlo as Jeff Burton (99) scoots by in turn three. This was the first of two mishaps for Pressley, who led briefly early in the event.

had never won, and was taken out in an accident that also damaged the chances of both Jarrett and Ernie Irvan, and opened the door to Gordon's victory.

Had Earnhardt not been involved in the accident, he certainly would have finished in the top three or four in the race — if he didn't win it — and the season would have been off to a great start. Instead he finished 31st at Daytona, was in a deep hole in the points after a single race, and had struggled since, although he had moved up to 16th place in the standings. Nearly everyone in the garage area at Darlington pointed to the "3" when asked who would be a favorite on Sunday. There is no denying Dale's brilliant work had turned the difficult track into his personal playground over the years.

As the cars rolled out for the first practice session, the Miller Lite Ford sat waiting for its driver. Rusty Wallace decided to fly to Darlington instead of making the two-hour drive from Charlotte, and when he left, he knew that the Florence, S.C., airport was reporting fog. He figured he would fly down, circle around for a little while, and wait for the early spring fog to burn off. Then he could land at the airport a few miles from the track, and zip over with plenty of time to prepare for the first practice session.

Unfortunately, the fog didn't dissipate according to his plan. After circling for a while, Rusty looked at his watch and called the Fayetteville, N.C., airport, the nearest one that was open. He also called for a rental car to be waiting for him when he got there. It took him an hour to negotiate the road between the airport and the track, and he arrived with the practice session already 30 minutes old.

Wallace quickly dialed into the car, and by the time the Busch Pole qualifying session began, Rusty had hopes he would be able to snatch a top-five starting position. It was not to be, however, as Rusty circled the track with a lap that was good enough for only the 15th spot on the starting grid.

Dale Jarrett was the driver who had everything right in his Quality Care/Ford Credit Ford, and zipped to his second straight Darlington pole. Jarrett's lap was a mere .008 seconds faster than Craven's run in the Budweiser Chevrolet, and both drivers needed to pull out all the stops to beat the lap turned by Bobby Labonte and his Interstate Batteries Pontiac. Geoff Bodine had a strong run to the fourth-fastest lap, while the third row was comprised of Roush Racing teammates Mark Martin and Jeff Burton. Hut Stricklin had another good qualifying run to put the Circuit City Ford on the inside of the fourth row, with Irvan on his right, and Sterling Marlin was ninth fastest. Gordon, who bobbled slightly in the second turn during his qualifying run, was 10th.

Mike Wallace ripped his way to his best qualifying lap of the year to claim the 17th-fastest time, ahead of Bill Elliott and his McDonald's Ford.

(Left) The Exide crew swarms Jeff Burton's Ford during a stop under green. With their help, Burton completed another impressive run, finishing fourth in the race and jumping from eighth to fifth in the point standings. (Below) Jimmy Spencer leads a pack that includes (in order) Jeremy Mayfield, Michael Waltrip, Johnny Benson and John Andretti.

Mike Wallace smacks the fourth-turn wall with his Spam Chevrolet, bringing out the race's third caution on lap 28. Kenny Wallace (81) jumps on the binders to avoid becoming involved and gets a nudge from Rick Mast (75), while Phil Parsons (42), subbing for Joe Nemechek, drops low and escapes unscathed.

Earnhardt was struggling once again with the qualifying setup on his GM Goodwrench Chevrolet. Dale eventually chose to use a former champion's provisional for the first time since the fall 1995 Charlotte race, and he signed on to start 43rd in the field. Bobby Hamilton, Ward Burton, Darrell Waltrip and Rick Mast also used provisionals to get into the field, the first time that current car owner points were used this year to determine the order of those using provisionals. Dick Trickle, who had been fourth on the grid at Atlanta, failed to make the field, as did Billy Standridge and Steve Grissom.

Jarrett rolled away at the point on Sunday afternoon, and once again put his Robert Yates Ford in the wind, establishing himself as the driver to beat in the race. But in an eerie moment almost exactly like the incident that ended his chase last September for the Winston Million, Jarrett slipped in oil in the third turn and clipped the wall. This time, it wasn't as serious, although Dale was forced to fall back into the top-10 pack and bide his time. His break came on lap 165, when his team turned him off pit road in the lead — and he led every lap for the remainder of the race.

It sounds like an easy victory, but the reality was that it was one of the most hard-fought of Dale's career. His crew kept him at the point with a crucial pit stop during the final caution of the event, but Ted Musgrave emerged to plant himself doggedly on Jarrett's tail and give Dale everything he could handle in the closing laps. In the final 10 circuits, Jarrett's worn tires left him manhandling the Ford to keep it in the lead, and he chopped Musgrave at every opportunity to keep the PRIMESTAR Thunderbird behind him. His victory was barely more than a car-length, and his second straight win bolstered his point lead.

Behind Musgrave, Gordon came home third, and Jeff Burton continued his strong performances with a solid run to fourth place, ahead of Bobby Labonte. Rusty rolled to a sixth-place finish, ahead of Michael Waltrip and Ken Schrader, while Geoff Bodine was ninth and Johnny Benson was 10th. Earnhardt, looking for a jump-start to his season, didn't find it, finishing 15th, a lap behind.

TranSouth Financial 400

Fin. Pos.	Start Pos.	Car #	Driver	Team
1	1	88	Dale Jarrett	Quality Care/Ford Credit Ford
2	21	16	Ted Musgrave	Family Channel/PRIMESTAR Ford
3	10	24	Jeff Gordon	DuPont Refinishes Chevrolet
4	6	99	Jeff Burton	Exide Batteries Ford
5	3	18	Bobby Labonte	Interstate Batteries Pontiac
6	15	2	Rusty Wallace	Miller Lite Ford
7	27	21	Michael Waltrip	CITGO Ford
8	13	33	Ken Schrader	Skoal Bandit Chevrolet
9	4	7	Geoff Bodine	QVC Ford
10	36	30	Johnny Benson	Pennzoil Pontiac
11	41	17	Darrell Waltrip	Parts America Chevrolet
12	23	1	Morgan Shepherd	Delco Remy America Pontiac
13	12	5	Terry Labonte	Kellogg's Corn Flakes Chevrolet
14	30	81	Kenny Wallace	Square D Ford
15	43	3	Dale Earnhardt	GM Goodwrench Service Chevrolet
16	18	94	Bill Elliott	McDonald's Ford
17	19	37	Jeremy Mayfield	Kmart/RC Cola Ford
18	40	22	Ward Burton	MBNA America Pontiac
19	42	75	Rick Mast	Remington Arms Ford
20	25	36	Derrike Cope	Skittles Pontiac
21	8	28	Ernie Irvan	Texaco Havoline Ford
22	26	23	Jimmy Spencer	Camel Cigarettes Ford
23	16	10	Ricky Rudd	Tide Ford
24	5	6	Mark Martin	Valvoline Ford
25	33	98	John Andretti	RCA Ford
26	7	8	Hut Stricklin	Circuit City Ford
27	32	97	Chad Little	John Deere Pontiac
28	20	71	Dave Marcis	Realtree Camouflage Chevrolet
29	24	20	Greg Sacks	Hardee's Ford
30	34	31	Mike Skinner	Lowe's Chevrolet
31	29	42	Phil Parsons	BellSouth Chevrolet
32	9	4	Sterling Marlin	Kodak Film Chevrolet
33	28	44	Kyle Petty	Hot Wheels Pontiac
34	38	40	Robby Gordon	Coors Light Chevrolet
35	31	11	Brett Bodine	Close Call Phone Card Ford
36	11	9	Lake Speed	Melling Engine Parts Ford
37	39	43	Bobby Hamilton	STP Pontiac
38	14	19	Gary Bradberry	Child Support Recovery Ford
39	35	29	Robert Pressley	Cartoon Network Chevrolet
40	2	25	Ricky Craven	Budweiser Chevrolet
41	22	96	David Green	Caterpillar Chevrolet
42	37	77	Bobby Hillin	Jasper Engines/Federal-Mogul Ford
43	17	91	Mike Wallace	Spam Chevrolet

Interstate Batteries 500

(Texas Motor Speedway • April 6, 1997)

When teams found their way from Dallas and Ft. Worth to the speed palace rising in a field near Interstate 35, almost two years had passed since the formal groundbreaking was held for Bruton Smith's new Texas Motor Speedway.

During those two years, the massive construction project had progressed from the earthmoving mode to a nearly finished product that promised to be state of the art in every way. And it was, but Mother Nature decided to test the mettle of the tens of thousands of fans who turned out to see the first NASCAR Winston Cup race in Texas since 1981.

It was almost perfect. The facility gleamed, the garage area was superb, the attention to detail was outstanding. Then the rain came.

This was not a normal, misting shower. It was a frog-choker that went on and on, hour after hour, and turned the acreage around the track intended for parking into a quagmire. Despite management's outstanding efforts, including importing hundreds of tons of gravel and running shuttle busses to and from other parking lots, the traffic was a nightmare. Fans parked anywhere they could. It was testimony to the faith of the fans and their love for the sport, that they would find a way to get to the track, even if it meant walking a good distance along the highway.

(Left) The Wood Brothers crew rolls their CITGO Ford, in qualifying trim, through the garage area on Thursday morning. Unfortunately, they would not have a chance to qualify, as rain pounded the vicinity throughout most of the weekend.

(Right) Jeff Burton is chased by (in order) Chad Little, Dale Jarrett, Jeff Gordon and Terry Labonte in a single file draft on the new 1.5-mile superspeedway.

DU PONT
Quality Care
JOHN DEERE
EXIDE
BATTERIES
Ford
ROUSH RACING
99

A crowd of more than 150,000 cheer wildly as the NASCAR Winston Cup cars roar through the frontstretch after taking the green flag to start the Interstate Batteries 500. The field lined up according to 1997 owner points after rain washed out qualifying.

A year from now, when the NASCAR Winston Cup teams return, the episode will have been forgotten. The sodded grass will have grown in, the roads will do their job of moving traffic, the facility will be totally completed, and everyone will chuckle as they play "remember when?"

After winning two-on-the-trot, Dale Jarrett brought his 87-point lead in the point standings over Jeff Gordon to the 1.5-mile quad-oval, and the Labonte brothers, Terry and Bobby, were proud to return to their native state in third and fourth place, respectively. For Bobby, this race provided the opportunity to show off the special paint scheme honoring Texas on his Interstate Batteries Pontiac. At the same time, the heat was on car owner Joe Gibbs and his crew. Interstate Batteries sponsored the inaugural race, and the company's corporate headquarters is in Dallas.

Jeff Burton held down fifth place in the point standings, ahead of Mark Martin, Geoff Bodine and Ricky Rudd. Rusty Wallace finally had cracked the top 10 and held ninth place. Ernie Irvan was 10th, just ahead of Ted Musgrave, who had used his second place at Darlington to move up in the standings.

Jarrett and the rest of the Cup regulars found themselves the focus of a week-long celebration of speed in the Ft. Worth area, ranging from downtown street festivals to charity fund-raisers at Billy Bob's, one of the most famous attractions in Texas. Thursday morning, it appeared that the weather would at least cooperate with the teams, and allowed a Busch Pole qualifying session that would sort the starters from the 51 cars on hand to battle for the maximum 43 positions in the rich, $3.8-million race.

But 10 minutes before the scheduled start of the first qualifying session, the rains began, and when they finally abated two days later, more than five inches of water had fallen on the track and the sur-

John Andretti waits out the rain in the garage area, hoping to get some meaningful practice time in before racing on the new track for the first time.

rounding area. The fields planned for parking became unusable, and tractors and tow trucks began pulling stranded cars from the muck. In the garage area, the competitors stood by, unable to make a single qualifying lap. Saturday, the rain stopped, and it appeared there would be one round of qualifying, but those plans changed when many competitors lobbied for practice time in hopes of getting their cars dialed in to help present a competitive race on Sunday.

That decision meant for the second time this year, the starting field would be determined by car owner points and race entry postmarks. The top 35 cars were allocated positions according to the car owner points accumulated in the first five races of the season, and the final eight places were awarded according to the postmarks on the entry forms the teams had returned to NASCAR officials.

Bobby Labonte shows off the commemorative paint scheme on his Pontiac, honoring his team's sponsor, Interstate Batteries, who also sponsored the inaugural event.

53

Dale Earnhardt muscles the Goodwrench Chevrolet ahead of Dale Jarrett and Ward Burton. Despite front-end damage suffered on the first lap of the race, Earnhardt drove to a sixth-place finish, his best of the season, with Burton right behind him in seventh.

Those who didn't make the field included Robert Pressley, Ed Berrier, Randy LaJoie, David Green, Mike Bliss in ASE Racing's Ford, Gary Bradberry, Rick Wilson in David Blair's Ford, Wally Dallenbach, and H.B. Bailey, who had hoped to start in the inaugural race in his native Texas.

The Coca-Cola 300 became the first competitive race on the new track, and when it was over, Mark Martin had streaked to his fourth NASCAR Busch Series victory in six 1997 starts. It was the 30th NASCAR Busch Series victory in Mark's career, and the triumph moved him to within one of tying Jack Ingram for the most career victories in the history of the series. While hoisting the trophy, Mark also hoped the experience gained on the tight-cornered track would do him good in the upcoming NASCAR Winston Cup race.

With three top-five finishes in the last four races, someone should have been paying attention to the Exide Batteries team and driver Jeff Burton. Instead of walking around the garage area beating their chests with pride, however, the Buddy Parrott-led crew simply went about

(Right) *Hendrick drivers Terry Labonte and Jeff Gordon team up to put the pressure on Geoff Bodine (7) in the early stages of the event. Gordon would finish in 30th place after being involved in an accident, and dropped from second to fifth in the standings.* **(Below)** *The field had yet to complete one lap when this 13-car incident ensued in the middle of the pack. Darrell Waltrip's chrome Monte Carlo (17) got the worst of it, forcing the three-time champion out of the race in 43rd place.*

their jobs quietly, knowing they had a horse capable of running at the front, given the right circumstances.

On Sunday, those circumstances all came into play. Dale Jarrett struggled with no third gear or clutch. Ernie Irvan took himself out in a hard crash with Greg Sacks, as he tried to make up a lost lap in a frantic run to the yellow flag. Earnhardt was involved in a first-lap accident and had to fight furiously to come home sixth with a strong driving performance. Jeff Gordon was involved in the Irvan-Sacks conflagration. Bill Elliott's McDonald's Ford was involved in the first-lap accident that included Earnhardt, Darrell Waltrip and others. Todd Bodine, substituting for Ricky Craven after his Darlington accident, had the tools to win and ran at the front in the Budweiser Chevrolet, but he lost the air off his car when Burton went past him and slid into the wall. Jimmy Spencer crunched his Camel Ford. Martin had engine failure. Wallace was involved in the same wreck that ended Irvan's day.

In the end, Burton, who smoothly fought his way back from a lap down due to a pair of green-flag stops for tires, fuel and some loose lug nuts, had all it took in the closing laps of the race. He took command with

Ricky Rudd discusses chassis settings with crew chief Jim Long. Rudd may not have hit the setup perfectly for the race, but he managed to avoid problems and brought the Tide Ford home in fifth place, his second top-five finish of the season.

58 laps remaining and built a four-second victory over Jarrett to claim the first NASCAR Winston Cup visit to victory lane at the new speedway.

It was also the first career victory for the Virginian, and it gave team owner Jack Roush his first win since Martin took the checkers at Charlotte in the fall of 1995. Jarrett fought his way to second place despite his problems, while Bobby Labonte responded to the Interstate Batteries challenge and beat older brother Terry to the line to claim third place. Rudd stayed out of trouble and worked his way to a solid fifth-place finish with his Tide Ford, while Ward Burton overcame sheet metal damage to finish seventh behind the strong-driving Earnhardt. Sterling Marlin and Michael Waltrip were eighth and ninth, respectively, with Michael posting his third top-10 finish of the season. Steve Grissom returned to his early season form and claimed the final top-10 position after being forced to miss the Darlington event when he failed to qualify.

While Burton celebrated his first NASCAR Winston Cup victory, the approximately 200,000 fans began filing out, having witnessed history in the making as the NASCAR Winston Cup Series made its return to the great state of Texas.

A jubilant Jeff Burton declares victory after scoring his first NASCAR Winston Cup win. The race marked his 96th career start.

Interstate Batteries 500

Fin. Pos.	Start Pos.	Car #	Driver	Team
1	5	99	Jeff Burton	Exide Batteries Ford
2	1	88	Dale Jarrett	Quality Care/Ford Credit Ford
3	4	18	Bobby Labonte	Interstate Batteries Pontiac
4	3	5	Terry Labonte	Kellogg's Corn Flakes Chevrolet
5	8	10	Ricky Rudd	Tide Ford
6	15	3	Dale Earnhardt	GM Goodwrench Service Chevrolet
7	12	22	Ward Burton	MBNA America Pontiac
8	22	4	Sterling Marlin	Kodak Film Chevrolet
9	21	21	Michael Waltrip	CITGO Ford
10	35	41	Steve Grissom	Kodiak Chevrolet
11	16	94	Bill Elliott	McDonald's Ford
12	30	98	John Andretti	RCA Ford
13	31	81	Kenny Wallace	Square D Ford
14	7	7	Geoff Bodine	QVC Ford
15	36	71	Dave Marcis	Realtree Camouflage Chevrolet
16	24	9	Lake Speed	Melling Engine Parts Ford
17	42	91	Mike Wallace	Spam Chevrolet
18	27	33	Ken Schrader	Skoal Bandit Chevrolet
19	26	11	Brett Bodine	Close Call Phone Card Ford
20	17	43	Bobby Hamilton	STP Pontiac
21	43	78	Billy Standridge	Diamond Rio Ford
22	25	31	Mike Skinner	Lowe's Chevrolet
23	32	90	Dick Trickle	Heilig-Meyers/Simmons Ford
24	19	1	Morgan Shepherd	Delco Remy America Pontiac
25	18	25	Todd Bodine	Budweiser Chevrolet
26	38	97	Chad Little	John Deere Pontiac
27	23	44	Kyle Petty	Hot Wheels Pontiac
28	13	30	Johnny Benson	Pennzoil Pontiac
29	40	42	Joe Nemechek	BellSouth Chevrolet
30	2	24	Jeff Gordon	DuPont Refinishes Chevrolet
31	28	75	Rick Mast	Remington Arms Ford
32	20	37	Jeremy Mayfield	Kmart/RC Cola Ford
33	34	8	Hut Stricklin	Circuit City Ford
34	29	40	Robby Gordon	Coors Light Chevrolet
35	11	16	Ted Musgrave	Family Channel/PRIMESTAR Ford
36	10	28	Ernie Irvan	Texaco Havoline Ford
37	9	2	Rusty Wallace	Miller Lite Ford
38	6	6	Mark Martin	Valvoline Ford
39	33	23	Jimmy Spencer	Camel Cigarettes Ford
40	39	20	Greg Sacks	Hardee's Ford
41	37	36	Derrike Cope	Skittles Pontiac
42	41	77	Bobby Hillin	Jasper Engines/Federal-Mogul Ford
43	14	17	Darrell Waltrip	Parts America Chevrolet

NASCAR WINSTON CUP SERIES 1997

Food City 500

(Bristol Motor Speedway • April 13, 1997)

Dale Jarrett rolled into Bristol Motor Speedway with a 95-point lead and a smile on his face. In the first six races of the season, Jarrett had posted five top-five finishes, including a pair of wins, and had it not been for Dale Earnhardt's late-race accident at Daytona that damaged Jarrett's car, the mark would be a perfect six for six.

No one had to tell the Quality Care/Ford Credit Ford driver that those were the kind of performances that took Terry Labonte to the NASCAR Winston Cup championship last season. Consistent finishes in the top five or six, while the other drivers beat and battered themselves on their way to victory lane, have been Labonte's hallmark for his entire career. That style of driving has brought Terry a pair of titles — and Jarrett is one of the quickest studies in the NASCAR garage. His two-race winning streak had been snapped at Texas, but he posted a runner-up finish and gained points over his closest pursuers in the process.

Labonte's consistency was almost as good as Jarrett's. Terry had taken the Kellogg's Chevrolet to five top-10 finishes in the first six races, but therein lay the difference in points. Jarrett's finishes had been mostly in the top five, and, in several races, included leading the most laps and gaining the bonus points that go with that accomplishment. Only two of Terry's finishes had been in the top five, and he had yet to win this season.

(Right) Sterling Marlin brings his Kodak Chevrolet to a stop while his crew hurdles pit wall with new tires and fuel. Marlin qualified on the front row next to pole-winner Rusty Wallace, and led briefly near the midpoint of the race.

(Below) In the closing laps of the Food City 500, Rusty Wallace (2), Jeff Gordon (24) and Terry Labonte (5) run nose to tail, all three looking for a way to seal the victory at Bristol.

56

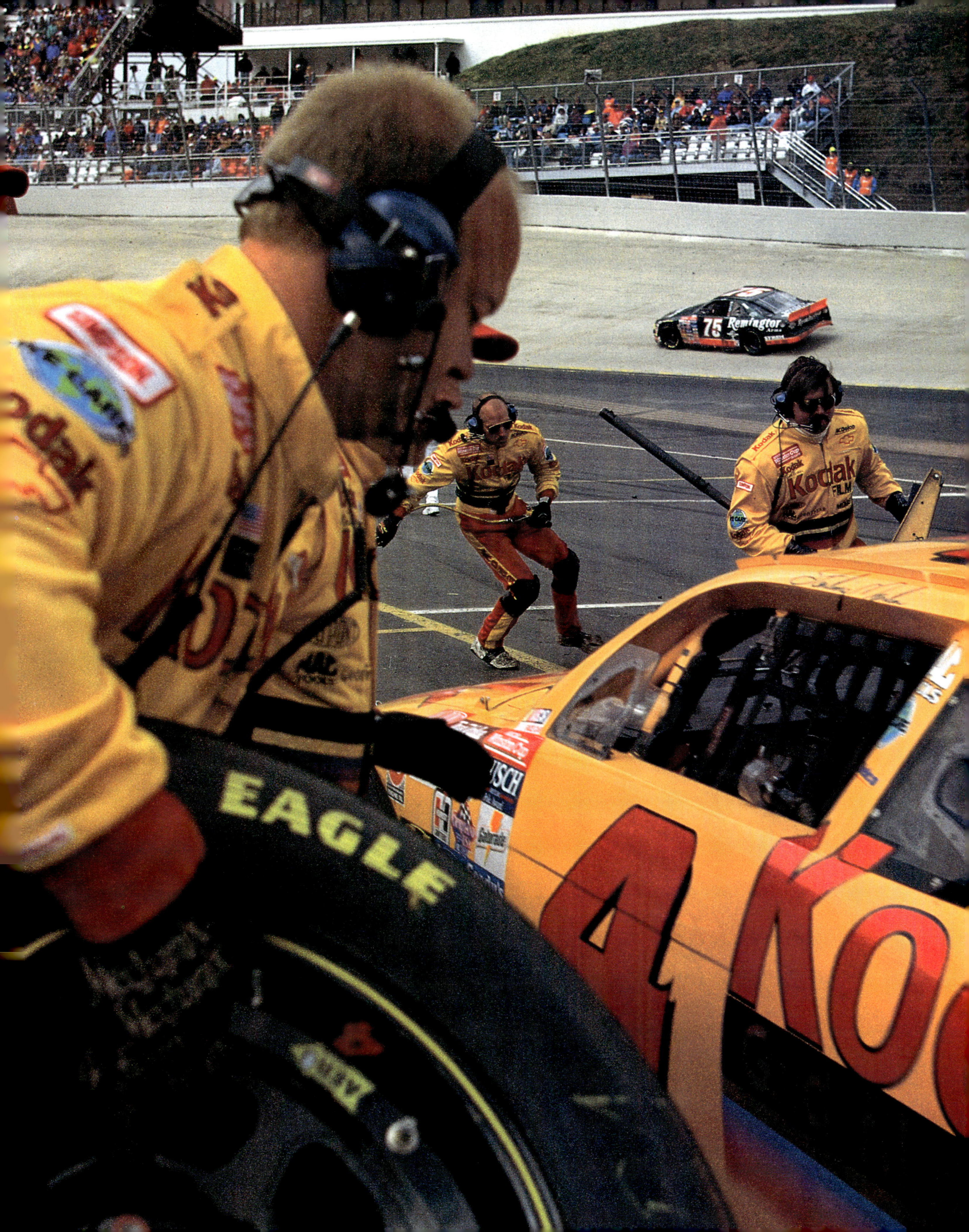
EAGLE
75
Remington
Kodak
FILM

(Above) The McDonald's Ford sits in its designated 18th starting position on Sunday morning. When driver Bill Elliott climbed aboard, he took the Thunderbird to the front of the field to dice with the leaders, before eventually settling to a seventh-place finish. *(Left)* Winless on the short tracks in his NASCAR Winston Cup career, point-leader Dale Jarrett attempts to unlock the secret of running on the bullrings with crew chief Todd Parrott. *(Below Left)* Jeff Burton (left) and Jimmy Spencer give a wave to the enthusiastic Bristol crowd during driver introductions. This was the best part of Burton's day; his engine expired early in the race. Spencer led 36 laps during the event, but came home 15th, the first car one lap down.

Younger brother Bobby Labonte was right on track with Terry, as well. He was 41 points behind the Kellogg's driver, but his third place at Texas had underscored the growing competitiveness of the Pontiac Grand Prix. There were few who thought Bobby would go much deeper into the season before posting a victory.

Jeff Gordon's involvement in the wreck at Texas had begun when Greg Sacks slowed as he headed for a caution flag and was hit by a hard-charging Ernie Irvan, who was trying to beat the leaders back to the yellow to regain a lost lap. Jeff's resulting 30th place sent the DuPont Chevrolet driver to fifth in the standings. He trailed Jarrett by 184, and was 27 points behind Texas winner Jeff Burton. Separated by only 35 points, Ricky Rudd and Geoff Bodine were locked in a tight battle for sixth place, and Mark Martin was doing his best to close on seventh-place Bodine. Ward Burton's seventh place in Texas moved him to ninth in the standings, and for the first time this year, Dale Earnhardt's name appeared in the top 10.

Earnhardt, still looking for his first top-five finish, knew his long winless streak, now reaching back to the spring race at Atlanta in 1996, had to end soon. He had plenty of trophies at home with Bristol's name on them. He was a long way off from the lead in the points race — trailing by 291 — but he also knew that there was plenty of time to make those points up, if he could get back to the winner's circle and the frontrunners had a bit of poor racing luck.

Earnhardt hoped his season would turn at Bristol and his team would continue the progress it had shown at Darlington and Texas. But when the first round of qualifying was completed on the steeply banked half-mile, Earnhardt was disappointed with his

(Above) It's hard to keep your nose clean at Thunder Valley, as Derrike Cope's Skittles Pontiac and Dick Trickle's Heilig-Meyers Ford clearly show. (Left) The Miller crew delivers another flawless pit stop during one of the race's 20 caution periods. Their consistent performances kept Wallace among the leaders throughout the afternoon.

time, good enough for only 29th on the speed list. He felt the car would race well, but he was 2.5 miles per hour off the pace of the pole-winner, Rusty Wallace.

With four consecutive Bristol poles in the back pocket of his Valvoline driver's suit, Mark Martin came to Thunder Valley hoping to make it five in a row. Problems throughout the practice sessions, including a broken starter and an engine miss, plagued the Ford driver, and, during his qualifying lap, the power steering malfunctioned, leaving him in a split-second wrestling match with the steering wheel of the Thunderbird. He was 23rd on the list.

Martin's problems left the door open for Rusty, and the Miller Lite Ford driver capitalized on it, beating Sterling Marlin's effort by .022 seconds. Ted Musgrave slapped the Family Channel/PRIMESTAR Ford on the inside of the second row, and Kenny Wallace put the Square D Ford in the fourth starting position. Gordon and Jarrett were right in the hunt, taking the third row positions, just better than the laps

59

posted by Hut Stricklin and Geoff Bodine, both continuing their strong qualifying efforts. Steve Grissom and Jimmy Spencer made up the fifth row, just nipping Texas winner Jeff Burton and a good effort from Brett Bodine and his BDR Motorsports camp.

Darrell Waltrip, running his Parts America Monte Carlo in the red-and-white color scheme that was featured on his 1985 Budweiser Chevrolet, had hopes of putting the car at the front of the pack at Bristol, where he had gone to victory lane 12 times in his career. His qualifying lap, however, mirrored the frustrations of his practice session, and he was 42nd fastest among the 47 cars taking times. He used a former champion's provisional to start the race, falling in line behind Michael Waltrip, Jack Sprague (driving for the still-injured Ricky Craven), Morgan Shepherd and Dave Marcis, all of whom were in the field via provisional starts. Bobby Hillin, Billy Standridge, Mike Wallace and Greg Sacks all failed to make the field when the second round of qualifying was washed out and the field was set by the times recorded in the first session.

(Above Left) Robby Gordon spins on the backstretch bringing out the race's sixth caution flag. Brett Bodine escapes unharmed on the outside and continued on to pick up his first top-10 finish of the year. (Left) Ward Burton (22), Bobby Labonte (18) and John Andretti tangle off the fourth turn bringing out the 14th caution on lap 259. Despite the damage, Burton stayed in the race and finished 18th, just one lap off the pace.
(Below) After giving Wallace a nudge on the final lap of the race, Jeff Gordon jumps to the lead and sets sail for the checkered flag.

The front of Dale Earnhardt's Goodwrench Chevrolet shows the rigors of his struggle from the 29th starting position to a solid sixth-place, lead-lap finish, tying his best run of the season so far.

With a huge crowd of more than 118,000 fans packed into the seats surrounding the half-mile oval, Wallace and Gordon established themselves as the leading contenders for victory from the drop of the green flag. Between them, they eventually led 365 of the 500 laps, seldom letting another driver see anything but the television panels on the rear of the Miller Light Ford and the DuPont Chevrolet.

While the focus of the crowd was on the leaders, Earnhardt began battling from the rear of the field and eventually got all the way to sixth place, recovering from a lost lap in the process. There was no question that the fire for victory still burned in his belly.

As the race wound down to the closing laps, three champions were at the head of the field, as Wallace led Gordon, and Terry Labonte chomped at his Hendrick Motorsports teammate's rear bumper. The last 15 laps of the race were worth every penny of the admission price, with Gordon repeatedly looking for a way past Wallace. Labonte simply lurked behind, watching and waiting for a single mistake from either of the drivers ahead of him that would catapult him into victory.

Gordon stuck his nose under Wallace twice before the event moved into its final 10 laps, and each time, Wallace slammed the door on the 1995 champion. Then, with seven laps left in the race, Labonte attacked Gordon, and it was Jeff's turn to turn left and pinch the Kellogg's Chevrolet off rather than yield the second-place position. With one lap to go, Terry tried again, and again, but Gordon fended him off.

Wallace was approaching the slower car of Jimmy Spencer and had to take a higher line into the first turn. It slowed his momentum slightly, and Gordon erased the car-length lead Rusty had built. Headed down the backstretch, Gordon tapped the rear bumper of the Ford with the nose of his Chevrolet. Immediately, Gordon dove for the inside of the track as Rusty fought for control, and, in that brief instant, the DuPont Chevrolet had the preferred line.

They barreled through the fourth turn, and Gordon emerged as the leader as the two sprinted for the checkered flag. Gordon got there first, posting his third victory of the young season, and Wallace was forced to settle for second, while Labonte barely held off the charges of Jarrett and Martin for third place.

Earnhardt was pleased, to a certain extent, with his second straight sixth place, beating Bill Elliott and Chad Little to the line. Jeremy Mayfield finished ninth, and Brett Bodine was 10th, posting his first top-10 finish of the season.

Food City 500

Fin. Pos.	Start Pos.	Car #	Driver	Team
1	5	24	Jeff Gordon	DuPont Refinishes Chevrolet
2	1	2	Rusty Wallace	Miller Lite Ford
3	17	5	Terry Labonte	Kellogg's Corn Flakes Chevrolet
4	6	88	Dale Jarrett	Quality Care/Ford Credit Ford
5	23	6	Mark Martin	Valvoline Ford
6	29	3	Dale Earnhardt	GM Goodwrench Service Chevrolet
7	18	94	Bill Elliott	McDonald's Ford
8	21	97	Chad Little	John Deere Pontiac
9	32	37	Jeremy Mayfield	Kmart/RC Cola Ford
10	12	11	Brett Bodine	Close Call Phone Card Ford
11	19	90	Dick Trickle	Heilig-Meyers/Simmons Ford
12	16	33	Ken Schrader	Skoal Bandit Chevrolet
13	34	43	Bobby Hamilton	STP Pontiac
14	15	29	Robert Pressley	Cartoon Network Chevrolet
15	10	23	Jimmy Spencer	Camel Cigarettes Ford
16	36	36	Derrike Cope	Skittles Pontiac
17	25	75	Rick Mast	Remington Arms Ford
18	35	22	Ward Burton	MBNA America Pontiac
19	24	42	Joe Nemechek	BellSouth Chevrolet
20	2	4	Sterling Marlin	Kodak Film Chevrolet
21	39	21	Michael Waltrip	CITGO Ford
22	27	96	David Green	Caterpillar Chevrolet
23	30	95	Ed Berrier	Feed The Children Chevrolet
24	26	98	John Andretti	RCA Ford
25	43	17	Darrell Waltrip	Parts America Chevrolet
26	7	8	Hut Stricklin	Circuit City Ford
27	22	10	Ricky Rudd	Tide Ford
28	41	1	Morgan Shepherd	Cruisin' America Phone Card Pontiac
29	14	44	Kyle Petty	Hot Wheels Pontiac
30	42	71	Dave Marcis	Realtree Camouflage Chevrolet
31	33	30	Johnny Benson	Pennzoil Pontiac
32	9	41	Steve Grissom	Kodiak Chevrolet
33	8	7	Geoff Bodine	QVC Ford
34	13	18	Bobby Labonte	Interstate Batteries Pontiac
35	28	31	Mike Skinner	Lowe's Chevrolet
36	31	9	Lake Speed	Melling Engine Parts Ford
37	37	19	Gary Bradberry	Child Support Recovery Ford
38	3	16	Ted Musgrave	Family Channel/PRIMESTAR Ford
39	38	28	Ernie Irvan	Texaco Havoline Ford
40	40	25	Jack Sprague	Budweiser Chevrolet
41	4	81	Kenny Wallace	Square D Ford
42	11	99	Jeff Burton	Exide Batteries Ford
43	20	40	Robby Gordon	Coors Light Chevrolet

NASCAR WINSTON CUP SERIES 1997

Goody's Headache Powder 500

(Martinsville Speedway • April 20, 1997)

Jeff Gordon's "bump-and-run" victory at Bristol gave him three victories in the first seven races of the season, but it did little to cut into the point lead held by Ford-driving Dale Jarrett, with the Quality Care Thunderbird driver coming home a solid fourth, just a few car lengths behind the DuPont Chevrolet.

Gordon's gain was 20 points, but he was third in the standings when the teams arrived at Clay Earles' and Clay Campbell's spiffy half mile in the southern portion of Virginia for the Goody's Headache Powder 500. Sandwiched between the two combatants was the defending NASCAR Winston Cup champion, and Terry Labonte was going about his usual program of taking whatever the car would give him week after week, and piling up the points.

Labonte had been third at Bristol, and he gained but five points on Jarrett, cutting the difference to 90 markers as the teams prepared for the eighth race of the season. Bobby Labonte, Jeff Burton and Mark Martin occupied fourth, fifth and sixth place in the standings, ahead of Ricky Rudd in their furious battle for fourth place. The margin between Bobby and Ricky was just 62 points, and Rudd merely had to look at the next line of the standings to see who had been picking his way through the points.

(Right) Kenny Wallace has a look of intensity before leading the field off the line to start the Goody's Headache Powder 500. Wallace followed his first career NASCAR Winston Cup pole with a sixth-place finish, his best of the season so far.

(Below) A capacity crowd packs the stands on a beautiful spring day at the pristine half mile in southern Virginia. Note the new exit road from the pits, forcing cars to re-enter traffic on the straightaways rather than at the entrance to the turns.

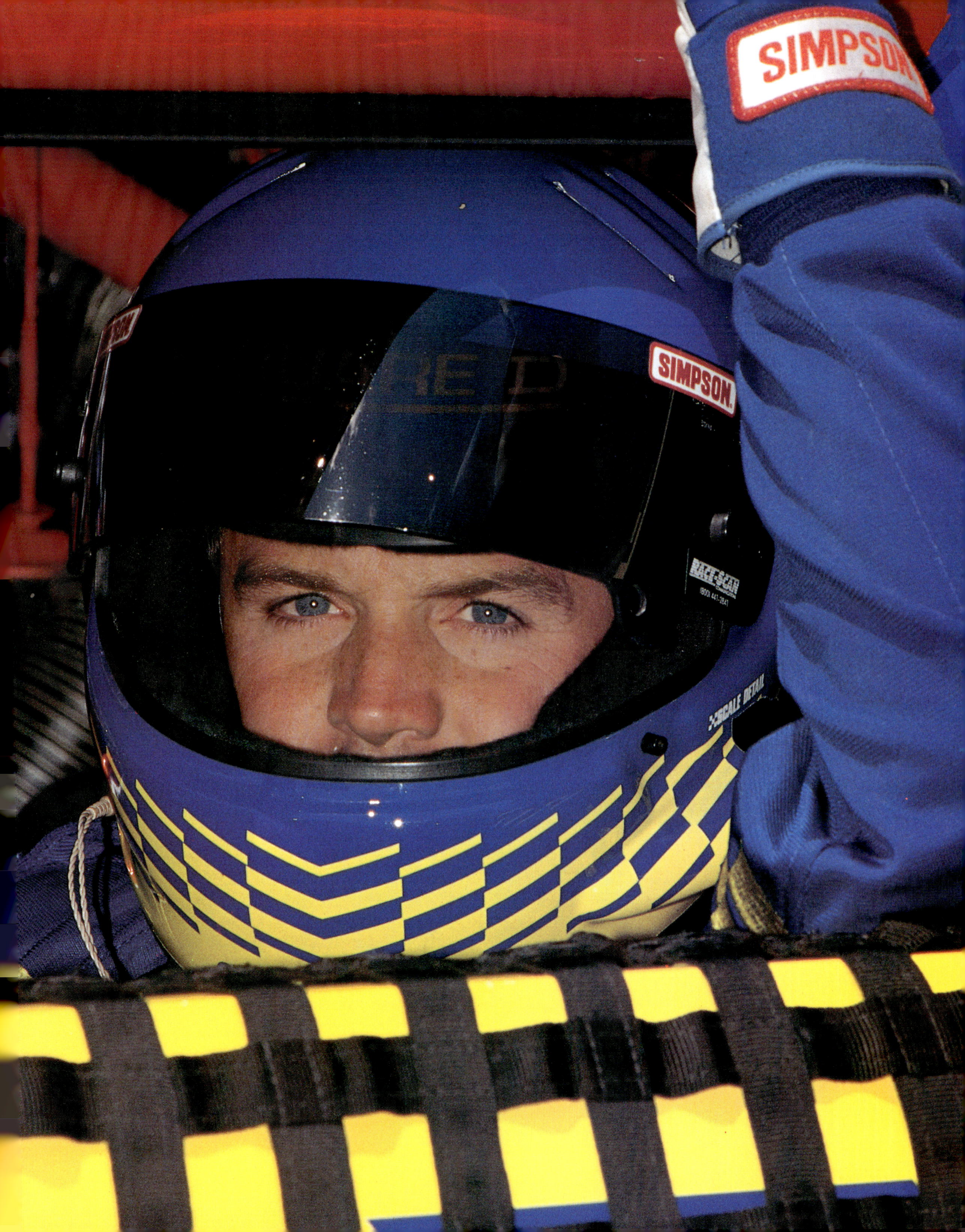
SIMPSON
SIMPSON

Lined up and ready to go, the field prepares to pull off pit road and begin warm-up laps. Note the additional openings in the front of the Square D Thunderbird, allowing extra air for cooling the brakes — an essential element of a car's setup at Martinsville.

Dale Earnhardt, after his 31st-place finish at Daytona, had marched toward the front, and now was eighth, just four points behind Rudd. Bill Elliott and Rusty Wallace occupied the ninth and 10th positions, and for the first time in several races, Geoff Bodine was not in the top 10. At Bristol, he and Jimmy Spencer had tangled more than once, and after the race, Geoff made a couple of comments regarding the on-track contretemps with Spencer. The statement cost him a $10,000 fine from NASCAR officials for his choice of words, and although Geoff apologized to the fans, it had been costly both in the wallet and in the point standings. His 33rd-place finish dropped him to 12th place in the standings. An innocent victim in the Bodine/Spencer crash was Steve Grissom, who was "stumping" around Martinsville with a walking boot on his right foot. He had suffered a stress fracture in his foot when he hit the wall after being collected in the accident.

One of the surprises at Martinsville involved the crews and crew chiefs working on the Felix Sabates-owned cars driven by Robby Gordon and Joe Nemechek. Neither driver had gotten off to a good start this season, and although Gordon won the Atlanta pole, he was 32nd in the point standings in the Coors Chevrolet. Nemechek's situation was even worse as he was 39th in the standings in the BellSouth Monte Carlo. Joe had missed the Bristol race, and Phil Parsons had substituted at Darlington while Joe attended to personal matters following the death of his brother, John.

In the days between Bristol and Martinsville, Sabates had swapped crews with the drivers. Tony Glover and his personnel now were working with Nemechek, while Mike Hillman and his mates were preparing the machines for Gordon. Switching the entire crews came as a surprise, although all three Sabates teams had struggled in the opening races of the season, with Gordon's best finish a 14th at Atlanta, and with Nemechek's 19th place as his best result. Wally Dallenbach, behind the wheel of the First Union Monte Carlo in what was originally slated as a limited season of competition, had failed to make the field four times, and in the only race he had competed in, he finished 42nd at Daytona. Still, First Union had put more money into the pot, and the team was now preparing to run nearly every race for the remainder of the season.

Ricky Craven was back behind the wheel of the Budweiser Chevrolet after recovering from a broken shoulder blade and broken ribs received in a testing crash at Texas. Harry Ranier nominated NASCAR Winston West champion Lance Hooper to drive the Hardee's Ford after regular runner Greg Sacks broke several bones in his foot during a crash at Greenville-Pickens Speedway during a testing session. Hooper had moved east and was working as a crew member and mechanic for the Ranier team.

(Above) William Elliott discovers something interesting to point out to his father, Bill, on Sunday morning, before Daddy has to climb in his car and go to work. *(Below)* Ricky Rudd gets the "go" sign to exit his pit and return to the track. Pit road was a very busy place as the race was slowed by 11 caution flags.

Ernie Irvan (28), Sterling Marlin (4) and Robby Gordon (40) dice for position on the track, their cars showing evidence of the tight quarters on the Virginia short track.

however, it was the Square D Ford of Kenny Wallace that was the fastest in the session, and he nailed down his first career NASCAR Winston Cup pole in his 97th start. He became the sixth different pole-winner in the first eight races of the season, and was the third first-time pole-winner this season, matching Mike Skinner at Daytona and Robby Gordon at Atlanta.

On Kenny's right was the revamped Chevrolet of Nemechek, who had an early qualifying run, and had held the pole until Kenny's blue-and-yellow Ford rolled off the line late in the session.

With 47 cars on hand for Busch Pole qualifying, it was clear that, once again, the battle for a starting position would be just as crucial as the final laps of the race on Sunday. When the session was completed, a Wallace was on the pole, just like Bristol the week before. This time,

Geoff Bodine, one of the winningest drivers in the long and glorious history of Martinsville, was on form, claiming the third-fastest lap and relegating Jeff Gordon to the outside of the second row. Rudd

(Above) The only problem Gordon had all day was when he was tagged by Jimmy Spencer (23) midway through the event. While Spencer spins to the inside, Gordon stands on the throttle and loops the DuPont Chevrolet in a 360-degree recovery, which enabled him to continue in the race after losing only two positions on the track. (Left) Bobby Hamilton (43) challenges Gordon for the lead on the outside with Rusty Wallace (2) ready to capitalize on a mistake by either driver. After Gordon took the lead for the first time on lap 22, Hamilton was the only other driver to reach the point, and eventually finished second.

grabbed the fifth spot from Hut Stricklin, whose Circuit City Ford had another solid qualifying effort. Terry Labonte and Bobby Hamilton lined up in the fourth row, and behind them, Bill Elliott and Kyle Petty filled the final positions in the top 10.

One of the surprises during the qualifying session was the failure of Dale Jarrett to make the top 10, bringing to an end his

The Hot Wheels Pontiac cools off in the garage area after Kyle Petty parked it with handling problems before completing 400 laps.

string of 11 straight races with a top-10 start. Worse, Mark Martin needed a provisional to make the field, and Sterling Marlin crashed during practice and his team couldn't get the spare car ready for the qualifying session. Marlin made the field during the second round. Earnhardt was the final qualifier in the first round, starting 25th, but his pit would be on the backstretch. Robby Gordon and Dave Marcis also used provisionals to get into the race, as did Bobby Hillin, who was the final starter based on 1996 car owner points when all of the other current top 40 car owners had their mounts in the race. Randy MacDonald, Billy Standridge, Hooper, David Green and Gary Bradberry all were unable to make the field.

Unlike the previous race, there was no reason for Jeff Gordon to do any bumping on the final lap to seal the victory on Sunday afternoon in Virginia. His only trouble during the 500-lap event came when he was tagged and spun by Jimmy Spencer. Gordon merely did a 360, nailed the throttle, and recovered in third place, falling just two positions during the spin. Other than that, Martinsville belonged to the 1995 NASCAR Winston Cup champion.

He led a total of 432 of the 500 laps, erasing the old event record of 427 laps led set by Cale Yarborough in 1974. His lead was as much as a straightaway through much of the race, and when the final green flag waved with 18 laps remaining, Gordon was at the point, able to hold off a strong challenge from Hamilton in the closing laps to post a .356-second margin of victory.

Martin put on a great showing in the event, despite pitting on the backstretch, and finished third, ahead of the ever-present Terry Labonte and Rusty Wallace. Younger brother Kenny fought with his brother in the final stages of the race and finished sixth, ahead of Jeremy Mayfield and Bobby Labonte. Darrell Waltrip rolled to ninth place, ahead of Ken Schrader.

The Spam Chevrolet sits behind the wall getting some much-needed service on it's overheated brakes. Driver Mike Wallace eventually finished the race, but was listed 39th, 86 laps down.

Goody's Headache Powder 500

Fin. Pos.	Start Pos.	Car #	Driver	Team
1	4	24	Jeff Gordon	DuPont Refinishes Chevrolet
2	8	43	Bobby Hamilton	STP Pontiac
3	39	6	Mark Martin	Valvoline Ford
4	7	5	Terry Labonte	Kellogg's Corn Flakes Chevrolet
5	15	2	Rusty Wallace	Miller Lite Ford
6	1	81	Kenny Wallace	Square D Ford
7	29	37	Jeremy Mayfield	Kmart/RC Cola Ford
8	14	18	Bobby Labonte	Interstate Batteries Pontiac
9	17	17	Darrell Waltrip	Parts America Chevrolet
10	26	33	Ken Schrader	Skoal Bandit Chevrolet
11	11	23	Jimmy Spencer	Camel Cigarettes Ford
12	25	3	Dale Earnhardt	GM Goodwrench Service Chevrolet
13	5	10	Ricky Rudd	Tide Ford
14	6	8	Hut Stricklin	Circuit City Ford
15	19	99	Jeff Burton	Exide Batteries Ford
16	23	88	Dale Jarrett	Quality Care/Ford Credit Ford
17	22	30	Johnny Benson	Pennzoil Pontiac
18	18	22	Ward Burton	MBNA America Pontiac
19	2	42	Joe Nemechek	BellSouth Chevrolet
20	28	41	Steve Grissom	Kodiak Chevrolet
21	38	4	Sterling Marlin	Kodak Film Chevrolet
22	35	25	Ricky Craven	Budweiser Chevrolet
23	13	29	Robert Pressley	Cartoon Network Chevrolet
24	12	16	Ted Musgrave	Family Channel/PRIMESTAR Ford
25	20	9	Lake Speed	Melling Engine Parts Ford
26	34	21	Michael Waltrip	CITGO Ford
27	37	11	Brett Bodine	Close Call Phone Card Ford
28	27	98	John Andretti	RCA Ford
29	3	7	Geoff Bodine	QVC Ford
30	31	90	Dick Trickle	Heilig-Meyers/Simmons Ford
31	30	28	Ernie Irvan	Texaco Havoline Ford
32	16	31	Mike Skinner	Lowe's Chevrolet
33	42	77	Bobby Hillin	Jasper Engines/Federal-Mogul Ford
34	24	36	Derrike Cope	Skittles Pontiac
35	21	1	Morgan Shepherd	Cruisin' America Phone Card Pontiac
36	32	75	Rick Mast	Remington Arms Ford
37	9	94	Bill Elliott	McDonald's Ford
38	41	71	Dave Marcis	Realtree Camouflage Chevrolet
39	36	91	Mike Wallace	Spam Chevrolet
40	10	44	Kyle Petty	Hot Wheels Pontiac
41	40	40	Robby Gordon	Coors Light Chevrolet
42	33	97	Chad Little	John Deere Pontiac

NASCAR WINSTON CUP SERIES 1997

Save Mart Supermarkets 300

(Sears Point Raceway • May 4, 1997)

After the deluge that seemed to last forever in Talladega and forced the postponement of the Winston 500 until the Saturday before Mother's Day, the smiles were back on the faces of the drivers and crew members when they arrived in the Bay Area for the running of the Save Mart Supermarkets 300 at Sears Point Raceway.

In addition to the rainout, the extra day spent at Talladega trying to get the race into the books had scrambled the schedules and required the teams to work even harder than normal to get the cars and transporters loaded and on site in California in time. There was still time, however, for some of the members of the NASCAR Winston Cup family to enjoy the myriad of sights in the Bay Area and the city of San Francisco.

(Left) Road-racing aficionados Rusty Wallace (2) and Terry Labonte (5) snake their way through the second turn at the 2.52-mile California road course. Wallace, the defending race-winner, jumped to the lead on lap four, but would suffer engine problems and fall to 40th in the final rundown.

(Right) Mark Martin gathers intensity while waiting for the start of the Save Mart Supermarkets 300. Would this be the day he would finally end his 48-race winless streak dating back to the 1995 season?

68

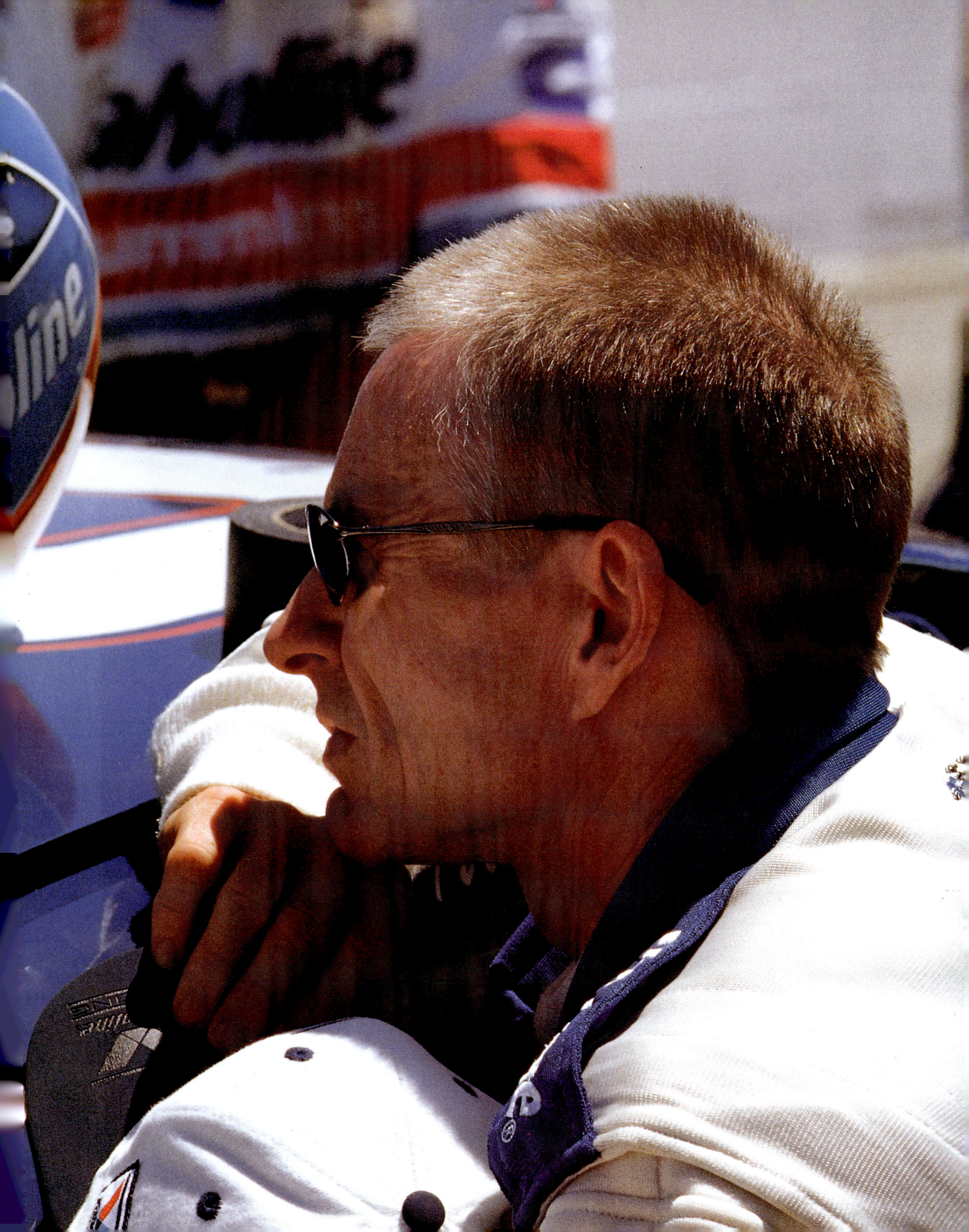

the island of Alcatraz, where media members and drivers were treated to a tour of the famous prison before settling into the day's question-and-answer period.

One of the highlights of the week was an effort by the track's management and NASCAR to draw attention to the 45-mph speed limit on the Golden Gate Bridge. A total of 15 NASCAR Winston Cup show cars — complete with police escort — lined up on the Sausalito side of the bridge and paraded across the famous span at 45 miles per hour. They then wound their way through the city for some seven miles before pulling into Justin Herman Plaza, where fans and other curious onlookers had the chance to examine real NASCAR Winston Cup race cars up close.

Among the pre-event favorites to win the Save Mart Supermarkets 300 were former winners Ricky Rudd, Dale Earnhardt, Geoff Bodine and Rusty Wallace, and all expected to run well again on the twisting road course. But there were others who figured to be in the hunt for victory, including Mark Martin; road racers Wally Dallenbach and Robby Gordon; Jeff Gordon, who had improved his expertise on the road courses; and Bill Elliott, who missed this same race last year while recovering from the broken leg he suffered at Talladega. Terry Labonte,

(Top) Chad Little was hoping to run well for his home-state fans in California, but failed to qualify his backup John Deere Pontiac after damaging the primary car in Friday's practice session. (Above) Steve Grissom is a picture of concentration between practice runs on the road course. Although he did not race among the leaders during the event, he maintained position on the lead lap and brought his Kodiak Chevrolet home in 17th place. (Right) Using the pole-winner's option, Mark Martin (6) prepares to start the race from the right lane, moving second-place starter Rusty Wallace to the inside for the drop of the green flag. All other rows on the starting grid remain in the traditional inside-outside formation.

Some drivers were seen walking the boardwalk at Fisherman's Wharf, while others were glimpsed hanging from the side of a cable car or climbing the steep hills of the city. Others spent their time walking through the picturesque streets of Sausalito, and the wineries in the Sonoma and Napa valleys also drew some Cuppers and their families. The track's annual press conference and media day was spent on

Sterling Marlin uses his Kodak Chevrolet to lean on Robby Gordon's Coors Monte Carlo as the two drivers battle for position on the third lap of the race. Gordon's strong road-racing background went for naught in this race; his engine expired near the halfway mark.

with a history as one of the best road racers on the tour and with Riverside victories and poles to his credit, was another driver who had to be considered a strong contender for victory.

Considerable changes were evident to spectators as they began arriving at Sears Point for the race. The track was purchased last year by Bruton Smith's Speedway Motorsports, and one of the first things done was to grade a portion of the hillside located inside the loop between turns two and six. The work enabled spectators to see more of the action (previously the cars had simply disappeared from sight) and improved the area on the hillside. In fact, the vistas enabled fans to see virtually the entire circuit, a unique feature for a road course, where most spectators only see the stretch of track in front of them. A wide range of other improvements were under way, and Smith promised that by the time the Series returned to Sears Point in 1998, fans would have one of the finest facilities in the world to attend.

As it has been in the past, the Save Mart Supermarkets 300 was a combination event for the NASCAR Winston Cup and NASCAR Winston West series, and there were numerous cars on hand seeking spots in the event. Because of the NASCAR Winston West entries, the field would be expanded to a maximum of 46 cars, with the first 38 to be determined by qualifying times. Four spots were guaranteed to

71

NASCAR Winston Cup provisional starters, two were given to NASCAR Winston West provisional starters, and two places were saved for past champions from each series. As it turned out, 44 cars made the race, and when the first qualifying session was completed, Martin had relied on his tried and true road-racing mount from the Jack Roush stable to notch the pole. The Valvoline Ford driver, winless since the fall 1995 race at Charlotte, was nearly three-tenths of a second faster than Wallace and led a Ford charge to seven of the top-10 starting slots. Jeff Gordon and Terry Labonte claimed the second row, followed by strong qualifying runs by Brett Bodine and Michael Waltrip, with Geoff Bodine and Dale Jarrett taking the fourth-row slots ahead of Dallenbach and Rudd.

The first day of activity was not without its dramas. Jeff Gordon spun in the practice session but didn't hit anything with his DuPont Chevrolet, and Chad Little bent his John Deere Pontiac, also during practice, and was forced to go to his backup car. In the qualifying session, Darrell Waltrip spun during a very fast lap and was forced to qualify in the second round. He did — with a lap that was the sixth-fastest in the field. Ol' DW grinned afterward, saying that this was the first time his team had built and brought a real road-racing car to Sears Point and he felt he could figure into the final results — if he could avoid trouble in the race on Sunday.

(Top) Darrell Waltrip puts the heat on John Andretti through The Carousel. *(Middle)* On two wheels or four, Mark Martin had the Valvoline Thunderbird flying around the course, leading all but five laps on the way to a stirring, and long overdue, victory. *(Right)* Fastest second-round qualifier Darrell Waltrip chases his brother, Michael (21), working his way to an outstanding fifth-place finish — his first top five of the season. *(Below)* Jeff Gordon (24), Terry Labonte (5) and Dale Jarrett (88) keep the heat on Mark Martin in the closing laps, waiting for the Valvoline Ford driver to make the slightest mistake, opening the door to victory lane. But Martin was perfect, and the quartet crossed the finish line without breaking ranks.

Tom Hubert, a frequent NASCAR Southwest Tour competitor now working as a tire changer for the Pennzoil team, was asked to drive Billy Standridge's Diamond Rio Chevrolet in qualifying. When he was more than a second quicker in practice than Standridge, Hubert found himself making the start in Sunday's race. Defending NASCAR Winston West champion Lance Hooper was behind the wheel of Harry Ranier's Hardee's Ford while Greg Sacks recovered from a broken foot, and he put the car into the field. Jeff Davis, driving a Ford entered by Harry Melling, was one provisional starter, while the others were Jeremy Mayfield, Ricky Craven and Morgan Shepherd. Those missing the race included Rick Mast, Joe Nemechek, Robert Pressley, Chad Little, David Green, Dick Trickle, and NASCAR Winston West drivers R.K. Smith and Gary Smith. Green worked a deal to put Caterpillar's colors on Larry Gunselman's Ford.

72

The largest crowd in the history of Sears Point Raceway greeted the rumbling rainbow of NASCAR Winston Cup cars as the field snaked around the track behind the pace car, headed for the green flag. When it dropped, the red-white-and-blue Valvoline Ford bolted to the lead under Martin's heavy right foot. Mark had the measure of the field, but yielded the point to a charge by Rusty on the fourth lap. Two laps later, Wallace made a mistake in the entry to turn seven and slid off into the dust.

Martin then turned the event into a Valvoline parade, leading 69 of the 74 laps around the serpentine circuit. Although he was the dominant driver, Martin drove an extremely careful race. There was never a moment that another car was not gnawing at his rear bumper, and a single slip, a missed shift or a tiny error upon entering a corner, and his chance for the win would have been gone.

In the end, Jeff Gordon emerged as the primary challenger to Martin's lead and he made a last-lap effort to pass Mark in the final corner. Martin's expertise, gained by three consecutive victories at Watkins Glen, kept him at the point and left Gordon to settle for second place.

Terry battled to third place ahead of Jarrett, who posted the best road-course finish of his career. Darrell Waltrip's run was brilliant, bringing him home fifth as he showed flashes of the form that brought him victories at Riverside in the past. Brett Bodine drove to a solid sixth place, his best finish of the year, and Michael Waltrip posted another top 10 for the Wood Brothers and CITGO. Ernie Irvan came home eighth in front of his home crowd, while Jeff and Ward Burton claimed the final top-10 positions.

Geoff Bodine, after running in the top five, lost the engine in the QVC Ford and finished last. The finish was tough to swallow for Geoff, particularly because he wanted to run well for Dawn Gillis, the winner of a national QVC sweepstakes. Dawn's likeness and name appeared on the black Ford, and Geoff was extremely disappointed he was unable to give her a ride to victory lane.

Tom Hubert (78) chases Darrell Waltrip (17) and Mike Skinner (31) through Sears Point's sweeping turn six. Hubert earned the ride in the Diamond Rio Ford by posting outstanding lap times during practice while subbing for the team's regular driver, Billy Standridge.

Save Mart Supermarkets 300

Fin. Pos.	Start Pos.	Car #	Driver	Team
1	1	6	Mark Martin	Valvoline Ford
2	3	24	Jeff Gordon	DuPont Refinishes Chevrolet
3	4	5	Terry Labonte	Kellogg's Corn Flakes Chevrolet
4	8	88	Dale Jarrett	Quality Care/Ford Credit Ford
5	26	17	Darrell Waltrip	Parts America Chevrolet
6	5	11	Brett Bodine	Close Call Calling Card Ford
7	6	21	Michael Waltrip	CITGO Ford
8	24	28	Ernie Irvan	Texaco Havoline Ford
9	20	99	Jeff Burton	Exide Batteries Ford
10	14	22	Ward Burton	MBNA America Pontiac
11	12	16	Ted Musgrave	Family Channel/PRIMESTAR Ford
12	32	3	Dale Earnhardt	GM Goodwrench Service Chevrolet
13	11	44	Kyle Petty	Hot Wheels Pontiac
14	25	23	Jimmy Spencer	Camel Cigarettes Ford
15	9	46	Wally Dallenbach	First Union Chevrolet
16	19	31	Mike Skinner	Lowe's Chevrolet
17	33	41	Steve Grissom	Kodiak Chevrolet
18	21	36	Derrike Cope	Skittles Pontiac
19	23	43	Bobby Hamilton	STP Pontiac
20	29	18	Bobby Labonte	Interstate Batteries Pontiac
21	35	30	Johnny Benson	Pennzoil Pontiac
22	34	91	Mike Wallace	Spam Chevrolet
23	41	1	Morgan Shepherd	Delco Remy America Pontiac
24	28	38	Butch Gilliland	Genuine Gear Ford
25	30	71	Dave Marcis	Realtree Camouflage Chevrolet
26	16	4	Sterling Marlin	Kodak Film Chevrolet
27	39	37	Jeremy Mayfield	Kmart/RC Cola Ford
28	27	78	Tommy Hubert	Diamond Rio/Hanes Ford
29	22	8	Hut Stricklin	Circuit City Ford
30	17	98	John Andretti	RCA Ford
31	15	33	Ken Schrader	Skoal Bandit Racing Chevrolet
32	13	94	Bill Elliott	McDonald's Racing Ford
33	43	07	Sean Woodside	Cinema Vehicle Service Pontiac
34	10	10	Ricky Rudd	Tide Ford
35	31	77	Bobby Hillin	Jasper Engines/Federal-Mogul Ford
36	36	81	Kenny Wallace	Square D Ford
37	42	9	Jeff Davis	Melling Engine Parts Ford
38	44	35	Larry Gunselman	Caterpillar Ford
39	40	25	Ricky Craven	Budweiser Chevrolet
40	2	2	Rusty Wallace	Miller Lite Ford
41	18	40	Robby Gordon	Coors Light Chevrolet
42	37	20	Lance Hooper	Hardee's Ford
43	38	19	Gary Bradberry	Child Support Recovery Int'l Ford
44	7	7	Geoff Bodine	QVC Ford

NASCAR WINSTON CUP SERIES 1997

Winston 500

(Talladega Superspeedway • May 10, 1997)

What was scheduled to be the ninth race of the season became the 10th race after the Winston 500 was rained out for two days and rescheduled to follow the Save Mart Supermarkets 300 at Sears Point. The date selected by NASCAR for the resumption of activities at the longest oval on the circuit was Saturday, the day before Mother's Day, and it created some problems for several of the NASCAR Winston Cup drivers who were scheduled to compete in the NASCAR Busch Series race at New Hampshire International Speedway the same day.

The Winston 500 was the second round in this year's edition of the Winston Million, the bonus posted by R.J. Reynolds payable to any driver able to win three of the four "crown jewel" events in a single season. The Daytona 500, the Coca-Cola 600 at Charlotte and the Mountain Dew Southern 500 at Darlington join the Winston 500 at Talladega in making up the races for the Winston Million. These races were chosen because they were the richest, the longest, the oldest and the fastest races on the schedule. In 1985, the program's first year, Bill Elliott triumphed in the Daytona 500, the Winston 500 and the Southern 500 to earn the nickname "Million Dollar Bill." Try as they have in the years since, no other drivers have been able to duplicate Bill's feat of winning the Winston Million.

Following his Daytona 500 victory this year, Jeff Gordon came to Talladega hoping to find a way to put the second event of the Winston Million in his pocket. He was a good bet to win at Darlington, but Charlotte had been a problem to him throughout his career. If Jeff was to win the Winston Million, he said, he would like to get the second part of the deal done right here.

(Right) Terry Labonte wears his game face while preparing to run the Winston 500, a race he knows will be a challenge based on his 36th-fastest qualifying effort. In the race, Terry worked his way to a sixth-place finish — good enough to take the point lead for the first time this season.

(Below) Holding the inside on Bobby Labonte (18), John Andretti sets the early pace, proving his blistering pole speed of more than 193 miles per hour was no fluke. Andretti would hold is own among the leaders all day and finish a solid fourth in Cale Yarborough's Thunderbird.

6
Kellogg's
Kellogg's
NASCAR
Winston Cup
1996 Champion
GMAC
Hendrick
Labonte

John Andretti, driving Cale Yarborough's RCA Ford, had ripped off a lap good enough to unseat Earnhardt, but John had his own worries about claiming his second career NASCAR Winston Cup pole. His concerns were bolstered when Bobby Hillin rolled under the checkered flag, but Hillin's speedy lap in his Jasper Engines Ford was good only for the second-place starting spot.

Their laps put Earnhardt on the inside of the third row, but he was actually delighted just to start in the top five after the problems he had encountered during qualifying in the first third of the season. He had another reason to smile at Talladega, as well. He represented his father, Ralph, as he was inducted into the International Motorsports Hall of Fame on Thursday night. Ralph was one of six inductees in 1997, and was in a class that will be long remembered for its accomplishments in motorsports. Also inducted that night were Buddy Baker, Richard Petty, Rick Mears, Jim Hall, and drag racer Don Garlits.

That night was special for Dale, who presented the Hall of Fame medal to his mother, and the pleasure carried over into Friday's qualifying session. On his right was Rusty Wallace, whose restrictor-plate

(Above) Greg Sacks climbs aboard the Hardee's Ford for his sixth start of the season, returning to action after suffering a foot injury earlier in the year. *(Right)* A NASCAR official checks spoiler angles during pre-race inspection. The critical measurement is checked prior to each practice session and qualifying round, as well as before and after the race.
(Below Right) Killing time before the start of the Winston 500, fourth-row starters Ernie Irvan (middle) and Bobby Labonte (right) engage in conversation, while Mark Martin, fresh off his win in California, listens in.

When the teams first assembled at the mammoth superspeedway two weeks ago, Gordon was back on a tear following his victory at Martinsville. A total of 49 cars were on hand trying to win a starting spot in the Winston 500, and when the Busch Pole qualifying session was completed, a stunned garage area looked at the scoring pylon and saw the numbers 98 and 77 at the top of the pole.

For most of the qualifying session, the number 3 had been at the top as Dale Earnhardt turned in a sizzling lap to lead the session. In the middle of a 36-race winless streak — the longest since he and car owner Richard Childress had been together — Earnhardt, the winningest driver in Talladega's history, showed that he and the Goodwrench team had not given up. But Dale knew his qualifying lap wasn't quite good enough, and when the roar went up from the grandstand dwellers as "98" flashed to the top of the pylon, Dale knew he had not won the pole.

races have given him problem after problem in the last several years. This time, Wallace said the motor and the chassis were "perfect," and his lap put Daytona 500 pole-sitter Mike Skinner on the inside of the third row. Ken Schrader had his Skoal Bandit primed for the weekend and took the outside of the third row, while Ernie Irvan and Bobby Labonte beat Dale Jarrett and Bill Elliott for the fourth row. Gordon and Derrike Cope, having a strong qualifying run in his Skittles Pontiac, just missed the top 10.

The final first-day qualifier was Ward Burton, and when the second qualifying session fell victim to Saturday's rain, the field was filled with times taken during the first day.

(Left) NASCAR officials impound the roof from Jeff Burton's Exide Ford after roof-flap placements were found to be out of spec during pre-qualifying inspection. Burton was forced to enter the backup car, and ended up using a provisional to get into the field. *(Below)* Dale Earnhardt takes a familiar place for him at Talladega - at the front of the field - while Jeff Gordon and Sterling Marlin pace the rest of the lead pack through the tri-oval. Earnhardt led on seven different occasions during the event, but could not overtake Martin in the closing laps, settling for second, his first top-five finish of the season.

Ken Schrader puts the Skoal Bandit into the wind, taking his turn at the front in a race that featured 26 official lead changes among 13 different drivers.

Terry Labonte's first-day time kept him mired in 36th place for the start of the race, and Jeff Burton, Jeremy Mayfield, Morgan Shepherd and Chad Little had to use provisionals to make the field. Helping Little into the field, Darrell Waltrip celebrated the 25th anniversary of his debut in NASCAR Winston Cup racing by taking a former champion's provisional and would start 43rd.

Unable to make a second run, and thus missing an opportunity to make the field, were Gary Bradberry, Joe Nemechek, Phil Barkdoll, Ed Berrier and Mike Wallace. Nemechek, however, found himself pressed into service when the rescheduled date of the race caused a conflict for SABCO teammate Robby Gordon. Gordon was entered in the Indianapolis 500, and his presence was required there for qualifying. Nemechek would drive at Talladega for Gordon, who had earned the 32nd starting position.

Two days of rain followed the setting of the grid, forcing the postponement of the event, but when teams returned, they were treated to superb weather. Nearly every fan returned two weeks later and they packed into the grandstands to see who would triumph in the event. Most fans thought the race would feature at least one multicar accident since the field would be so tightly bunched because of the restrictor plates used to control the speeds of the cars on the huge track.

No one knew what was in store.

The Jimmy Makar-led Interstate Batteries crew makes a two-tire change for left-side rubber and fuel for driver Bobby Labonte. Labonte had, by far, the fastest Pontiac in the field, and drove to a third-place finish to maintain fifth in the point standings.

In a race with no cautions — and on a restrictor-plate track — the leaders pitted as a group so as not to risk losing the lead draft. Here, Jeff Gordon leads Mark Martin (6), John Andretti (98) and Terry Labonte (5), among others, onto pit road. Gordon, Martin, Labonte and Andretti all finished in the top six.

The field took the green flag, and the usual slicing and dicing ensued. Drivers pulled out to pass only to find themselves immediately sliding back through the pack when no one else pulled out to help them. The race cycled through the first set of green-flag stops, and then another, with not a single yellow flag being shown. It went on like that for the entire race — and the 1997 Winston 500 became the fastest 500-mile stock car race in the history of the sport.

When it was all over, Mark Martin, who, at Sears Point, had ended his personal winless streak that dated back to the fall of 1995, had held off four challengers — Earnhardt, Bobby Labonte, Andretti and Jeff Gordon — over the final laps to notch his second straight victory of the season and the 20th triumph of his NASCAR Winston Cup career. The average speed of the race was 188.354 mph, erasing the old mark set by Elliott in 1985 when he rocketed from nearly two laps behind to win at 186.288 mph in the years prior to restrictor-plate regulations.

The race was the first caution-free NASCAR Winston Cup race since the North Wilkesboro event held in October of 1992 and won by Geoff Bodine, ironically in another rain-delayed event.

Terry Labonte fought all the way from 36th place to finish sixth in the race, while Jimmy Spencer claimed seventh, ahead of Jeff Burton, Johnny Benson and Ernie Irvan.

Series point leader Dale Jarrett struggled throughout the day with engine problems in his Quality Care/Ford Credit Ford. With no cautions to help solve the problems, he was forced to settle for a 35th-place finish, four laps behind. With the combination of Gordon's fifth place and Terry's sixth place, both Hendrick Motorsports drivers pushed by Jarrett in the point standings following the race. Terry took over the lead, 39 markers ahead of Jeff, while Jarrett now trailed the defending NASCAR Winston Cup champion by 52 points.

Earnhardt's smile continued to show even at the race's conclusion. His fighting second place had been his first top-five finish of the season and it moved him to sixth place in the point standings.

Winston 500

Fin. Pos.	Start Pos.	Car #	Driver	Team
1	18	6	Mark Martin	Valvoline Ford
2	3	3	Dale Earnhardt	GM Goodwrench Service Chevrolet
3	8	18	Bobby Labonte	Interstate Batteries Pontiac
4	1	98	John Andretti	RCA Ford
5	11	24	Jeff Gordon	DuPont Refinishes Chevrolet
6	36	5	Terry Labonte	Kellogg's Corn Flakes Chevrolet
7	20	23	Jimmy Spencer	Camel Cigarettes Ford
8	39	99	Jeff Burton	Exide Batteries Ford
9	17	30	Johnny Benson	Pennzoil Pontiac
10	7	28	Ernie Irvan	Texaco Havoline Ford
11	29	10	Ricky Rudd	Tide Ford
12	6	33	Ken Schrader	Skoal Bandit Chevrolet
13	12	36	Derrike Cope	Skittles Pontiac
14	28	21	Michael Waltrip	CITGO Ford
15	26	90	Dick Trickle	Heilig-Meyers Ford
16	5	31	Mike Skinner	Lowe's Chevrolet
17	27	46	Wally Dallenbach	First Union Chevrolet
18	10	94	Bill Elliott	McDonald's Ford
19	32	40	Joe Nemechek	Coors Light Chevrolet
20	2	77	Bobby Hillin	Jasper Engines/Federal-Mogul Ford
21	14	9	Lake Speed	Ace Hardware Ford
22	15	75	Rick Mast	Remington Arms Ford
23	40	37	Jeremy Mayfield	Kmart/RC Cola Ford
24	38	16	Ted Musgrave	Family Channel/PRIMESTAR Ford
25	13	20	Greg Sacks	Hardee's Ford
26	30	81	Kenny Wallace	Square D Ford
27	33	25	Ricky Craven	Budweiser Chevrolet
28	41	1	Morgan Shepherd	Crusin' America Phone Card Pontiac
29	22	29	Robert Pressley	Cartoon Network Chevrolet
30	37	71	Dave Marcis	Realtree Camouflage Chevrolet
31	35	43	Bobby Hamilton	STP Pontiac
32	43	17	Darrell Waltrip	Parts America Chevrolet
33	31	11	Brett Bodine	Close Call Phone Card Ford
34	42	97	Chad Little	John Deere Pontiac
35	9	88	Dale Jarrett	Quality Care/Ford Credit Ford
36	23	8	Hut Stricklin	Circuit City Ford
37	4	2	Rusty Wallace	Miller Lite Ford
38	34	96	David Green	Caterpillar Chevrolet
39	16	4	Sterling Marlin	Kodak Film Chevrolet
40	21	44	Kyle Petty	Hot Wheels Pontiac
41	24	41	Steve Grissom	Kodiak Chevrolet
42	25	22	Ward Burton	MBNA America Pontiac
43	19	7	Geoff Bodine	QVC Ford

NASCAR WINSTON CUP SERIES 1997

The Winston

(Charlotte Motor Speedway • May 17, 1997)

With back-to back victories to his credit at Sears Point and Talladega, Mark Martin's long winless string was forgotten when the teams arrived at Charlotte Motor Speedway for the 13th running of The Winston, the sport's all-star event.

While many expected the momentum of the Valvoline team to continue on the track it had taken in California and Alabama, Mark was much more realistic. He had seen streaks come and go in the past, and he had often said, with a voice of experience, that when you had the horse, you rode it until it quit — but that eventually it would quit.

(Left) Riding a winning horse into Charlotte, Jack Roush was hoping that his driver, Mark Martin, could continue his winning ways and pick up a lucrative victory in The Winston, a feather still missing from Jack's hat.

(Right) A jubilant Jeff Gordon declares victory in Charlotte's winner's circle after conquering the all-star field, winning in excess of $200,000 in the process.

NASCAR
Winston
THE WINSTON
DUPONT
QUAKER STATE
JURASSIC PARK THE RIDE
ACDelco
GMAC
Coca-Cola

(Above) Chad Little and Lake Speed (9) bring the field to the stripe to start the Winston Open. Only one driver in the field of 30 would advance to The Winston in the 50-lap sprint race. (Right) Setting the pace for the Winston Open was Chad Little, who accepts the pole-winner's trophy after turning a lap at 181.220 miles per hour in his John Deere Pontiac, and giving his team a much-needed morale boost.

The weekend of The Winston is unlike any other in the sport. The events of the weekend paid cubic dollars, and there were no points awarded. Teams were able to "go for broke," and if the car or engine failed, no crucial NASCAR Winston Cup championship points would be lost. As a result, past runnings of The Winston had brought some of the biggest fireworks of the season, as drivers fought for the prestige of being the best of the best that night — not to mention the pocketful of cash that went with the huge trophy.

Unlike some years past, this running of the all-star race would see just a single car advance from the preliminary race, the Winston Open. There were 19 drivers and teams already in the main event, and the fact that just the winner of the Winston Open would advance put even more pressure on some of the best teams in the sport, whose drivers had not yet qualified for the all-star race.

Among those who would line up to do battle in the Winston Open were the likes of Ricky Craven, Ken Schrader, Chad Little, Wally Dallenbach, Rick Mast, Joe Nemechek, Steve Grissom, Dick Trickle, Robby Gordon, Lake Speed, Johnny Benson, Mike and Kenny Wallace, Brett Bodine, Mike Skinner, Robert Pressley, Ted Musgrave, Derrike Cope, Jeremy Mayfield, John Andretti, David Green, Morgan Shepherd, Bobby Hillin, Dave Marcis, Rick Wilson, Billy Standridge, Randy MacDonald and Ed Berrier. Joe Ruttman also was on hand, driving the first NASCAR Winston Cup car fielded by Michael Waltrip's NASCAR Busch Series team.

It was quite a cast to be narrowed down to a single car, so when Little out-qualified Speed to win the Winston Open pole, it was a huge boost to the morale of the John Deere crew. The team, up-scaled from Little's NASCAR Busch Series effort from the previous year, had started the year with no provisionals, and had struggled throughout the first part of the season. Chad said, after his pole-winning run, that he hoped this would point his team in the right direction.

Craven, who many in the garage area thought was on the verge of winning his initial NASCAR Winston Cup Series point race after his recent strong performances, took the inside of the second row, beating Dallenbach for the spot, while Pressley claimed the fifth starting position for the Winston Open.

Qualifying for The Winston is different than for any other event on the circuit. The format was chosen to bring the entire team into play to help determine the starting order, by incorporating a right-side, two-tire change on pit road into the three-lap test. The total time of the three laps, including the pit stop, would determine the average speed of each competitor,

(Left) *Ricky Craven spends some brief moments in victory lane after emerging victorious in the Winston Open. Craven's celebration was cut short as he had just 30 minutes before he would join his Hendrick teammates in the evening's main event.*
(Below) *Bobby Labonte gets off to a rough start by spinning down the frontstretch on the fourth lap of The Winston. Labonte recovered nicely by winning the second segment, and eventually finished second in the final 10-lap sprint.*

For the third consecutive year, Dale Earnhardt unveiled a special paint scheme for The Winston. This year, his Wheaties-sponsored Chevrolet started from the front row next to pole-winner Bill Elliott, and eventually finished fourth.

and, unlike NASCAR Winston Cup point races, there was no speed limit on pit road — either on the entrance to the two-tire stop or on the exit. Drivers spent several laps on the track practicing their entries onto pit road before the qualifying session, while crew chiefs clocked each entry with a stopwatch to help determine how much time would be gained or lost on pit road.

With $50,000 on the line for the pole-winner, Dale Earnhardt posted the best time of the session so far, when his crew cranked a 9.66-second stop on the specially painted, orange Wheaties Chevrolet. When his entire time on the track was computed, his average speed for the three laps was 141.887 miles per hour, more than enough to better Sterling Marlin's 141.466-mph speed.

But, it was the final qualifier who stole the thunder of the evening. Bill Elliott and crew chief Mike Beam had a surprise for the crowd, with Bill flat-footing in down pit road and coming to a perfect stop right against the pit wall. The closer the driver gets to the wall, the less distance the crew has to travel, and the faster the pit stop. The McDonald's Ford team tripped the clocks at 9.55 seconds, and Bill was gone. His speed of 143.272 mph ignited the crowd, and brought him to the winner's circle to accept the trophy and the cash.

During the qualifying session, Jeff Gordon, a favorite to win the pole with his Jurassic Park-painted Chevrolet, slid through his pit when he locked the right-front brake, sending him to a 19th-place starting position. Darrell Waltrip broke a rear gear when he tried to leave pit road after his stop, and Martin, after his crew gave him the fastest service of the night in 9.34 seconds, struggled leaving the pits, costing him a shot at the pole.

When it was over, Marlin and defending champion Michael Waltrip were lined up on the second row, with Bobby Labonte and Dale Jarrett

Jeff Gordon's Monte Carlo had much more than this paint job touting the movie, "The Lost World." Fresh from the Hendrick Motorsports R&D department, the brand new car thundered around the track devouring everything in its path.

84

Defending champion of The Winston, Michael Waltrip, also shows a new look with his CITGO Thunder-Dalmatian.

on the third. Rusty Wallace and Martin were seventh and eighth, ahead of Jeff Burton and Geoff Bodine. Terry Labonte and Ricky Rudd made up the sixth row, with Bobby Hamilton and Ward Burton behind them, and Kyle Petty and Ernie Irvan were 15th and 16th fastest. Jimmy Spencer started alongside Darrell Waltrip, with Gordon behind Darrell.

The 50-lap Winston Open saw Speed jump to an early lead, but Craven was obviously determined to find a way to join his other two Hendrick Motorsports teammates in The Winston, and on lap 29, he rocketed past the red Melling Ford. Three laps later, Grissom sent Speed to third place and set out after Craven, but Ricky had all he needed under the hood of the Budweiser Monte Carlo. He held off Grissom's determined charge the remainder of the way, claiming the $28,000 winner's share of the purse. His moment of triumph was brief, however, with the car immediately being swarmed by Andy Graves and the crew, who had just 30 minutes to prepare it for the main event.

At the front of the field when The Winston's first 30-lap segment took the green flag, Elliott and Earnhardt waged a war that kept the huge throng on its feet, trading the lead back and forth. While the focus was at the point, Gordon came ripping and snorting through the field, devouring cars like the dinosaur on the hood of the research and development car from Hendrick Motorsports. By the 10th lap he was in the top 10, and he continued to charge, taking third place from Elliott with three laps left in the segment. While Bill had faded slightly, Jarrett had moved to battle with Earnhardt, and after the lead swapped hands between the two, Jarrett held the point at the end of the first segment.

The field was inverted for the start of the second 30 laps, putting Jarrett, Earnhardt, Gordon and Elliott at the back of the field, while the Labonte brothers, Bobby and Terry, rocketed away from the pack to battle between themselves for the honor of claiming the second segment of the race. Bobby won the struggle, and behind the two Texans, Gordon came snorting through the pack again, eventually finishing fourth behind Craven, who had a fine run to third place. His finish put Gordon on the outside of the second row for the start of the final, 10-lap sprint to the big bucks, and when he saw the brothers battling for the lead when the green dropped, Gordon cracked a grin under his helmet.

He whipped past Bobby on the 61st lap and then got the run he needed exiting the second turn a lap later, to get under Terry. When the two entered the third turn, Gordon yanked the wheel left, the car settled on a rail in the third turn, and he pulled clear. He knew that once he moved to the front, no one could beat what he had under the skin of the Monte Carlo in a short sprint race — and he was right. He cruised to his second victory in the all-star race. Bobby eventually passed Terry, but could not close the gap on Gordon, while Earnhardt finished fourth, ahead of Spencer. Martin, who had continued his winning streak with the IROC round at Charlotte, saw it end with a sixth-place finish. Jarrett beat Craven for seventh, and Rudd and Elliott were the final top-10 finishers.

The Winston

Fin. Pos.	Start Pos.	Car #	Driver	Team
1	19	24	Jeff Gordon	DuPont Refinishes Chevrolet
2	5	18	Bobby Labonte	Interstate Batteries Pontiac
3	11	5	Terry Labonte	Kellogg's Corn Flakes Chevrolet
4	2	3	Dale Earnhardt	GM Goodwrench Service Chevrolet
5	18	23	Jimmy Spencer	Camel Cigarettes Ford
6	8	6	Mark Martin	Valvoline Ford
7	6	88	Dale Jarrett	Quality Care/Ford Credit Ford
8	20	25	Ricky Craven	Budweiser Chevrolet
9	12	10	Ricky Rudd	Tide Ford
10	1	94	Bill Elliott	McDonald's Ford
11	10	7	Geoff Bodine	QVC Ford
12	9	99	Jeff Burton	Exide Batteries Ford
13	14	22	Ward Burton	MBNA America Pontiac
14	15	44	Kyle Petty	Hot Wheels Pontiac
15	3	4	Sterling Marlin	Kodak Film Chevrolet
16	4	21	Michael Waltrip	CITGO Ford
17	17	17	Darrell Waltrip	Parts America Chevrolet
18	7	2	Rusty Wallace	Miller Lite Ford
19	16	28	Ernie Irvan	Texaco Havoline Ford
20	13	43	Bobby Hamilton	STP Pontiac

Segment 1

1. Dale Jarrett
2. Dale Earnhardt
3. Jeff Gordon
4. Bill Elliott
5. Mark Martin
6. Michael Waltrip
7. Jimmy Spencer
8. Darrell Waltrip
9. Ricky Rudd
10. Ward Burton
11. Jeff Burton
12. Kyle Petty
13. Rusty Wallace
14. Sterling Marlin
15. Geoff Bodine
16. Ricky Craven
17. Bobby Labonte
18. Terry Labonte
19. Ernie Irvan
20. Bobby Hamilton

Segment 2

1. Bobby Labonte
2. Terry Labonte
3. Ricky Craven
4. Jeff Gordon
5. Jimmy Spencer
6. Dale Jarrett
7. Dale Earnhardt
8. Jeff Burton
9. Geoff Bodine
10. Mark Martin
11. Bill Elliott
12. Ricky Rudd
13. Kyle Petty
14. Sterling Marlin
15. Ward Burton
16. Michael Waltrip
17. Rusty Wallace
18. Darrell Waltrip
19. Ernie Irvan
20. Bobby Hamilton

NASCAR WINSTON CUP SERIES 1997

Coca-Cola 600

(Charlotte Motor Speedway • May 25, 1997)

Jeff Gordon's runaway victory in the final segment of The Winston bore immediate fruit for his team. The win gave him a sweep of the season's special non-points events (he had won the Busch Clash in February at Daytona) and brought the DuPont team a huge share of the winner's purse — more than $200,000.

The Hendrick Motorsports team brought a different car from the stable for the running of the Coca-Cola 600, giving the beleaguered Ford forces some hope after the Blue Ovals watched their best efforts get whipped into submission in The Winston.

After technical inspection following The Winston, the DuPont team was told not to bring the winning car back to the track until some changes were made to it, so the team chose to use a different chassis for the longest race of the season, given the limited amount of time between events. Gordon had called the Jurassic Park car he used in The Winston "the car of the future," but the future would have to wait a few more weeks. Instead, one of the team's tried and true Monte Carlos was rolled into the garage area in preparation for the Coca-Cola 600.

NASCAR officials notified teams that the Fords would be allowed to add one-quarter inch of rear spoiler to the Thunderbirds for the 600, and the decision, of course, was met with mixed reviews, depending on which camp the comments came from. The Ford folks said the quarter inch wasn't enough, but the Chevrolet teams howled that it was too much. The Pontiac teams merely shrugged their shoulders.

In the days between The Winston and the Coca-Cola 600, NASCAR Busch Series rookie Steve Park faced the media and was announced as the driver of a five-race NASCAR Winston Cup

(Right) Jeff Gordon cranks the wheel of the DuPont Chevrolet in the opening laps of the Coca-Cola 600. His win from the pole in the longest race of the year would complete a sweep of the events at Charlotte, and close the gap on point-leader Terry Labonte.

(Below) Morning and afternoon showers did not deter the huge crowd that turned out for the Coca-Cola 600, which took the green flag under overcast skies, just 30 minutes after the scheduled starting time.

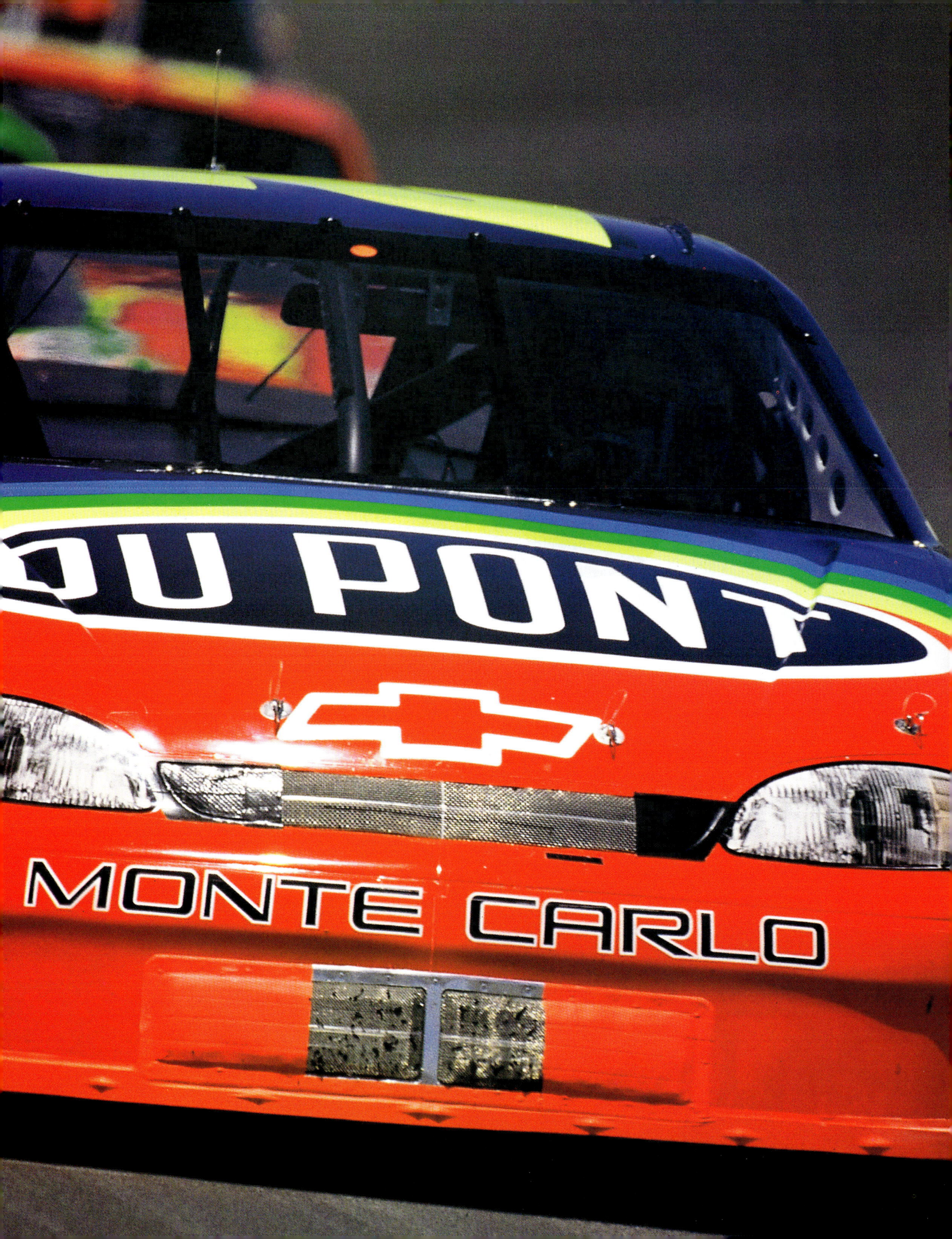
DU PONT
MONTE CARLO

(Left) What's left of Geoff Bodine's QVC Ford (top) is carried back to the garage after Bodine backed it into the wall during practice. For the race, Geoff enlisted younger brother Todd (above) to assume the driving duties in the backup Thunderbird. *(Right)* Outfitted in a commemorative driver's suit, Ernie Irvan stands beside the Texaco Havoline Ford, painted in nostalgic white and black to celebrate Texaco's 10 years with Robert Yates Racing.

schedule behind the wheel of a car owned by Dale and Teresa Earnhardt and sponsored by Burger King. There was little doubt where this program was headed in 1998. Park, with his brilliant performances in the NASCAR Busch Series this year, was clearly on the fast track.

With Harry Ranier's team struggling and ready to cease operation when the Hardee's sponsorship suffered problems, Ranier/Walsh Racing's Tom Baldwin signed on as the new crew chief for Junie Donlavey's Richmond-based team with driver Dick Trickle. The Coca-Cola 600 would serve as a milestone for two NASCAR Winston Cup drivers: Caterpillar Chevrolet driver David Green and wife Diane celebrated the birth of their first child, daughter Kaylie Rae, prior to the race, and Darrell Waltrip prepared to make his 700th career start when he went to the line.

Robert Yates Racing had its own celebration to mark the 10th anniversary of the team. When the crew rolled out the Texaco Thunderbird, Ernie Irvan's car carried the same paint scheme that had graced the Thunderbird 10 years ago when Davey Allison was behind the wheel. The appearance of the car in its white-black-and-gold colors stopped many people short in the garage and brought to mind many of the great moments — and victories — that the Yates-Allison combination had enjoyed in the past.

Whether it used a new car or an old one, the DuPont team had little to worry about. There was no question who would be the favorite to win the Busch Pole for the Coca-Cola 600 when qualifying began. Gordon, with three consecutive 600 poles under his belt, was one of the fastest drivers during practice and was the odds-on favorite to pick up a fourth straight bundle of dough. Gordon's only concern, it seemed, was that he

Back in black for the Coca-Cola 600, Dale Earnhardt climbs aboard his Goodwrench Chevrolet. As has become his pattern at Charlotte, Dale would start near the rear, this time in 33rd position, and then slice his way through the field to dice with the leaders — all to the delight of the Charlotte fans.

drew the 18th position, and he felt the track might cool down more as the session ran later into the evening and aid some teams in their quest for the inside of the front row.

Despite these thoughts, Gordon ripped off a lap of 184.3 mph, and then watched and waited, expecting to be beaten. Hendrick Motorsports teammate Ricky Craven, running 45th in line, almost beat Gordon, but failed by .017 of a second. Jeff had claimed his fourth straight Coca-Cola 600 Busch Pole. That put two of the Hendrick cars on the front row, while Dale Jarrett emerged as the fastest Ford with a lap that earned him the inside of the second row. Jeff Green, promoted from his Busch ride and given the opportunity to drive the Cartoon Network Chevrolet after Robert Pressley was released from the team after The Winston weekend, responded with the fourth-fastest lap for the Diamond Ridge team.

Joe Nemechek, who would go on to claim the NASCAR Busch Series victory on Saturday, grabbed the inside of the third row, and Ken Schrader was alongside him. Bobby Hamilton was the fastest Pontiac driver, posting the seventh-fastest time and barely beating the lap posted by Darrell Waltrip. Terry Labonte and Bill Elliott made up the fifth row, just ahead of Mark Martin, who was looking for his third consecutive points win, and rookie Mike Skinner.

Missing from the action was Geoff Bodine after he crashed hard during the opening practice session. Although he was all right, the QVC Ford was history, and Geoff nominated younger brother Todd to drive another of the stable's black Thunderbirds for the rest of the weekend. Geoff's decision brought an end to his string of 180 consecutive starts that dated back to 1991.

Robby Gordon, hoping to complete a doubleheader of action on the same day with the Indianapolis 500 in the morning and the Coca-Cola 600 in the evening, barely missed locking a spot during the first qualifying session, but his time was more than good enough to ensure a spot in the field. He left the track to fly to Indianapolis knowing he had a chance to join John Andretti in the record books as the only drivers to run in both races on the same day.

No driver who ran improved his time during the second session, and Ward Burton, Johnny Benson, Todd Bodine and Hut Stricklin were forced to use provisionals to make the field. Chad Little, Mike Wallace, Ed Berrier, Bobby Hillin, and Dave Marcis were sent home for the weekend. Hillin then found himself in a strange position. After failing to qualify for the race, he was told he would be replaced in the Jasper Engines Ford — but he was to continue driving the car until the team found a replacement driver.

With the Indianapolis 500 rained out and the Coca-Cola 600 starting almost 30 minutes late due to track drying efforts after a storm, Robby Gordon had plenty of time to make the trip back to Charlotte and was in the field when it rolled under the flagstand, where NASCAR starter Doyle Ford was flagging his final event prior to retirement.

With 400 laps to run, there would be plenty of time for drama, and Jeff Gordon was one of the first drivers to give fans a thrill. During an early-race pit stop, the car fell off the jack on pit road, and Gordon

With darkness beginning to set in, the field rumbles toward anxious pit crews under one of seven cautions during the race.

was red-flagged at the end of lap 185, at 8:41 p.m., and drivers, crews and an enormous gathering of fans were all forced to wait and see if the race would be restarted.

After two and a half hours, the drivers finally were back in their seats and the cars were rolling again. For 20 laps, they circled the track under yellow behind the pace car as track officials put the finishing touches on the drying job. At 11:46 p.m., and on lap 216, the race went green again — and the drama began. Rusty immediately rocketed to the head of the field, and made up his lap when the next caution came out. As the leaders shuffled back and forth during the course of green- and yellow-flag pit stops over the last

(Above) Ernie Irvan (28) holds the outside through the frontstretch quad-oval, working past Jeff Burton (99) as he hunts down the leaders. Irvan took the lap-leader bonus for the race, but fell to 13th place by the time the checkered flag fell. *(Right)* Dale Jarrett's engine erupts while taking the white flag alongside Bobby Hamilton's STP Pontiac, dropping Jarrett to 27th in the final rundown.

emerged in 30th place. A second stop to make hasty repairs to his car moved him back to 39th place, and his fight back through the field began. Rusty Wallace, with one of the hottest cars in the field, lost a lap when the lug nuts loosened on his right-front wheel on lap 45. He spent the next three hours battling back to the front of the pack. Jarrett was sent to the end of the line for a restart after a tire rolled away from his crew on pit road.

As the halfway mark approached, another line of storms rolled toward Charlotte, and the race became a dash to see if the field could make the magical halfway point at 200 laps — enough to put the race into the record books if it was rained out. Bobby Labonte and crew chief Jimmy Makar gambled for track position by changing only two tires during a stop, putting Bobby into the lead, but the rain arrived before the field reached the 200-lap mark. The event

hour of the race, the event turned into a war between Wallace, Gordon, the Labonte brothers, Elliott and Martin.

Knowing the event could not be completed at a reasonable hour, NASCAR officials notified the teams that, at 12:45 p.m., the race would continue for only 20 more laps. When the 20-lap shootout started,

After returning to Charlotte from the rained-out Indianapolis 500, Robby Gordon's day goes from bad to worse as he loops the Coors Chevrolet in turn four on lap 184.

In the early morning hours, Jeff Gordon and Rusty Wallace contest the victory in the rain-shortened event. Gordon would prove to be the stronger of the two, and edged Wallace for his fifth win of the season.

Wallace led Gordon, with Jeff Burton, Martin and Elliott tucked in right behind. The race would end on lap 333, and Gordon was determined not to wait around to see what might happen. He dove under Wallace on lap 317 and never looked back, pulling clear of the Miller Ford and easing to a half-second victory over Rusty. The two had raced to the yellow flag on the final lap after Jarrett blew an engine. Martin saw his winning streak end but beat Elliott for third place, and Jeff Burton came home ahead of Bobby Labonte. Dale Earnhardt drove to a solid seventh place, and Terry Labonte, Morgan Shepherd and Ricky Rudd claimed the final top-10 positions.

The victory gave Gordon a brilliant sweep of the Charlotte events, including The Winston, the pole for the Coca-Cola 600, and then the Coca-Cola 600 win. More importantly, the victory made Gordon eligible to battle for the Winston Million during the Mountain Dew Southern 500 at Darlington during Labor Day weekend — an event he has won for the last two years.

Rookie David Green goes to school on Mark Martin, who muscles his Valvoline Ford through the fourth turn in the early stages of the race. Martin was never able to lead a lap in the event, but finished the evening solidly in third.

Coca-Cola 600

Fin. Pos.	Start Pos.	Car #	Driver	Team
1	1	24	Jeff Gordon	DuPont Refinishes Chevrolet
2	21	2	Rusty Wallace	Miller Lite Ford
3	11	6	Mark Martin	Valvoline Ford
4	10	94	Bill Elliott	McDonald's Ford
5	16	99	Jeff Burton	Exide Batteries Ford
6	14	18	Bobby Labonte	Interstate Batteries Pontiac
7	33	3	Dale Earnhardt	GM Goodwrench Service Chevrolet
8	9	5	Terry Labonte	Kellogg's Corn Flakes Chevrolet
9	25	1	Morgan Shepherd	Delco Remy America Pontiac
10	18	10	Ricky Rudd	Tide Ford
11	27	41	Steve Grissom	Kodiak Chevrolet
12	24	36	Derrike Cope	Skittles Pontiac
13	13	28	Ernie Irvan	Texaco Havoline Ford
14	31	44	Kyle Petty	Hot Wheels Pontiac
15	40	30	Johnny Benson	Pennzoil Pontiac
16	32	96	David Green	Caterpillar Chevrolet
17	22	21	Michael Waltrip	CITGO Ford
18	19	23	Jimmy Spencer	Camel Cigarettes Ford
19	5	42	Joe Nemechek	BellSouth Chevrolet
20	17	75	Rick Mast	Remington Arms Ford
21	8	17	Darrell Waltrip	Parts America Chevrolet
22	4	29	Jeff Green	Cartoon Network Chevrolet
23	37	16	Ted Musgrave	Family Channel/PRIMESTAR Ford
24	30	9	Lake Speed	Melling Engine Parts Ford
25	42	8	Hut Stricklin	Circuit City Ford
26	36	11	Brett Bodine	Close Call Phone Card Ford
27	3	88	Dale Jarrett	Quality Care/Ford Credit Ford
28	35	37	Jeremy Mayfield	Kmart/RC Cola Ford
29	7	43	Bobby Hamilton	STP Pontiac
30	26	98	John Andretti	RCA Ford
31	38	19	Gary Bradberry	Child Support Recovery Ford
32	34	78	Billy Standridge	Hanes Ford
33	15	90	Dick Trickle	Heilig-Meyers/Simmons Ford
34	12	31	Mike Skinner	Lowe's Chevrolet
35	20	46	Wally Dallenbach	First Union Chevrolet
36	39	22	Ward Burton	MBNA America Pontiac
37	2	25	Ricky Craven	Budweiser Chevrolet
38	6	33	Ken Schrader	Skoal Bandit Chevrolet
39	23	81	Kenny Wallace	Square D Ford
40	29	4	Sterling Marlin	Kodak Film Chevrolet
41	28	40	Robby Gordon	Coors Light Chevrolet
42	41	7	Todd Bodine	QVC Ford

NASCAR WINSTON CUP SERIES 1997

Miller 500

(Dover Downs International Speedway • June 1, 1997)

The grins on the faces of Jeff Gordon and his Rainbow Warrior team members when they arrived at Denis McGlynn's ever-expanding "Monster Mile" in Dover's capital city were understandable. The DuPont team had put together a brilliant two weeks at Charlotte, winning The Winston and then sweeping both the pole and the win in the Coca-Cola 600. During the course of the 10 days, nearly $500,000 had been added to the number following Gordon's name in the money-won column of the season's statistics.

As if that wasn't enough reason to smile, the team arrived at the one-mile concrete roller coaster as the three-time defending champion of races at Dover Downs International Speedway. Beginning with the fall race in 1995, no one but Gordon had been to Dover's victory lane, much to the delight of the thousands of DuPont employees who made the short trip south from the Wilmington corporate headquarters.

A walk through the Dover garage area found Richard Jackson's team sporting a new name on his Pontiac, with R&L Carriers, one of the largest family-owned trucking companies in the country, emblazoned on the car. The financial assistance had come at the right time, with Jackson needing additional financing to help the team continue to run at every race. Morgan Shepherd, as usual, would be behind the wheel.

(Right) The thrill of victory is manifest in the Tide crew on Dover's pit road after their boss, Ricky Rudd, emerged with the lead in the waning laps and took the win.

(Below) The Hot Wheels crew provides fresh rubber and fuel for their driver Kyle Petty. Their swift service on pit road helped Petty score the new team's first ever top-five finish.

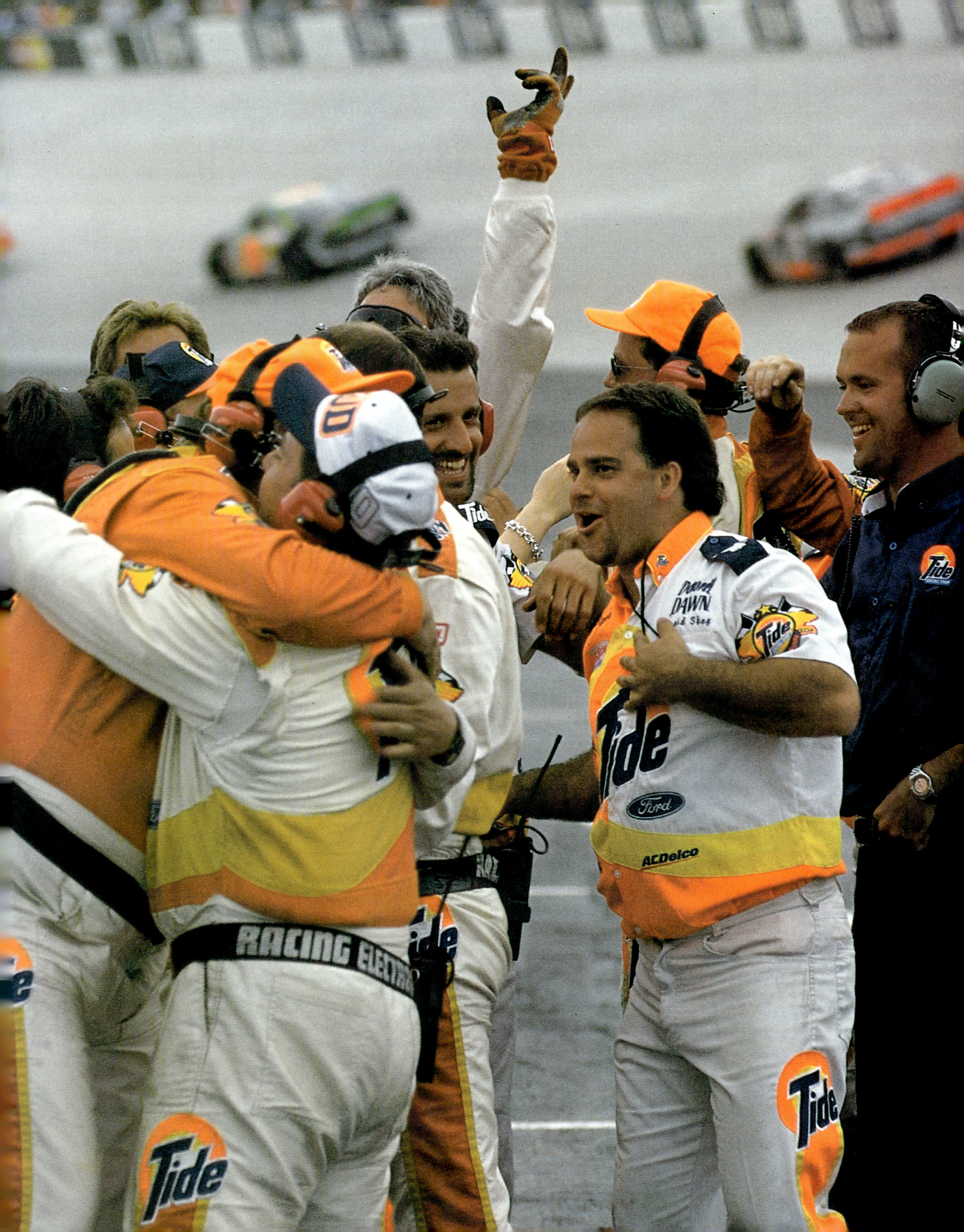
Tide
DAWN
Ford
ACDelco
RACING ELECTR
Tide
Tide
Tide

(Above) Mike Wallace describes how his Spam Chevrolet reacts on Dover's concrete surface to Geoff Bodine, who returned to the wheel of his QVC Ford after sitting out the Coca-Cola 600 last week at Charlotte.
(Above Right) Earplugs and gloves are two pieces of essential equipment for drivers. *(Right)* Wally Dallenbach, filling in for Robby Gordon in the Coors Chevrolet, keeps track of qualifying times as he sits on pit road waiting for his turn on the track.

Busch Series, and also released team manager Eddie Jones. Veteran crew chief David Ifft was on hand at Dover as a temporary replacement to guide the FILMAR team and driver Kenny Wallace.

The rain-shortened Coca-Cola 600 victory, coupled with Terry Labonte's eighth place, had moved Gordon into second place in the standings, and he arrived at Dover just six points behind his Hendrick Motorsports teammate. Dale Jarrett's 27th place at Charlotte – a result of the engine blowing in his Quality Care Ford as he crossed the line to take the white flag for the final lap of the race — sent him to third place, and he now trailed Labonte by 112 points. Mark Martin's third place boosted him to fourth, 20 points behind Jarrett. Bobby Labonte held fifth, 75

There was also some bad news. Harry Melling's team was missing in action, deciding to take the Dover weekend off after running the first third of the season without a primary sponsor. Lake Speed and the remainder of the red Ford team had been hoping that some financial assistance would come their way, but with none arriving before the trip to Dover, the team remained at home.

Geoff Bodine, after being forced from his QVC Ford during the Charlotte weekend following his practice accident, was back behind the wheel of the black Thunderbird. Nearby, Wally Dallenbach was fitting himself into the Coors Light Chevrolet fielded by the SABCO Racing stable. Dallenbach was available to substitute for SABCO teammate Robby Gordon who was injured during the Indianapolis 500 and was unable to compete at Dover.

Also in the headlines were Jeff Green and the FILMAR organization that fields Square D Fords for Kenny Wallace. Green, in third place in the points and one of the contenders for the NASCAR Busch Series championship, had moved into the Diamond Ridge Cartoon Network Chevrolet at Charlotte. By the time the teams arrived at Dover, the decision had been made by Diamond Ridge to put all its efforts with Green into the NASCAR Winston Cup program. Green would compete in Cup for the remainder of the season, rather than split his duties between the two series. FILMAR management released crew chief Gil Martin, the only crew chief the team had known since it began in the NASCAR

94

behind Martin, and 46 ahead of a steadily-improving Dale Earnhardt. Jeff Burton trailed Earnhardt by only six points, while Ricky Rudd held eighth place, 49 points ahead of Rusty Wallace. Michael Waltrip was 10th in the standings after Charlotte, 15 points ahead of Bill Elliott.

By the time the Busch Pole qualifying session rolled around at Dover, the "Monster Mile" had lived up to its reputation. No less than six NASCAR Busch Series drivers had found the wall during the opening day, and Cuppers Shepherd, Billy Standridge and Bobby Hamilton had their own encounters with the concrete. The incidents, combined with a slightly harder compound Goodyear tire provided for the race, had the drivers on edge when the first car rolled out for the qualifying session.

(Right) Teammates in the garage but competitors on the track, Ernie Irvan (28) and Dale Jarrett get together at the end of pit road after pitting under caution. Jarrett edged Irvan to the line to maintain his lead for the ensuing restart. (Below) Dick Trickle (90) and Jeff Burton (99) drift out of the racing groove on Dover's 24-degree banks, while Sterling Marlin (4) stays glued to the bottom, trying to sneak past Jeff Green (29), Johnny Benson (30) and Wally Dallenbach (40).

When it was completed, Bobby Labonte had whipped his Interstate Batteries Pontiac to the marque's first Busch Pole of the season and his second straight at Dover. It was the eighth of his short career, and gave Pontiac its first pole since September 1996.

The only driver to keep Bobby's lap in sight was Gordon, who was forced to settle for the outside of the front row. Behind the two, the remainder of the top 10 saw several drivers record their best starting positions of the season. Kyle Petty and Joe Nemechek claimed the second row, with Dave Marcis stunning the garage area with his fifth-fastest lap. Dale Jarrett was alongside the Realtree Camouflage

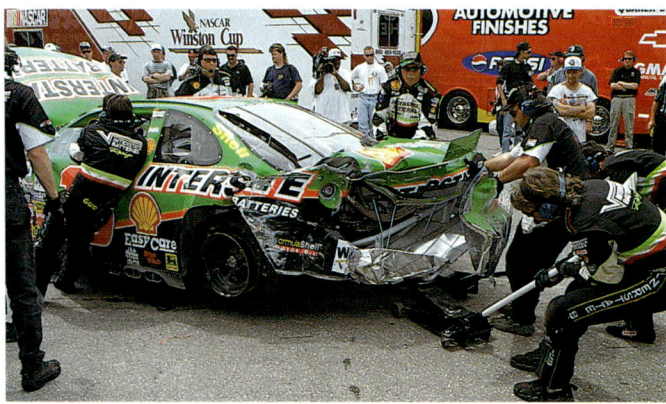

(Left) A dejected Bobby Labonte sits alone in the garage while his crew works on the Interstate Batteries Pontiac. The pole-winner led the first 30 laps of the race before he hit the second-turn wall, ending his hopes for victory. (Right) Crew members waste no time (top) beginning repairs to Labonte's car upon its return to the garage area. Their work complete, Bobby returns to the track (above) able to complete 283 laps during the 500-mile event.

Chevrolet, with Martin and David Green right behind. Ward Burton and Ernie Irvan completed the top 10. Dover would be the best starts of the season for Labonte, Petty, Marcis, Green and Burton.

With overcast skies and cooler temperatures, Sterling Marlin led the second-day assault, nailing down the second-fastest speed in the field. Hamilton, Mike Skinner, Kenny Wallace and Gary Bradberry used provisionals to make the race, while Dale Earnhardt, 44th fastest in the 45-car field, took a former champion's provisional. Standridge and Ed Berrier were the only drivers not to make the race.

All indications were that this would be the final 500-mile race at Dover as teams lined up for the Sunday afternoon start. Dover's usual race-happy fans piled into every seat in the place, putting a broad smile on McGlynn's face.

This event was running the full 500 laps. Had it ended at 400, Jarrett would have claimed his third victory of the season. But the track saved its action for the final 50 laps of the race, and the finish had the huge throng on its feet, applauding the unexpected winner.

On lap 450, with race leader Jarrett eyeing a fast-closing Gordon, John Andretti spun in the RCA Ford after being tapped by Skinner. The ensuing accident ended with Gordon hammering the rear of Jarrett's Ford, sending the Thunderbird driver into a spin. Gordon's radiator was smashed, and he went behind the wall for repairs, while Jarrett surfaced back in the lead. Seven laps after the green flag flew, Jarrett saw the second motor in as many weeks erupt, and he was out, coasting to the garage.

The lead went to Irvan, and Ernie looked set to win his first race of the season. But 28 laps from the end, Irvan slipped in the first turn and

Ernie Irvan leads the field to the stripe on the restart after the second caution of the race with Sterling Marlin on the inside, trying to regain a lap.

96

Ricky Rudd takes the checkered flag with Mark Martin nipping at his bumper. Martin struggled furiously in the closing laps to get past the Tide Ford, but Rudd was able to protect his lead and extend his personal string of winning seasons to 15.

drilled the wall while leading. That turned the lead over to a surprised Rudd, and when the field formed for the final restart with 20 laps left in the event, Rudd looked in his mirror and saw a hungry Martin in his red-white-and-blue Valvoline Ford.

In the final 10 laps, Martin gave Rudd all he could handle, pasting the Valvoline Ford on the Tide Thunderbird's rear bumper. He had Rudd so loose the final two laps that Ricky said he didn't know how he kept the car under him, but Martin never applied the chrome horn. Ricky beat Mark to the line by a car-length, and extended his record of winning at least one race a year to 15 straight seasons.

Jeff Burton rolled to third place, while Jeremy Mayfield and Petty posted solid and strong runs to grab fourth and fifth. Ken Schrader, Michael Waltrip and Elliott fought for sixth, seventh and eighth places, one lap down, ahead of Skinner, who won a two-laps-behind battle with Marlin.

The Rainbow Warriors affect repairs to the DuPont Chevrolet after driver Jeff Gordon drilled Dale Jarrett from behind. Gordon lost just 10 laps while repairs were made and finished the race in 26th place.

Miller 500

Fin. Pos.	Start Pos.	Car #	Driver	Team
1	13	10	Ricky Rudd	Tide Ford
2	7	6	Mark Martin	Valvoline Ford
3	34	99	Jeff Burton	Exide Batteries Ford
4	25	37	Jeremy Mayfield	Kmart/RC Cola Ford
5	3	44	Kyle Petty	Hot Wheels Pontiac
6	11	33	Ken Schrader	Skoal Bandit Chevrolet
7	24	21	Michael Waltrip	CITGO Ford
8	12	94	Bill Elliott	McDonald's Ford
9	40	31	Mike Skinner	Lowe's Chevrolet
10	26	4	Sterling Marlin	Kodak Film Chevrolet
11	17	16	Ted Musgrave	Family Channel/PRIMESTAR Ford
12	30	75	Rick Mast	Remington Arms Ford
13	19	25	Ricky Craven	Budweiser Chevrolet
14	21	5	Terry Labonte	Kellogg's Corn Flakes Chevrolet
15	4	42	Joe Nemechek	BellSouth Chevrolet
16	43	3	Dale Earnhardt	GM Goodwrench Service Chevrolet
17	39	43	Bobby Hamilton	STP Pontiac
18	8	96	David Green	Caterpillar Chevrolet
19	14	8	Hut Stricklin	Circuit City Ford
20	15	36	Derrike Cope	Skittles Pontiac
21	29	30	Johnny Benson	Pennzoil Pontiac
22	22	23	Jimmy Spencer	Camel Cigarettes Ford
23	33	91	Mike Wallace	Spam Chevrolet
24	28	41	Steve Grissom	Kodiak Chevrolet
25	5	71	Dave Marcis	Realtree Camouflage Chevrolet
26	2	24	Jeff Gordon	DuPont Refinishes Chevrolet
27	41	81	Kenny Wallace	Square D Ford
28	37	17	Darrell Waltrip	Parts America Chevrolet
29	23	98	John Andretti	RCA Ford
30	10	28	Ernie Irvan	Texaco Havoline Ford
31	16	97	Chad Little	John Deere Pontiac
32	6	88	Dale Jarrett	Quality Care/Ford Credit Ford
33	20	11	Brett Bodine	Close Call Phone Card Ford
34	9	22	Ward Burton	MBNA America Pontiac
35	42	19	Gary Bradberry	Child Support Recovery Ford
36	31	40	Wally Dallenbach	Coors Light Chevrolet
37	27	29	Jeff Green	Cartoon Network Chevrolet
38	36	1	Morgan Shepherd	R&L Carriers/Cruisin' America Pontiac
39	18	2	Rusty Wallace	Miller Lite Ford
40	1	18	Bobby Labonte	Interstate Batteries Pontiac
41	32	90	Dick Trickle	Heilig-Meyers/Simmons Ford
42	35	7	Geoff Bodine	QVC Ford
43	38	77	Bobby Hillin	Jasper Engine/Federal-Mogul Ford

NASCAR WINSTON CUP SERIES 1997

Pocono 500

(Pocono Raceway • June 8, 1997)

Ricky Rudd was still on cruise control when the NASCAR Winston Cup teams arrived at Drs. Rose and Joe Mattioli's unique triangular superspeedway in the splendid Pocono Mountains.

Rudd's Dover victory just a few days before had been an unexpected one for the Virginian and his team. In recent years, the triumphs that helped him stretch a string that included at least one victory in each of the last 14 seasons, had come late in the year. There had been considerable changes within his team during the off-season, and they were continuing to contest the NASCAR Winston Cup Series with a tightly knit group of crewmen. Without the hordes of bodies that some teams feel are necessary for research and development, Rudd admitted he had been surprised to find himself in victory lane this early in the season. He meant no disrespect to his team and crew, but he had felt that the team would need longer to come together to challenge for a victory this year.

(Left) After getting together last week at Dover in an accident that knocked both drivers out of winning contention, Jeff Gordon and Dale Jarrett (88) are nose to tail once again, vying for the Pocono victory.

(Right) Bobby Hamilton has a look of concern in the Pocono garage, having arrived there with a new and untested STP Pontiac. He shouldn't have worried; Hamilton was the fastest in qualifying and claimed his third career pole.

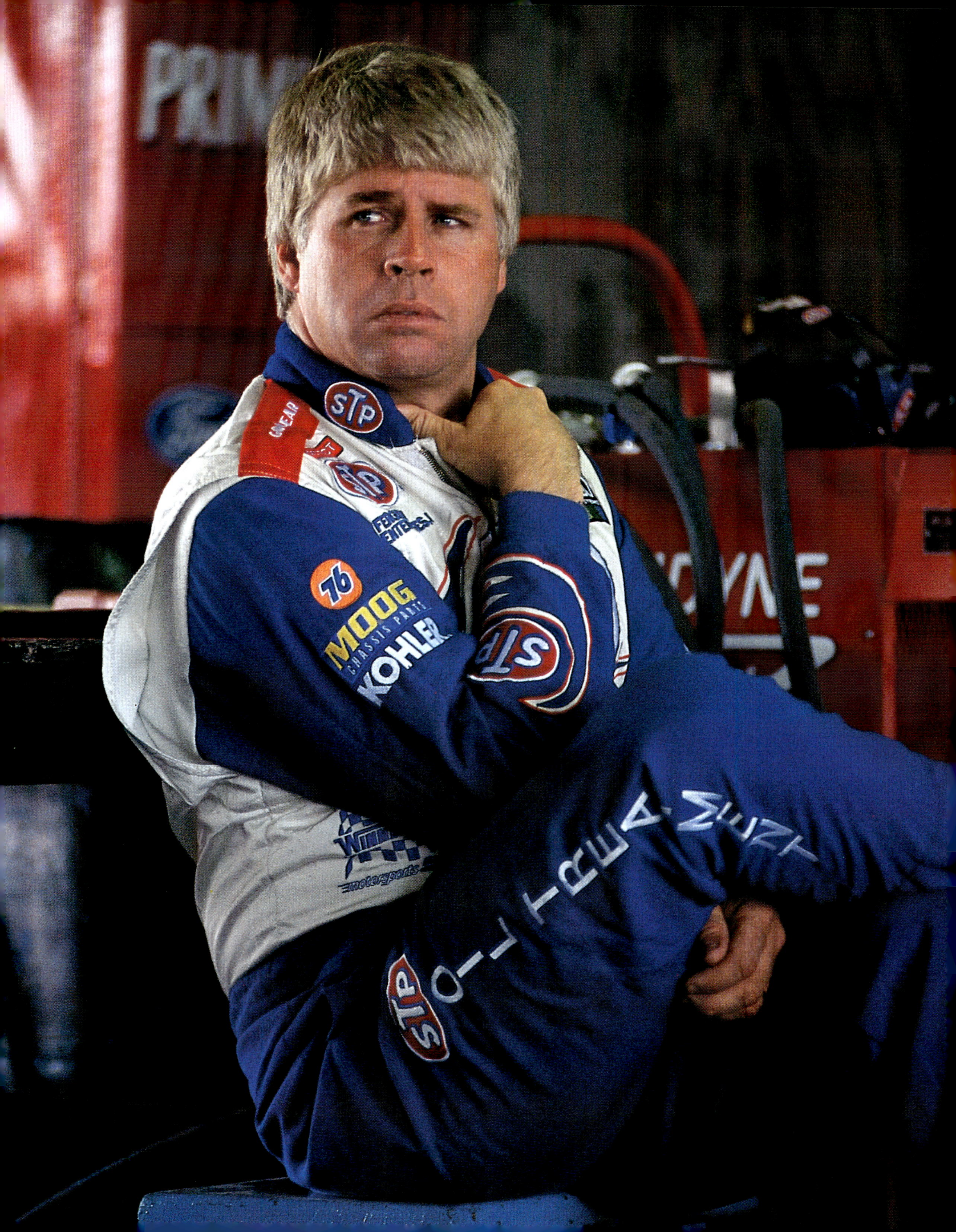
STP
76
MOOG
CHASSIS PARTS
KOHLER

Instead, Rudd had watched in amazement as the cards fell his way at Dover, and he rolled into the winner's circle to lengthen his string to a remarkable 15 straight years with a victory.

While Rudd was streaking to the win with his Tide Ride and climbing to eighth in the point standings, Jeff Gordon's day at Dover had turned to ashes when he collided with Dale Jarrett. Gordon finished 26th and lost points to teammate Terry Labonte, who maintained the point lead despite his 14th-place Dover finish. Mark Martin's second place at Dover moved him to within 41 points of Gordon, as the teams prepared for Pocono. Dale Jarrett's engine problems, relegating him to a 32nd-place finish, pushed the Ford driver even further behind in the standings.

(Left) Sterling Marlin has a good laugh on pit road while he waits for the start of the Pocono 500. *(Below)* Surrounded by photographers and swarmed by his fans, Jeff Gordon is happy to sign autographs as he works his way down pit road for his qualifying run.

(Above) Rick Mast (75) slips past Ken Schrader (33) and Jimmy Spencer (23) as the three drivers drag race down Pocono's lengthy frontstretch. Mast had started 10th, his best qualifying effort of the season so far.
(Right) Jeff Gordon tucks in behind Bobby Hamilton at the entrance to Pocono's first turn as the two drivers dice for the lead in the opening laps. Hamilton's fine run from the pole was cut short by an accident on lap 132.

Jeff Burton continued to impress with his third place at Dover, which he used to hold fifth in the standings, ahead of Dale Earnhardt and Bobby Labonte. Michael Waltrip (seventh at Dover) and Bill Elliott (eighth at the "Monster Mile") were ninth and 10th in the point standings, ahead of a furious battle involving Bobby Hamilton, Jeremy Mayfield and Rusty Wallace.

The Pocono race marked the final time that Morgan Shepherd would be behind the wheel of Richard Jackson's Pontiac. Shepherd had agreed to switch to the Jasper Motorsports team beginning with the upcoming Michigan race, sending Bobby Hillin to the sidelines. There was no early indication at Pocono about who would move into the Jackson Pontiac, now carrying the colors of R&L Carriers.

With Jeff Green now concentrating on the NASCAR Winston Cup side of things for the Diamond Ridge team, it meant that two brothers would be competing for the Rookie-of-the-Year title at stock car racing's highest level. Jeff joined brother David Green in the battle for the tyro title, and both Owensboro, Ky., natives would have their hands full with the likes of Robby Gordon and Mike Skinner, the other top rookies in the struggle for supremacy this season.

Robby, out of the Coors Chevrolet while recovering from burns received in his Indianapolis 500 accident, found himself the center of interest. Car owner Felix Sabates had told media members that he felt Robby had to make the decision whether he wanted to be a NASCAR Winston Cup driver, or to continue being a stock car driver and an Indy Racing League competitor. Things obviously weren't

101

rosy in the SABCO Racing camp. With Gordon still on the sidelines, Sabates had Greg Sacks on hand to drive the Coors Monte Carlo after Harry Ranier's effort had folded.

The Busch Pole qualifying session was a strange one — and yielded even stranger results. Normally, when the temperature drops during a session, the average speeds go up, so most drivers like to pull a big number, meaning they will go late in the session when speeds should be optimized. It worked in reverse at Pocono. The qualifying session began under sunny skies, but as it moved on, clouds rolled into the Pocono Mountains and cooled the track. However, only one driver who ran late in the session was able to use the cooler temperatures to his advantage and crack the top 10.

When the clocks were finished, Bobby Hamilton had claimed his third career pole and given Pontiac its second straight. It also put Hamilton's name alongside Dover Busch Pole winner Bobby Labonte as the only Grand Prix pole-winners for the season thus far. Hamilton's quick time came as a surprise to him, with a new car hastily put together in the Petty Enterprises shop and brought to the track untested. He claims he doesn't like flat tracks — but his performance in the STP Pontiac belied that statement.

Dale Jarrett joined Hamilton on the outside of the front row, and behind the two, the top 10 took on an unusual configuration. Ward Burton, the only driver to run late and make the top 10, grabbed the inside of the second row, ahead of Sacks, who hustled the Coors car to the fourth-fastest time of the afternoon. Bill Elliott and Ricky Rudd claimed the third row, ahead of Terry Labonte and Darrell Waltrip. John Andretti and Rick Mast completed the top 10, ahead of Jeff Gordon and Dale Earnhardt.

(Right) Two lanes of tight, side-by-side traffic drift through the six-degree-banked turn three, gaining momentum before fanning out on Pocono's roomy frontstretch.
(Below) Jeff Gordon makes his final pit stop on lap 174, temporarily giving up the lead. Another fine stop by the DuPont crew helped Gordon maintain track position and retake the point for good after the leaders cycled through their green-flag stops.

One of the casualties of the first session was Joe Nemechek, who lost the engine in his BellSouth Chevrolet during his qualifying lap. With a new motor installed, however, he ripped a lap good enough for third fastest overall in the field and easily was the fastest second-round qualifier.

At the other end of the spectrum, Chad Little's first-day lap was 27th fastest, usually more than enough to guarantee entry into the field. Not this time, however. A dozen drivers ran faster in the second round, and Little was left to load his John Deere Pontiac for the long

Jeff Burton (99) stalks Dale Jarrett through the third turn in a late-race duel for position. Burton eventually got past to finish second in the race; Jarrett came home third.

haul home. Also missing the race were Billy Standridge and Dave Marcis, with Ken Schrader, Kyle Petty, Mike Skinner and Dick Trickle being forced to use provisionals to make the field.

For the first three-quarters of the race, it appeared that Ward Burton was the driver who would climb out of his MBNA America Pontiac and greet the Mattiolis in victory lane. The Pontiac driver bolted to five-second leads at times, and seemed headed for his second career victory. When Jeff Gordon headed for pit road to replace a flat tire on lap 21, it looked as though the Rainbow Warriors would not win their second straight June Pocono race. But Gordon fought back. Burton lost the engine in his Pontiac, and when the clouds returned later in the afternoon, Gordon had the car for the moment.

He waited until Ted Musgrave pitted for fuel to claim the lead for the final time with 16 laps left in the race. He then kept Jeff Burton at bay in the closing laps to grab his sixth victory in 13 point races this season. Elliott, Rudd and Ernie Irvan all struggled with brake problems, eliminating them from contention.

When the 200 laps were completed, Gordon rolled to a 1.4-second victory over the Exide Ford driver. Jarrett, Martin and Mayfield completed the top five, with Musgrave fighting back for sixth place, ahead of Darrell Waltrip and Geoff Bodine. Terry Labonte and Earnhardt completed the top 10.

While Gordon was celebrating in the winner's circle, there was a quiet session of high-fives around the QVC Ford. Despite cutting a tire and falling out of sequence in pit stops early in the race, Bodine's eighth place had broken a string of poor finishes that had plagued him since Bristol. He had fallen all the way to 27th place in the standings, but Bodine hoped this race had turned the corner for his team, and he would be able to climb back into the hunt for a top-10 spot by the end of the season.

Gordon's victory, combined with Terry's ninth place, moved him into a tie with the Kellogg's driver for the lead in the point standings.

Pocono 500

Fin. Pos.	Start Pos.	Car #	Driver	Team
1	11	24	Jeff Gordon	DuPont Refinishes Chevrolet
2	18	99	Jeff Burton	Exide Batteries Ford
3	2	88	Dale Jarrett	Quality Care/Ford Credit Ford
4	14	6	Mark Martin	Valvoline Ford
5	27	37	Jeremy Mayfield	Kmart/RC Cola Ford
6	31	16	Ted Musgrave	Family Channel/PRIMESTAR Ford
7	8	17	Darrell Waltrip	Parts America Chevrolet
8	24	7	Geoff Bodine	QVC Ford
9	7	5	Terry Labonte	Kellogg's Corn Flakes Chevrolet
10	12	3	Dale Earnhardt	GM Goodwrench Service Chevrolet
11	38	36	Derrike Cope	Skittles Pontiac
12	20	1	Morgan Shepherd	R&L Carriers/Cruisin' America Pontiac
13	32	21	Michael Waltrip	CITGO Ford
14	40	44	Kyle Petty	Hot Wheels Pontiac
15	28	4	Sterling Marlin	Kodak Film Chevrolet
16	22	25	Ricky Craven	Budweiser Chevrolet
17	13	46	Wally Dallenbach	First Union Chevrolet
18	35	41	Steve Grissom	Kodiak Chevrolet
19	34	23	Jimmy Spencer	Camel Cigarettes Ford
20	10	75	Rick Mast	Remington Arms Ford
21	6	10	Ricky Rudd	Tide Ford
22	16	2	Rusty Wallace	Miller Lite Ford
23	39	33	Ken Schrader	Skoal Bandit Chevrolet
24	15	8	Hut Stricklin	Circuit City Ford
25	37	11	Brett Bodine	Close Call Phone Card Ford
26	42	90	Dick Trickle	Heilig-Meyers/Simmons Ford
27	21	30	Johnny Benson	Pennzoil Pontiac
28	25	96	David Green	Caterpillar Chevrolet
29	19	28	Ernie Irvan	Texaco Havoline Ford
30	17	91	Mike Wallace	Spam Chevrolet
31	23	18	Bobby Labonte	Interstate Batteries Pontiac
32	5	94	Bill Elliott	McDonald's Ford
33	36	19	Gary Bradberry	Child Support Recovery Ford
34	30	81	Kenny Wallace	Square D Ford
35	29	29	Jeff Green	Cartoon Network Chevrolet
36	26	42	Joe Nemechek	BellSouth Chevrolet
37	33	77	Bobby Hillin	Jasper Engines/Federal-Mogul Ford
38	3	22	Ward Burton	MBNA America Pontiac
39	1	43	Bobby Hamilton	STP Pontiac
40	9	98	John Andretti	RCA Ford
41	41	31	Mike Skinner	Lowe's Chevrolet
42	4	40	Greg Sacks	Coors Light Chevrolet

103

NASCAR WINSTON CUP SERIES 1997

Miller 400

(Michigan Speedway • June 15, 1997)

Jeff Gordon's Pocono trophy — the sixth of the season for the DuPont driver and his Rainbow Warrior crew — had barely found a place in the collection, when it was time for the teams to leave the comfy confines of their shops and head north for the first race of the season at Roger Penske's two-mile Michigan Speedway.

The track was its usual immaculate self when the crews rolled through the tunnel — not a blade of grass uncut, and not a scrap of paper to be found — and since the NASCAR Winston Cup teams had been there last August, Gene Haskett and his troops had been hard at work. Two temporary grandstands in the fourth turn had been replaced with permanent seats, and a 5,000-seat grandstand had been erected in the third turn, bringing the total

(Left) Ernie Irvan claims his trophy at Michigan in an emotional win to post his first victory of the season.

(Right) Ernie Irvan (28) uses the middle of the track to work his way around early leaders Ricky Craven (25) and Ted Musgrave (16) on his way through the field from the 20th starting spot. Dale Earnhardt, who started directly behind Irvan in 22nd, tags along toward the front.

MONTE CARLO
Havoline
28
Family
PRIMESTAR
16
Ford
THUNDERBIRD
MOOG
SIMPSON
76
WISECO
25

number of seats to more than 107,000 — and every one had long since been sold out.

Michigan has always taken the lead in providing amenities for everyone — including the drivers — and this year, Haskett had a little surprise for the Cuppers. The motorhome area, where competitors park their weekend homes, had been expanded, and a playground had been installed there for youngsters to use. Competitors agreed it was the little things such as this that made coming to Michigan such a pleasurable experience. Michigan Speedway had another nice touch

(Above) A crew member performs some spot welding on John Andretti's RCA Thunderbird in the Michigan garage. Despite the adjustments, Andretti failed to qualify for the race on speed and was forced to use a provisional to make the field. (Left) Tony the Tiger graces the hood of Terry Labonte's Monte Carlo in a promotion for sponsor Kellogg's. Labonte was hoping that last year's charm of running special colors would rub off this season and break him out of his tie with Gordon at the top of the point standings. (Below) After a 38th-place qualifying effort, Michael Waltrip sits quietly in the garage while the Wood Brothers Ford is converted to race trim. His setup for the race proved to be an improvement, allowing Michael to stay on the lead lap and finish 16th.

for the fans. Members of the Michigan AAA were cruising the parking lots throughout the weekend, ready to offer immediate assistance to fans having problems with their vehicles before, during or after the event.

There were some new combinations at Michigan when practice opened. Morgan Shepherd was on hand for his first outing in the Jasper Motorsports Ford, and, when asked, he gushed about the way the car handled. In Richard Jackson's Pontiac camp, the newly liveried R&L Carriers Grand Prix was being driven for the first time by New England's Jerry Nadeau. Nadeau was immediately fast — the third fastest in practice, no less — raising eyebrows up and down pit road.

Lake Speed and Harry Melling's team, after missing two races, were back for the race in Melling's backyard. Dave Marcis' Chevrolet was painted in colors hyping a new video about Richard Childress and his team, and Dale Earnhardt carried Goodwrench Service Plus on his familiar black Chevrolet as part of a special Goodwrench promotion.

The biggest news, however, was the blue-orange-and-white Chevrolet in the garage area for defending NASCAR Winston Cup Champion Terry Labonte. As part of a special two-race promotion, Kellogg's Corn Flakes was gone, and

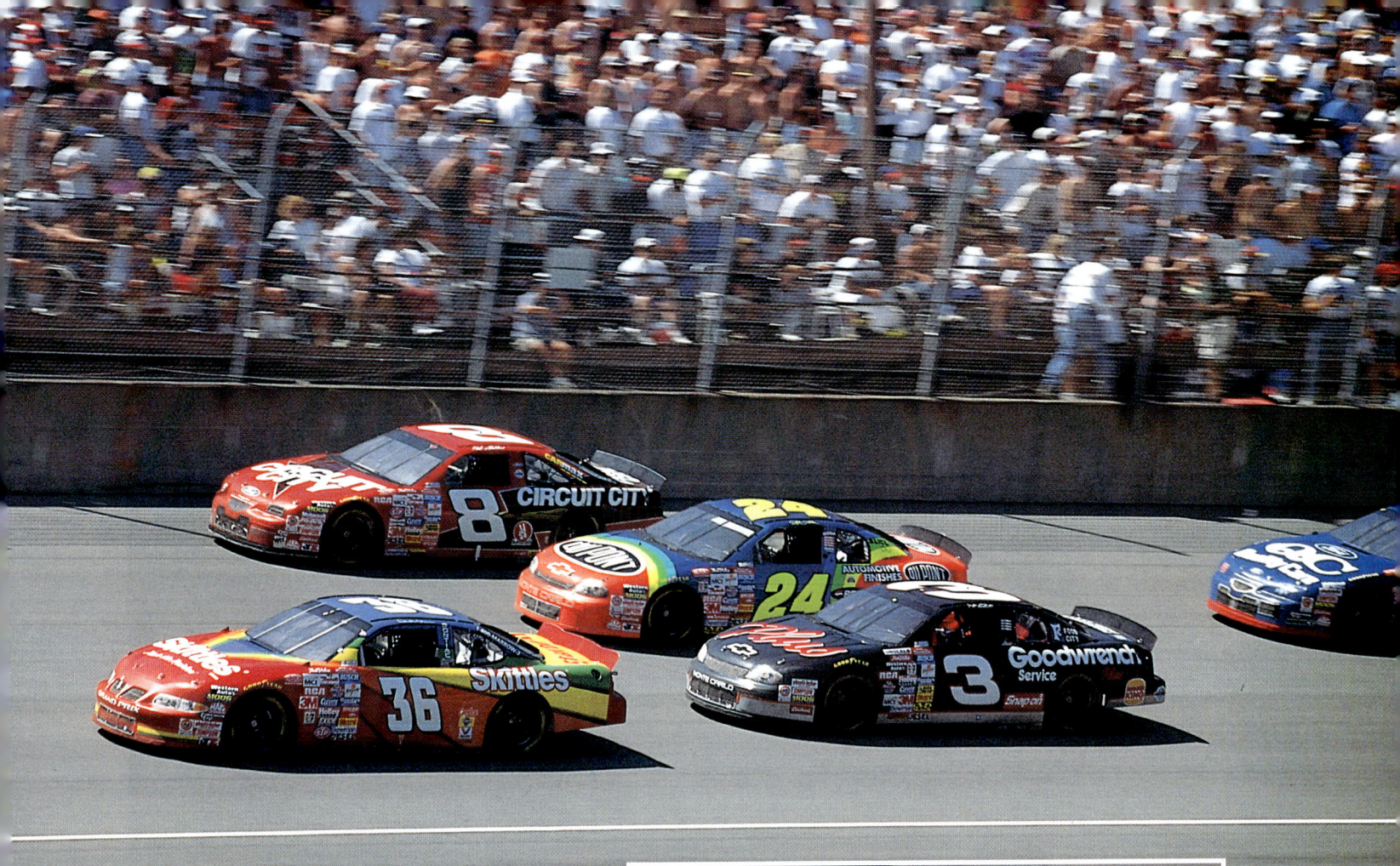

(Above) Using the entire width of Michigan's frontstretch, Derrike Cope (36), Dale Earnhardt (3), Jeff Gordon (24) and Dale Jarrett shuffle underneath Hut Stricklin (8) in their battle for position. Cope would have an outstanding run from his 42nd-place starting position to finish 8th in the race.
(Right) Ernie Irvan, Mark Martin and Ted Musgrave form a draft behind Bill Elliott at the front of the field. The four drivers all took their turns at the point during the second half of the race, before Irvan claimed it for good.

the Monte Carlo carried the famous tiger and Kellogg's Frosted Flakes on its hood and flanks. No one had forgotten that Terry had driven cars with special paint schemes twice last year — and had notched his season's two victories in them.

Gordon's Pocono victory, combined with Labonte's ninth place, had moved the two drivers into a tie atop the NASCAR Winston Cup point standings, with Gordon snaring the Winston bonus money at Pocono by virtue of his number of victories. Labonte remained the picture of consistency, however, with 11 top-10 finishes in the first 13 races of the season. It was the same type of consistency that had brought him his title in 1996, and Terry felt his team was on track for its first victory of the year.

Surging Mark Martin found himself in third place in the standings. His fourth at Pocono had moved him to within 61 points of the lead. Dale Jarrett, third at Pocono, was fourth in the standings, 58 points behind Martin, and Jeff Burton, second the previous week, was solidly in fifth place, 85 points ahead of Earnhardt.

Bobby Labonte and Ricky Rudd occupied seventh and eighth places in the standings, ahead of Michael Waltrip and Jeremy Mayfield, whose fifth-place Pocono finish pushed Bill Elliott out of the top 10.

With the cars on pit road in the qualifying line, driver after driver stopped to chat briefly with Joe Nemechek — and Joe immediately

Bobby Labonte (18) inches around Wally Dallenbach (46) while pole-winner Dale Jarrett looks for an opening of his own.

mean good luck for Jarrett, who claimed his third Busch Pole of the season. He streaked to a lap of 183.669 miles per hour, six-hundredths of a second faster than the lap posted by Nemechek. Ricky Craven, despite a miss in his Budweiser Chevrolet's motor, was third fastest, with Sterling Marlin on his right. Marlin's qualifying run was fraught with drama. The engine in his Kodak Chevrolet blew while idling on pit road, forcing the Kodak Gold-clad crew to scramble and install another one before the qualifying session was completed.

found himself the focus of attention, as he proudly flashed pictures of his new baby, John Hunter. This Father's Day weekend would have special meaning to Joe and wife Andrea, who had become parents June 11, naming their son after his brother, John, who died earlier in the year.

The fact that qualifying was held on Friday the 13th seemed to

Ted Musgrave and Wally Dallenbach made up the third row, ahead of Johnny Benson and Bobby Labonte, driving the fastest Pontiacs in the field. Jeff Burton and Jimmy Spencer claimed the final positions in the top 10, barely edging Martin and Jeff Gordon.

*(**Below left**) The Texaco Havoline crew gives Ernie Irvan right-side tires and fuel in a spectacular late-race pit stop, sending Irvan back on the track in a position to seal the win. (**Below Right**) Crew chief Mike Beam looks through the wheel well to direct repairs to the front end of Bill Elliott's McDonald's Ford. The damage was minor, and Elliott was able to stay in contention and eventually finish second. (**Bottom**) Ted Musgrave (16) fights off hard charging Mark Martin (6) in their fight for the lead midway through the event. Musgrave led the most laps in the race, but would finish fourth, one spot behind his Roush Racing teammate.*

Ken Schrader (33), Wally Dallenbach (46) and Hut Stricklin (8) use the spacious Michigan oval to make a three-wide formation in their race for position.

The second qualifying session seemed as crucial as the first. Bill Elliott, one of the biggest favorites ever to get into a car at Michigan, turned a lap that would have been good enough for third place on the grid had he done it the first day. A total of 22 drivers took laps, and Nadeau prepared to make his NASCAR Winston Cup debut after putting the backup Jackson Pontiac in the field. He had crashed the primary car during the first qualifying session. Kyle Petty, John Andretti, Rick Mast and Derrike Cope were forced to use provisionals, and Darrell Waltrip took a former champion's provisional to allow another car into the field. With the field complete, Mike Wallace, Ed Berrier and Gary Bradberry would miss the race, as would Greg Sacks, driving Robby Gordon's Coors Chevrolet for Felix Sabates. Shepherd, who was unable to coax enough speed from the Jasper Ford, also watched the car being loaded in the garage area.

On Sunday, with a record crowd of more than 145,000 on hand, the Miller 400 took the green flag. Musgrave immediately bolted to the lead, hauling the field around for most of the first quarter of the race. Behind him, a dozen drivers were already showing they had the horses for the courses. Both Martin and Rusty Wallace ripped their way to the front of the field, but before half-distance, both had suffered cut tires. Mark was able to remain on the lead lap after a right-side change, but Rusty fell a lap behind when he was forced to change all four tires.

Ernie Irvan moved toward the front, as did Elliott, showing his qualifying lap was no fluke. By the time the event began winding down to the finish, it became clear that the crew that turned their driver out best in the final green-flag stop would be the one to make the joyous sprint to the winner's circle.

And that's the way it turned out. With 24 laps left in the race, Irvan headed for pit road, and the Robert Yates crew did fabulous work, giving him right-side tires and fuel in just 9.2 seconds. Elliott's team also did their work well — but took more than 11 seconds to service the McDonald's Ford. Those two extra seconds on pit road meant the difference between victory and second place.

When the stops were completed, Irvan found himself in the lead, and maintained his two-second advantage all the way to the end, beating Elliott to the checkered flag. Martin rallied to take third place, ahead of Musgrave, giving Ford a 1-2-3-4 sweep. Gordon's Chevrolet was fifth, ahead of Jarrett, and Earnhardt took seventh. Cope notched his best finish of the season, claiming eighth, ahead of Bobby Labonte and Benson.

Irvan's first victory of the season couldn't have come at a better time or place. In the final year of his contract with Yates, rumors had been circulating that Ernie would not be back in the "28" car in 1998. At the same time, his well-managed victory had come at the track where his career was nearly ended just three years ago. His feelings about the victory and where it occurred were obvious to everyone in the garage area and to the millions watching on television.

Miller 400

Fin. Pos.	Start Pos.	Car #	Driver	Team
1	20	28	Ernie Irvan	Texaco Havoline Ford
2	26	94	Bill Elliott	McDonald's Ford
3	11	6	Mark Martin	Valvoline Ford
4	5	16	Ted Musgrave	Family Channel/PRIMESTAR Ford
5	12	24	Jeff Gordon	DuPont Refinishes Chevrolet
6	1	88	Dale Jarrett	Quality Care/Ford Credit Ford
7	22	3	Dale Earnhardt	GM Goodwrench Service Plus Chevrolet
8	42	36	Derrike Cope	Skittles Pontiac
9	8	18	Bobby Labonte	Interstate Batteries Pontiac
10	7	30	Johnny Benson	Pennzoil Pontiac
11	36	9	Lake Speed	SaveTime/Mobil Ford
12	15	37	Jeremy Mayfield	Kmart/RC Cola Ford
13	34	10	Ricky Rudd	Tide Ford
14	9	99	Jeff Burton	Exide Batteries Ford
15	10	23	Jimmy Spencer	Camel Cigarettes Ford
16	38	21	Michael Waltrip	CITGO Ford
17	4	4	Sterling Marlin	Kodak Film Chevrolet
18	3	25	Ricky Craven	Budweiser Chevrolet
19	35	11	Brett Bodine	Close Call Phone Card Ford
20	6	46	Wally Dallenbach	First Union Chevrolet
21	31	27	Rick Wilson	David Blair Motorsports Ford
22	37	8	Hut Stricklin	Circuit City Ford
23	17	90	Dick Trickle	Heilig-Meyers/Simmons Ford
24	43	17	Darrell Waltrip	Parts America Chevrolet
25	23	97	Chad Little	John Deere Pontiac
26	39	44	Kyle Petty	Hot Wheels Pontiac
27	30	33	Ken Schrader	Skoal Bandit Chevrolet
28	29	96	David Green	Caterpillar Chevrolet
29	19	2	Rusty Wallace	Miller Lite Ford
30	41	75	Rick Mast	Remington Arms Ford
31	14	29	Jeff Green	Cartoon Network Chevrolet
32	24	43	Bobby Hamilton	STP Pontiac
33	28	78	Billy Standridge	Hanes Ford
34	25	71	Dave Marcis	Realtree Camouflage Chevrolet
35	27	22	Ward Burton	MBNA America Pontiac
36	32	1	Jerry Nadeau	R&L Carriers Pontiac
37	40	98	John Andretti	RCA Ford
38	21	41	Steve Grissom	Kodiak Chevrolet
39	18	5	Terry Labonte	Kellogg's Frosted Flakes Chevrolet
40	13	7	Geoff Bodine	QVC Ford
41	2	42	Joe Nemechek	BellSouth Chevrolet
42	16	31	Mike Skinner	Lowe's Chevrolet
43	33	81	Kenny Wallace	Square D Ford

109

NASCAR Winston Cup Series 1997

California 500 Presented by NAPA

(California Speedway • June 22, 1997)

It was the second new race of the season — at the second new superspeedway to open during 1997.

Instead of all the hype that accompanied the opening of Texas Motor Speedway in April, Roger and Greg Penske, along with Les Richter, chose instead to open the doors on the new two-mile superspeedway in Southern California, and let the competitors and fans make up their own minds about what had been built on the site of the old Kaiser steel mill.

Picture, if you will, an entrance, in the middle of one of the grimmest looking areas an exit of an interstate could bring, that looks as though it belongs at a five star resort. Imagine driving into a race track where the expanse of grass makes you think you have wandered into Augusta National by mistake. Think in terms of paved parking lots for 32,000 cars and extra-wide sidewalks, enabling fans to walk side by side. Contemplate, just for a moment, the concept of phones in the garages enabling crews to communicate with their shops without having to go back to their transporters.

(Right) A blur of cars flashes under the flagstand on a beautiful afternoon as NASCAR Winston Cup racing returns to Southern California at the immaculate California Speedway.

(Below) Team owner Felix Sabates cracks a smile as his driver Joe Nemechek gives the "thumbs up" to signal he's ready to lead the field to the green flag from the pole for the first time in his NASCAR Winston Cup career.

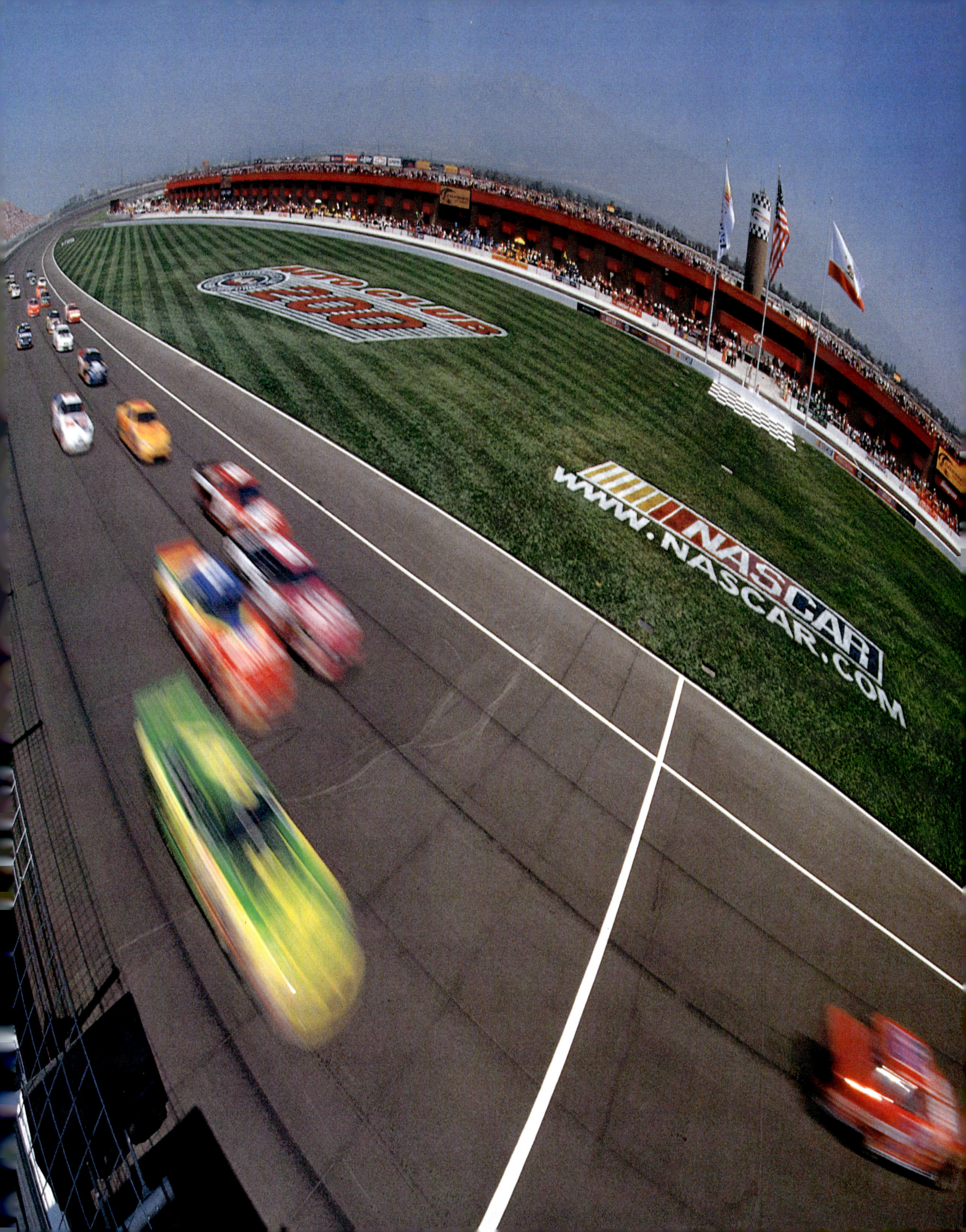
NASCAR
WWW.NASCAR.COM

What Penske and his troops had was a finished product, with every nut and bolt tightened, every plumbing fixture working properly, every blade of grass cut to a landscaper's fantasy.

It was all that way at California Speedway.

From the first stroke of the pencil on drafting paper, the facility was designed to be fan-friendly, and it succeeded in ways that Penske, Richter and their workers could not have imagined. First, seats were sold out for months in advance, and, during the weekend, Penske announced that additional seats would be built prior to next year's running of the California 500.

Two years ago, a group of competitors visited the bleak site, where parts of movies like "Terminator" had been filmed. No special effects were needed to make the landscape nightmarish. That's the way it was, according to Kyle Petty, who stood in one spot amidst a mountain of slag and cinders and shook his head, when Richter pointed out where the main grandstand would be.

(Top) With the list of drivers yet to qualify dwindling, Ernie Irvan signs autographs for the California fans, hoping his name will remain atop the leader board. At the end of that list, however, was Nemechek, who would bump Irvan to the outside of the front row. *(Left)* Kyle Petty has guarded emotions as he prepares to make his second-round qualifying attempt. With morning temperatures cooler than the afternoon heat of the previous round, Petty notched the 38th, and final, starting position based on speed. *(Below)* Intensity is etched on Steve Grissom's face as he prepares to roll off the line to begin the inaugural California 500.

Now it was state of the art — even more than that — and the teams were ready to do battle on an oval track in the rose-colored air of Southern California for the first time since Ontario Motor Speedway last hosted the Cuppers in 1980.

In the days between Michigan and Fontana, crew chief Tim Brewer and the Morgan-McClure team had parted company after

(Right) Jimmy Spencer drops his Camel Ford to the inside of Jeff Green (29) and Chad Little (97) along California Speedway's extremely fast backstretch. (Below) California Speedway's super-smooth racing surface allowed multiple grooves. Here, Dave Marcis tests the outside groove with his Realtree Chevrolet while Dale Earnhardt scrapes the apron in the Goodwrench Monte Carlo.

John Andretti was the first driver to test the concrete walls surrounding the two-mile oval during the open practice day, when his RCA Ford found the second-turn wall. It put the team into a hole it had

the first third of the season had brought less-than-desired results for driver Sterling Marlin and the Kodak cars. Beginning with the California race, Robert Larkins, a longtime team member, was acting as the interim crew chief. Also, Robby Gordon was set to return to the driver's seat of the Coors Chevrolet. He had been among the missing while recovering from an injury suffered during the Indianapolis 500.

hoped to avoid. John was all right, but now Cale Yarborough's team found itself with a single car for the remainder of the weekend. The emphasis changed from trying to win a pole and the race to trying to make the field and salvage the weekend.

On Friday, Robby Gordon, back behind the wheel, found himself the victim in a practice accident. During an examination at a local hospital, he failed a motor skills test and was out for the weekend. Greg Sacks, who had driven for the Coors team in Gordon's absence, zipped up his driver's suit and headed for the backup SABCO Chevrolet.

Nine days before the California race, Joe Nemechek had become a father for the first time, and, after barely missing the pole at Michigan, whistled the BellSouth Chevrolet to the fastest lap of the qualifying session, earning his first career NASCAR Winston Cup Busch Pole. In doing so, he became the fourth driver this season to win his first career pole, joining Mike Skinner, Robby Gordon and Kenny Wallace. Joe's quick lap sent California native Ernie Irvan to the other side of the front row, and relegated pre-race favorite Jeff Gordon to the inside of the second row for the start of the 250-lapper.

Wally Dallenbach was fourth fastest, while Ken Schrader, who would win the NASCAR Winston West race Saturday, was inside of Geoff Bodine. Geoff was walking with some new spring in his step now that it appeared the sale of majority interest in his team was imminent. Jeff Green continued to surprise in the Cartoon Network Chevrolet, claiming seventh. On his right was a high-fiving Darrell Waltrip, who had an outstanding qualifying run with his Parts America Chevrolet. Dale Jarrett and Terry Labonte made up the fifth row, ahead of Ricky Craven and Mark Martin, who would win the IROC round Saturday afternoon.

With 20 cars in search of the remaining 17 positions in the field, the second round of qualifying took on an added dimension. The second round was held in cooler, late-morning temperatures, and every team was forced to run to make the field. The temperature provided faster laps than Friday afternoon, and when the second round was completed, Sacks had led the way. The first four second-round qualifiers — Sacks, Hut Stricklin, Skinner and Marlin — all posted laps that would have won the pole a day earlier. Ricky Rudd, fighting with a chassis he admitted he should have left on the East Coast, was forced to take a provisional, as were Ward Burton, Steve Grissom and Dick Trickle. Kenny and Mike Wallace, along with Billy Standridge, all failed to make the field and were forced to watch their crews load up in preparation for the long trip home.

With a full house of spectators waving the field off, the green flag dropped on the California 500. The chase for the hardware, named the Les Richter Trophy in honor of the man who had been so instrumental in getting the Speedway built, was on. Nemechek led the first lap, and Dallenbach had the First Union Chevrolet at the front for the next six laps. But by the eighth lap, Jeff Gordon had moved to the point, hoping to write another chapter of the 1997 Rainbow Warrior's success story.

For several contenders, engine problems ended any hope of victory. Rick Mast, Irvan, Geoff Bodine and Schrader all succumbed to motor maladies of one sort or another. Bill Elliott cut a tire, and the shredded remains severed a brake line, ending a strong run to the front. Nemechek's hopes for his inaugural NASCAR Winston Cup victory ended with a pit road punch-up with another car.

Dale Jarrett came out to challenge for the victory in the Quality Care Ford, and Mark Martin's Valvoline Ford was extremely stout. Rudd's team found the handle on the Tide Ford during Happy Hour, changing the back-marker into a challenger. Jimmy Spencer charged to the front with his Camel Ford, and was able to challenge the leaders throughout the middle stages of the event, leading the field at times, in perhaps his best performance to this point in the season.

And Gordon kept motoring along.

The fourth and final caution flag of the day came with 100 laps left to run, and, as the event moved toward its completion, teams began making

Dale Jarrett (88) leads Terry Labonte, Rusty Wallace, Jeff Gordon and Ricky Craven around the outside in their hunt for race-leader Ernie Irvan after the final restart of the race.

Jeff Gordon applies the bumper of his DuPont Chevrolet to Ricky Rudd's Tide Ford along the sweeping frontstretch. Gordon was able to make the pass on his way to victory in the inaugural event, and Rudd finished third after having to take a provisional to make the race.

decisions regarding running to the finish with green-flag pit stops. The final round of fuel stops began with 57 laps left, and those who pitted at that point knew they would need another sprint to pit road for a quick splash of fuel to make it to the finish.

Gordon made his stop with 55 laps remaining in the event, and Rudd moved onto pit lane a lap later. Martin, Jarrett, Rusty Wallace and Dale Earnhardt had already made their stops by then, and clearly could not run to the flag. If the race remained green, they could not win.

Gordon started nursing his fuel, and, although he found himself at the point, he eventually allowed Martin by, letting Mark run hard, knowing that the Valvoline Ford really was not an issue, because it needed another stop.

It did — with 10 laps to go. When Mark headed for pit road, Gordon looked in the mirror and saw his Hendrick teammate, Terry Labonte, closing. Jeff was caught on the high wire. He had to run fast enough to stay ahead of Terry and slow enough to stretch the limited fuel he had for the final laps of the race.

He managed to do both, and posted a one-second victory to claim the Richter Trophy and notch his seventh win of the season, all to the delight of a partisan California crowd. If the race had been a single lap longer, Labonte would have scored his first victory of the season, as Gordon's DuPont Chevrolet sputtered and quit just after taking the checkered flag.

Terry was second, slightly frustrated at his luck, while Rudd's workmanlike drive netted a third place. Ted Musgrave came home fourth, ahead of Spencer, and Bobby Labonte claimed sixth. Jeff Green was a solid seventh in the best finish of his brief NASCAR Winston Cup career. Jarrett finished eighth, ahead of Craven. Martin had only a 10th-place finish for his weekend of work, after he ran out of fuel in the final laps, having failed to get enough fuel in the Ford during his brief visit to pit road with 10 laps to go.

California 500 Presented by NAPA

Fin. Pos.	Start Pos.	Car #	Driver	Team
1	3	24	Jeff Gordon	DuPont Refinishes Chevrolet
2	10	5	Terry Labonte	Kellogg's Frosted Flakes Chevrolet
3	39	10	Ricky Rudd	Tide Ford
4	20	16	Ted Musgrave	Family Channel/PRIMESTAR Ford
5	19	23	Jimmy Spencer	Camel Cigarettes Ford
6	15	18	Bobby Labonte	Interstate Batteries Pontiac
7	7	29	Jeff Green	Cartoon Network Chevrolet
8	9	88	Dale Jarrett	Quality Care/Ford Credit Ford
9	11	25	Ricky Craven	Budweiser Chevrolet
10	12	6	Mark Martin	Valvoline Ford
11	18	21	Michael Waltrip	CITGO Ford
12	21	37	Jeremy Mayfield	Kmart/RC Cola Ford
13	13	30	Johnny Benson	Pennzoil Pontiac
14	16	2	Rusty Wallace	Miller Lite Ford
15	8	17	Darrell Waltrip	Parts America Chevrolet
16	14	3	Dale Earnhardt	GM Goodwrench Service Plus Chevrolet
17	41	41	Steve Grissom	Kodiak Chevrolet
18	1	42	Joe Nemechek	BellSouth Chevrolet
19	24	97	Chad Little	John Deere Pontiac
20	22	9	Lake Speed	Melling Engine Parts Ford
21	35	98	John Andretti	RCA Ford
22	42	90	Dick Trickle	Heilig-Meyers/Simmons Ford
23	30	43	Bobby Hamilton	STP Pontiac
24	31	77	Morgan Shepherd	Jasper Engines/Federal-Mogul Ford
25	34	96	David Green	Caterpillar Chevrolet
26	36	11	Brett Bodine	Close Call Phone Card Ford
27	26	40	Greg Sacks	Coors Chevrolet
28	40	22	Ward Burton	MBNA America Pontiac
29	23	36	Derrike Cope	Skittles Pontiac
30	25	99	Jeff Burton	Exide Batteries Ford
31	38	44	Kyle Petty	Hot Wheels Pontiac
32	17	94	Bill Elliott	McDonald's Ford
33	28	31	Mike Skinner	Lowe's Chevrolet
34	5	33	Ken Schrader	Skoal Bandit Chevrolet
35	6	7	Geoff Bodine	QVC Ford
36	29	4	Sterling Marlin	Kodak Film Chevrolet
37	2	28	Ernie Irvan	Texaco Havoline Ford
38	33	1	Jerry Nadeau	R&L Carriers/Cruisin' America Pontiac
39	4	46	Wally Dallenbach	First Union Chevrolet
40	32	71	Dave Marcis	Realtree Camouflage Chevrolet
41	37	75	Rick Mast	Remington Arms Ford
42	27	8	Hut Stricklin	Circuit City Ford

NASCAR WINSTON CUP SERIES 1997

Pepsi 400

(Daytona International Speedway • July 5, 1997)

Jeff Gordon's "squeeze-it-until-its-dry" victory in Southern California had even more impact than just another triumph in an inaugural event at a track. True, it had matched his victory in the inaugural Brickyard 400 and made his the first name to be inscribed on both of the spectacularly designed trophies, but the California 500 win also allowed him to put just a little more distance between himself and his pursuers in the chase for the championship.

He emerged from Fontana with a 92-point lead over Mark Martin. Terry Labonte's fighting second place had pulled him to within 27 points of the Valvoline Ford driver in their ongoing battle to be the first to catch Gordon. Dale Jarrett's eighth place at California, after needing a late-race stop for fuel, put him 172 behind Gordon, and Jeff Burton's broken hub had cost him points in the struggle.

Dale Earnhardt, still searching for his first victory of the season, didn't find it at Fontana, and Bobby Labonte used that race to close on the GM Goodwrench driver. Ricky Rudd's third place moved him to just 20 points behind Labonte, while Michael Waltrip's alternator problems kept him ninth in the point standings. With six top-15 finishes in his last nine starts, Jeremy Mayfield had leap-frogged 10 positions in the point standings and had cracked the top 10 following the California race.

In the days between Fontana and the opening of practice for the Pepsi 400 on the other side of the country, Mike Wallace was released from his driving duties in the Spam Chevrolet, and Loy Allen was named as his replacement in a one-race deal.

(Right) John Andretti releases his emotions in victory lane after a convincing victory in the Pepsi 400. The win, a first for Andretti as well as car owner and three-time NASCAR Winston Cup Champion Cale Yarborough, came in John's 110th career start.

(Below) Jerry Nadeau (1), making his third NASCAR Winston Cup start for Richard Jackson, gets a lesson in three-wide racing from veterans Dave Marcis (71) and Darrell Waltrip (17). Nadeau had a good run going before he was collected in a multi-car accident on the last lap.

116

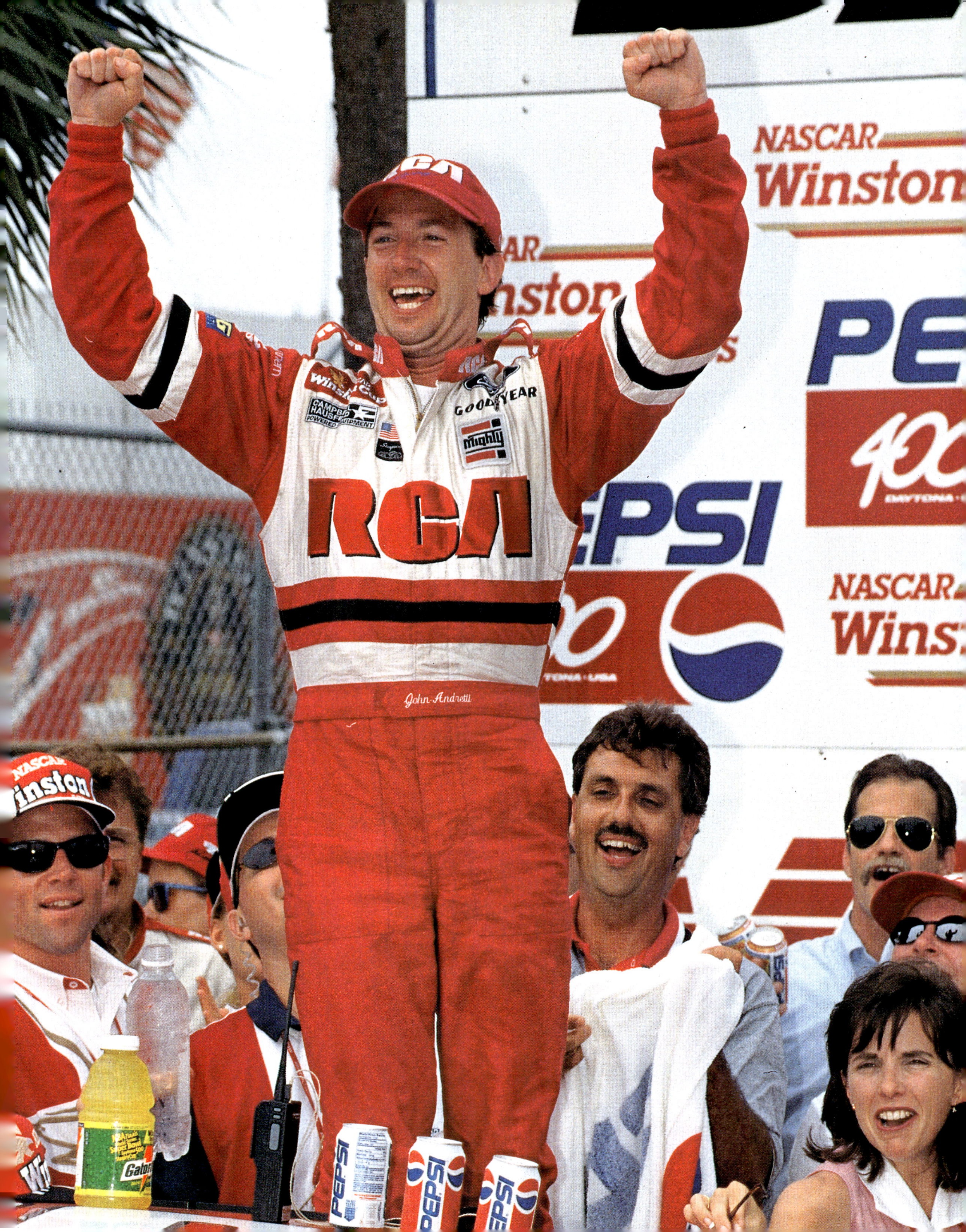
NASCAR
Winston
PEPSI
400
RCA
GOODYEAR
John Andretti
PEPSI

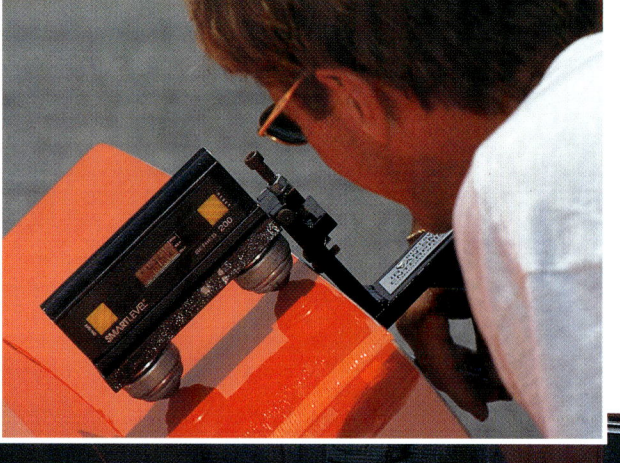

memories. After all, since then, the teams had journeyed across the country twice, to Michigan and Pocono, and the Daytona 500 pole had been forgotten by most. A variety of story lines had replaced the outstanding rookie achievement posted by Skinner.

The Childress team needed something to pull them out of the doldrums. Dale Earnhardt was still looking for his first victory of the season

(Left) As is the case at all restrictor-plate events, spoiler angles are checked and re-checked throughout the weekend to help ensure close competition and driver safety. (Below) The primary Cartoon Network Chevrolet sits alone in the garage area on jackstands after Jeff Green smacked the wall during practice. The crew pulled out the backup car, but Green was unable to gather the speed he needed to make the field.

When the teams unloaded in Daytona, ready to face three days of July's wilting Florida heat and humidity, there were some new looks around the garage area. Ricky Craven's Budmobile carried a "Louie the Lizard" graphic in keeping with Budweiser's new promotional program, and the Remington Ford fielded by Butch Mock for Rick Mast had seen its paint scheme changed to purple, teal and white to help promote Stren fishing line, another product in the Remington family.

In February, Mike Skinner slapped the Lowe's Chevrolet on the pole for the Daytona 500, getting his rookie season off to a spectacular start. At the time, Skinner gave the majority of the credit for his outstanding lap to the Richard Childress team that had prepared the Monte Carlo for the pole run. He was being slightly modest, but, at the same time, correct. "You are," he pointed out, "merely as good as your equipment."

In the months that followed, and in the half-season of races already on the books, his feat had been relegated to the dusty pages of a few

Ricky and Cathleen Craven get a good laugh from Terry Labonte along pit road before they begin the race on Saturday morning.

and was nearly 300 points out of the title chase. Skinner was leading the Rookie-of-the-Year battle, but was 28th in the point standings and had just a single top-10 finish to show for the first half of the season.

The team received what it needed during Busch Pole qualifying.

Skinner drew the first slot for qualifying, and he let it all hang out, afterward saying the car was as loose as he could drive it around the

(Left) Rookie Mike Skinner leads the field off pit road alongside teammate and two-time Pepsi 400 winner Dale Earnhardt. With his fast qualifying lap, Skinner completed a sweep of Daytona poles in 1997.

(Lower Left) Third-place starter John Andretti wasted little time in moving to the point, passing Mike Skinner on lap three. Andretti would lead 113 of 160 laps on his way to the victory.

Earnhardt gave his run everything he could, but came up just short, ensuring that Skinner would have his page in the Daytona record book as the first rookie to ever sweep the NASCAR Winston Cup poles in a season at the 2.5-mile tri-oval.

The Childress Racing one-two topped the list of first-day surprises that included John Andretti on the inside of the second row, with Jeff Gordon at his side, and a third row of Jimmy Spencer and Rusty Wallace. On the inside of the fourth row was another surprise. Billy Standridge had turned in his best qualifying performance of the year to claim the seventh-fastest time in the Hanes Ford. Michael Waltrip had the Wood Brothers' Thunderbird tweaked and grabbed the outside of the fourth row, ahead of Mast and Lake Speed.

track. His lap at 189.777 miles per hour set the early standard, and driver after driver tried to beat that speed, to no avail. Finally, the 41st driver in the line of 45 cars made his run, and he came the closest — missing by .004 seconds of tying his teammate for the pole.

That's right, his teammate.

Mark Martin (6), Bill Elliott (94) and Dale Earnhardt hook up in the draft to sweep past Michael Waltrip's CITGO Ford. Of the group, only Earnhardt managed to avoid problems, finishing fourth to pick up his second top-five finish of the year.

John Andretti leads the train into Daytona's third turn ahead of (in order) Rusty Wallace, Michael Waltrip and Jeff Gordon.

The slowest driver in the first round of times was Jeff Green, with good reason. After a practice crash, his team hurriedly pulled the backup Cartoon Network Chevrolet from the transporter and immediately sent Green into action.

With the majority of the field standing on times turned the previous day, only seven cars made runs during the second qualifying session. The increase in temperature held speeds down, and Chad Little posted the fastest lap of those who ran, grabbing the Busch "wild card" entry for the event. His time was good enough for 29th in the field. When the session was completed, provisional starts were claimed by Craven, Brett Bodine, Jerry Nadeau and Steve Grissom. That meant that Jeff Green and Loy Allen would not make the field for the Pepsi 400. They were joined by Geoff Bodine.

For Bodine, it appeared the bottom of the well had been reached. He had struggled throughout the year with financial problems within his team, and his anticipated sale of majority interest in his Ford effort had yet to materialize. Down on funding and low on staff, Bodine's failure to make the race marked the first time he hadn't qualified for a NASCAR Winston Cup race since he made his debut in 1982. It was a sad moment for the black-clad crew. However, Bodine remained optimistic that the infusion of funding from the sale of his team would happen at any time, allowing him to come back stronger than before.

While teams prepared for the running of the early morning 400-miler, Daytona's management had a surprise announcement. A permanent lighting system that would illuminate the entire 2.5-mile oval would be installed in time for next year's Pepsi 400. The $5 million project would enable next year's race to run in the evening, giving fans the opportunity to enjoy the race in less stifling conditions.

When the green flag dropped on the Pepsi 400, the majority of the huge throng was surprised to see Andretti bolt to the point with his RCA Ford. They were even more surprised to see him stay there.

Determined to prove that the red-and-white Thunderbird's superb qualifying lap had been no fluke, and even more determined to make up for what he called "letting the Daytona and Winston 500s get away," John pressed the advantage at the front of the field. He led all but six of the first 86 laps, but then pitted under green and lost a lap until the field cycled around through their green-flag stops.

As the race ground on, John worked his way back to the front, where he found himself working on Mark Martin for the lead. He couldn't find a way past the Valvoline Ford, and, finally, Bill Elliott gave him the boost he needed. Elliott, having been forced to pit to have a loose spark plug wire put back on, was fighting to recapture a lap. He had to make

Kyle Petty, holding the inside of Terry Labonte (5) and Ernie Irvan (28), had a strong run to seventh place, leading all Pontiacs for his third top-10 finish of the season.

the choice between Martin and Andretti. He chose to push John into the lead, hoping he could later pass the red-and-white Ford.

That put Andretti into the lead for the last time, but the journey to his initial NASCAR Winston Cup victory was not yet complete. Dale Earnhardt and Dale Jarrett had joined forces behind the RCA Ford and closed the gap, looking for a way past Andretti.

With four laps to go, Ricky Rudd cut a left-rear tire, triggering a multi-car wreck that included Morgan, Robby Gordon, Lake Speed, Hut Stricklin and Michael Waltrip. Figuring the race might not be restarted, and prompted by his crew in his radio earpiece, Andretti hustled to the yellow flag ahead of Earnhardt and Jarrett.

The clean-up crew made short work of the accident, and Andretti's suspicions that the race might end under yellow were history. The word reached him that the final lap would be a green-flag one, and, behind him, breathing fire and hoping to end his winless drought, Earnhardt narrowed his steel blue eyes. His chance had arrived.

Andretti paced the restart to his liking, keeping Earnhardt pasted to his bumper, and then nailed the throttle and got the start he wanted. Behind him, Earnhardt and Jarrett were suddenly joined by Terry Labonte and Sterling Marlin. Andretti watched in the rearview mirror — and saw chaos erupt.

Between the third and fourth turns, it happened — and Andretti changed his focus to the flagstand. He flashed under the checkered flag to gain the first victory for Cale Yarborough's team after 10 years and 293 races. Behind him, the multi-car accident claimed the likes of Mark Martin, Dick Trickle, Derrike Cope, Ward Burton, Lake Speed, Jerry Nadeau and Bobby Hamilton.

While Andretti rolled down pit road, accepting congratulations from the crew members of the cars he had beaten on the way to his first NASCAR Winston Cup victory, Labonte beat Marlin and Earnhardt to the line. Jarrett arrived in fifth place ahead of Rusty Wallace, Kyle Petty and Jeff Burton. Ernie Irvan and Bobby Labonte claimed ninth and 10th, with a total of 24 cars finishing on the lead lap.

Pepsi 400

Fin. Pos.	Start Pos.	Car #	Driver	Team
1	3	98	John Andretti	RCA Ford
2	35	5	Terry Labonte	Kellogg's Corn Flakes Chevrolet
3	30	4	Sterling Marlin	Kodak Film Chevrolet
4	2	3	Dale Earnhardt	GM Goodwrench Service Plus Chevrolet
5	16	88	Dale Jarrett	Quality Care/Ford Credit Ford
6	6	2	Rusty Wallace	Miller Lite Ford
7	38	44	Kyle Petty	Hot Wheels Pontiac
8	23	99	Jeff Burton	Exide Batteries Ford
9	24	28	Ernie Irvan	Texaco Havoline Ford
10	20	18	Bobby Labonte	Interstate Batteries Pontiac
11	27	81	Kenny Wallace	Square D Ford
12	22	16	Ted Musgrave	Family Channel/PRIMESTAR Ford
13	31	37	Jeremy Mayfield	Kmart/RC Cola Ford
14	34	17	Darrell Waltrip	Parts America Chevrolet
15	14	33	Ken Schrader	Skoal Bandit Chevrolet
16	15	30	Johnny Benson	Pennzoil Pontiac
17	37	71	Dave Marcis	Realtree Camouflage Chevrolet
18	9	75	Rick Mast	Stren/Remington Arms Ford
19	36	96	David Green	Caterpillar Chevrolet
20	25	43	Bobby Hamilton	STP Pontiac
21	4	24	Jeff Gordon	DuPont Refinishes Chevrolet
22	26	40	Robby Gordon	Coors Light Chevrolet
23	40	11	Brett Bodine	Close Call Phone Card Ford
24	11	42	Joe Nemechek	BellSouth Chevrolet
25	12	90	Dick Trickle	Heilig-Meyers Ford
26	21	22	Ward Burton	MBNA America Pontiac
27	18	6	Mark Martin	Valvoline Ford
28	28	36	Derrike Cope	Skittles Pontiac
29	10	9	Lake Speed	Melling Engine Parts Ford
30	41	1	Jerry Nadeau	R&L Carriers/Cruisin' America Pontiac
31	5	23	Jimmy Spencer	Camel Cigarettes Ford
32	32	77	Morgan Shepherd	Jasper Engines/Federal-Mogul Ford
33	17	94	Bill Elliott	McDonald's Ford
34	13	10	Ricky Rudd	Tide Ford
35	8	21	Michael Waltrip	CITGO Ford
36	19	8	Hut Stricklin	Circuit City Ford
37	39	25	Ricky Craven	Budweiser Chevrolet
38	42	41	Steve Grissom	Kodiak Chevrolet
39	33	46	Wally Dallenbach	First Union Chevrolet
40	7	78	Billy Standridge	Hanes Ford
41	1	31	Mike Skinner	Lowe's Chevrolet
42	29	97	Chad Little	John Deere Pontiac

NASCAR WINSTON CUP SERIES 1997

Jiffy Lube 300

(New Hampshire International Speedway • July 13, 1997)

There was little time for John Andretti to enjoy his first NASCAR Winston Cup victory, with the teams scheduled to compete just days later at the other end of the east coast. But when he walked into the garage area at Bob Bahre's one-mile oval, everywhere he went, Andretti was stopped by crew members, car owners, crew chiefs and other drivers, who gave him a pat on the back, a smile, a thumbs-up or a handshake of congratulations.

At the same time Andretti was collecting the handshakes, he was also saying a few words in defense of his team and the huge $50,000 fine levied on it by NASCAR for the offset bolts that held the carburetor on top of the intake manifold. The bolts allowed the carburetor to be moved an eighth of an inch backward, improving the airflow to the engine and boosting the power by about five horsepower. NASCAR had found the bolts during the pre-race inspection, and had them replaced for the event, eliminating any speculation that John's victory had been tainted in any way. The fine came from the use of the bolts at all, and Cale Yarborough's team immediately said it would protest the NASCAR decision and fine.

(Right) Tossing his water bottle into the crowd, an elated Jeff Burton begins the victory lane celebration. Coached by crew chief Buddy Parrott, Burton played the waiting game to score his second win of the season.

(Below) Ken Schrader leads the starting field under the green flag in front of a record crowd at New Hampshire International Speedway to start the Jiffy Lube 300. Schrader gave the Andy Petree-owned team a tremendous boost with their first Busch Pole of the season.

Hood
NEW HAMPSHIR
TIONAL SPEEDWA
Budweiser
EXIDE
BATTERIES
Western Auto
MOOG
76
OFFICIAL FUEL NASCAR
EXIDE BATTERIES
plasti-kote
SPRAY PAINT
SIMPSON
WISECO
COMPETITION CAMS
MAC TOOLS
WIX
FILTERS
Ford
THUNDERBIRD
99
GOODYEAR

Robert Yates listens to his driver, Ernie Irvan, in a rather subdued Texaco garage stall. Just days earlier, Yates had informed Irvan that his contract would not be renewed for the 1998 season.

Andretti's win wasn't the only topic of conversation in the garage area, however. Lots of the talk concerned the bombshell that had dropped on the NASCAR Winston Cup circuit following the Pepsi 400. Robert Yates, after months of soul-searching, had made the decision not to renew Ernie Irvan's driving contract, and had informed Irvan in the days between Daytona and New Hampshire. By the time the teams arrived for the next event, Ernie was looking for a ride for the coming year.

Rumors were already rife that the replacement for Irvan in the Havoline-sponsored Fords was none other than young Kenny Irwin, who had caught the eye of Yates and the Ford folks with his performances in the NASCAR Craftsman Truck Series. Yates was noncommittal about the Irwin rumors, but, clearly, he had already made his decision about who would be driving the "28" cars from his stable in 1998 and beyond.

One driver who was excited

Three lucky fans catch up with Bobby Labonte in time to collect autographs before Bobby reports to his car for the race.

about the New Hampshire event was Ken Schrader, who had joined Andy Petree's Skoal-sponsored Chevrolet team at the beginning of the season. Schrader's qualifying record at New Hampshire over the years was among the best of any in the sport. Since the circuit began running at Bahre's track, Schrader had not qualified out of the top 10 for any race, and Ken immediately established that the green-and-white Monte Carlo would contend for the Busch Pole. His was one of the two fastest cars in practice before qualifying, so it would come down to whether his team would make the right choices in the car's qualifying setup, and to whether Schrader would boot the Skoal car hard enough during his run.

Ken had drawn a mid-field qualifying position, and by the time he rolled off pit lane, Bobby Hamilton sat atop of the qualifying list. Schrader wheeled around the flat oval, and, when he was finished, he had beaten Hamilton's time by .011 of a second. As the line on pit road dwindled, Schrader's lap looked better and better.

When the session finished, Schrader claimed his first pole since June 1995. He also became the first driver to win a pole for Petree's team and the 12th entry of the season in the 1998 Busch Clash.

(Left) Ken Schrader (33) jumps out to an early lead over Bobby Hamilton (43) as second-row starters Ricky Craven (25) and Chad Little (97) lead the side-by-side pack into the first turn. (Below) A stoic Ray Evernham keeps an eye on his driver, Jeff Gordon, who suffered a flat tire and fell two laps off the pace during the unscheduled stop for new rubber. His 23rd-place finish also dropped him to second in the standings, three points behind Terry Labonte.

(Left) The Quality Care team outfits Dale Jarrett with four fresh tires in a stop under green. Jarrett was very strong over the first 200 laps, but engine woes once again dropped him well off the pace. (Below) Perhaps the best-known crew member along pit road each week, Danny "Chocolate" Meyers, joins the cyber age.

Hamilton would be on his right for the start of the 300-lapper. Ricky Craven gave the Northeastern fans reason to cheer by parking the Budweiser Chevrolet on the inside of the second row, just a tick faster than a surprising Chad Little. Chad notched the best qualifying performance of the season for the John Deere Pontiac.

Dale Jarrett became the fastest Ford driver, posting his 15th top-10 qualifying position in 17 races this season. Steve Grissom shared the third row with the Quality Care Ford driver. Kyle Petty and John Andretti were paired in the fourth row, while Jerry Nadeau put the R&L Carriers Pontiac on the inside of the fifth row, boosting his stature among his fans, and beating Terry Labonte for that position. Ernie Irvan and Rusty Wallace barely missed the top 10.

Behind them, Jeff Gordon missed the top 25 for the first time this year, when he blew his qualifying lap, and Dale Earnhardt also failed to make the field during the first round. The two decided to stand on their times during the second qualifying session. Jimmy Spencer was the fastest driver to run in the second session, grabbing the Busch Clash "wild card" slot for the Jiffy Lube 300. Brett Bodine, Hut Stricklin, Dave Marcis and Robby Gordon were forced to use provisionals to make the field, leaving Billy Standridge as the only driver not to make the race.

In the first two-thirds of the race, the rabbits had at it, with Schrader, Craven, Jarrett, Hamilton and Irvan fighting amongst themselves to establish their cars as the dominant ones in the field. Cruising along was Jeff Burton, who had qualified 15th. He picked his way toward the front, as he had all season. After an early-race brush with near disaster, when he tried to go three-wide and almost collected the concrete wall as a result, Burton settled into the race and followed crew chief Buddy Parrott's instructions in his earpiece.

Parrott reassured Burton over and over that he had the goods to win the race. He urged Burton to be patient, and the crew would help him get to the front. With a third of the race left to run, Parrott made good on his promise. The Exide crew turned Burton off pit road and into the lead after a two-tire stop.

From that point on, he was the dominant car, and, as the event ran the final third of the distance under the green, Jeff found himself able to stretch his advantage. With Earnhardt and Irvan battling behind him, Jeff moved a

Local favorite Ricky Craven brought Louie the Lizard to New Hampshire, hoping to show him victory lane at Ricky's home track. After a strong start, however, Craven fell off the pace and struggled to a 16th-place finish, one lap down.

Kimberle Burton joins her daddy in the winner's circle, a place she likely will get used to in the coming years.

fourth, ahead of Mark Martin and Bill Elliott. Labonte recovered from his late-race stop for fuel to finish seventh, while Irvan nursed his Ford to eighth place, ahead of Ricky Rudd and Geoff Bodine.

Where, you might ask, was the NASCAR Winston Cup point leader?

Gordon, who had struggled at Daytona with an ill-handling Chevrolet, found himself two laps behind, in 23rd place. A flat tire was the culprit at New Hampshire, and when the event was over, Gordon had dropped behind Labonte to second place in the point standings. The margin was a mere three points, but Labonte's consistency through the first 17 races had finally paid off.

little farther away. When Irvan's engine began to sour, as did Jarrett's, Earnhardt was left to make his move at Burton.

Jeff knew that he needed to make a quick stop for fuel before the event was over, but he was assured over his radio that all of the others also needed to stop. Burton heeded Parrott. He maintained his pace at the front of the field, and, with 15 laps to go, headed for pit road for the splash of Unocal that would carry him through the remainder of the race. He had rolled off the track with a seven-second advantage, and would now have to watch and wait to see if everyone else made their stops, as well.

Terry Labonte took the point when Burton headed for pit road, and when Jeff returned, the Kellogg's Chevrolet was still ahead of him. Jeff waited ... and waited ... and waited. As the laps wound down, he began to wonder if Terry really was going to need to stop — or if the defending NASCAR Winston Cup champion could somehow stretch his fuel into his first victory of the season.

With nine laps to go, Burton had his answer. Labonte headed for pit road, turning the lead back over to the Exide Ford driver. From then on, Jeff merely had to be careful and not make a mistake. Behind him, Earnhardt could not cut into the gap, and only a problem or an error by Burton would enable Earnhardt to move into a challenging position.

Burton chose his line carefully in the closing laps, never put a wheel wrong, and drove to a five-second victory over the black Chevrolet. Rusty Wallace fought his way to third place, while Grissom came home

Jiffy Lube 300

Fin. Pos.	Start Pos.	Car #	Driver	Team
1	15	99	Jeff Burton	Exide Batteries Ford
2	26	3	Dale Earnhardt	GM Goodwrench Service Plus Chevrolet
3	12	2	Rusty Wallace	Miller Lite Ford
4	6	41	Steve Grissom	Kodiak Chevrolet
5	16	6	Mark Martin	Valvoline Ford
6	23	94	Bill Elliott	McDonald's Ford
7	10	5	Terry Labonte	Kellogg's Corn Flakes Chevrolet
8	11	28	Ernie Irvan	Texaco Havoline Ford
9	18	10	Ricky Rudd	Tide Ford
10	14	7	Geoff Bodine	QVC Ford
11	1	33	Ken Schrader	Skoal Bandit Chevrolet
12	30	23	Jimmy Spencer	Camel Cigarettes Ford
13	7	44	Kyle Petty	Hot Wheels Pontiac
14	8	98	John Andretti	RCA Ford
15	40	8	Hut Stricklin	Circuit City Ford
16	3	25	Ricky Craven	Budweiser Chevrolet
17	22	37	Jeremy Mayfield	Kmart/RC Cola Ford
18	32	30	Johnny Benson	Pennzoil Pontiac
19	36	81	Kenny Wallace	Square D Ford
20	31	36	Derrike Cope	Skittles Pontiac
21	27	31	Mike Skinner	Lowe's Chevrolet
22	13	4	Sterling Marlin	Kodak Film Chevrolet
23	29	24	Jeff Gordon	DuPont Refinishes Chevrolet
24	21	96	David Green	Caterpillar Chevrolet
25	28	90	Dick Trickle	Heilig-Meyers Ford
26	25	16	Ted Musgrave	Family Channel/PRIMESTAR Ford
27	17	18	Bobby Labonte	Interstate Batteries Pontiac
28	24	75	Rick Mast	Remington Arms Ford
29	33	21	Michael Waltrip	CITGO Ford
30	4	97	Chad Little	John Deere Pontiac
31	2	43	Bobby Hamilton	STP Pontiac
32	34	29	Jeff Green	Cartoon Network Chevrolet
33	20	17	Darrell Waltrip	Parts America Chevrolet
34	42	40	Robby Gordon	Coors Light Chevrolet
35	41	71	Dave Marcis	Realtree Camouflage Chevrolet
36	35	22	Ward Burton	MBNA America Pontiac
37	38	77	Morgan Shepherd	Jasper Engines/Federal-Mogul Ford
38	5	88	Dale Jarrett	Quality Care/Ford Credit Ford
39	9	1	Jerry Nadeau	R&L Carriers/Cruisin' America Pontiac
40	19	42	Joe Nemechek	BellSouth Chevrolet
41	37	79	Randy MacDonald	T.R.I.X. Racing/NUCAR Conn. Chevrolet
42	39	11	Brett Bodine	Close Call Phone Card Ford

Pennsylvania 500

(Pocono Raceway • July 20, 1997)

How fleeting the NASCAR Winston Cup point lead can be!

Two races ago, following his victory in California, Jeff Gordon seemed in command of the point standings, holding a solid 92-point lead. However, problems in the Pepsi 400 and the Jiffy Lube 300 at New Hampshire, leading to mid-field finishes, dropped him into second place in the standings. As the teams unloaded in the Pocono Mountains for their second visit to the triangular Pocono Raceway, Gordon found himself trailing Hendrick Motorsports teammate Terry Labonte.

For all intents and purposes, the two were in a dead heat. Only three points separated the two drivers, and both looked at Pocono as a track where they would have to fight for every position, as they continued their quests for the championship.

The championship battle, with Mark Martin just 52 points behind in third place, was the focus at Pocono, but there was plenty of other news for media members to report. International Speedway Corporation announced it had purchased Phoenix International

(Right) The smiles are back on the faces of Dale Jarrett and his Quality Care teammates in Pocono's victory lane. With the team's recent engine problems seemingly behind them, Jarrett simply overpowered the rest of the field on the way to his third win of the season.

(Below) Dale Earnhardt and Jeff Gordon seem to be plotting their strategy for the start of the Pennsylvania 500. The two would line up together on the third row, with Earnhardt on the inside of Gordon.

NASCAR
Winston Cup
POCONO
POCONO
POCONO
CIRCLE
Budweiser
Budweiser
Quality Care

NASCAR Busch Series rookie standout Steve Park waits for his chance to qualify, hoping to make his NASCAR Winston Cup debut driving Dale and Teresa Earnhardt's Burger King Chevrolet.

Raceway, and that current president Buddy Jobe would remain in his role with the track. Jobe had purchased Phoenix in 1985, and his work at the track had made it a popular NASCAR Winston Cup venue over the years. He and ISC officials said the track would see continued improvement and growth under its new ownership, so Phoenix joined Darlington, Daytona, Talladega and Watkins Glen as ISC-owned tracks.

There was also some race team news. Spam officials said they were withdrawing sponsorship from the LJ Racing effort, although Greg Sacks would be behind the wheel of the team's Chevrolet at the track this weekend. Geoff Bodine, on the financial ropes with his team, said he had found two investors to provide the financial wherewithal that would keep his team racing, and allow him to return to a competitive mode. He anticipated introducing his investors before the end of the month.

With Bobby Hillin named as the new driver for the Hanes Ford, replacing Billy Standridge, the Triad Motorsports team hoped it had made the move that would allow the team to find the consistency it needed. And NASCAR Busch Series rookie star Steve Park, who

Fresh off their New Hampshire victory, Buddy Parrott, Jeff Burton and Jack Roush are in good spirits prior to the Pennsylvania 500. The second-year team had come together in the first half of the season and was now a weekly contender for wins.

130

made an outstanding impression on the series this year, was on hand in hopes of making his NASCAR Winston Cup debut in Dale and Teresa Earnhardt's Burger King Chevrolet.

Throughout the practice sessions, two of the SABCO team cars were at the top of the speed charts, with Wally Dallenbach and Joe Nemechek setting the pace for the 45 cars in the garage area. Some garage dwellers wondered if the two Chevrolet drivers could maintain the pace during qualifying, with Robert Yates Racing teammates, Ernie Irvan and Dale Jarrett, right on their heels in practice.

Dallenbach was the first of the two fast Bowtie drivers on the track. He notched a lap in his First Union Monte Carlo that many felt would be good enough to earn the second-generation driver the pole. Then Nemechek rolled out in the BellSouth machine. When he finished what he called, "A perfect lap, and one I don't believe I could run over again if I had to," he had claimed his second pole of the season and his third front-row start in the last five races.

(Right) Joe Nemechek accepts the Busch Pole Award after a blistering lap around the triangular superspeedway at 168.881 miles per hour, living up to his recently acquired nickname, "Front Row Joe." (Below) With Ernie Irvan on the outside, Joe Nemechek leads the field through turn one during pre-race warm-up laps. Joe took off at the drop of the flag to lead the first 11 laps before giving way to Jeff Gordon.

Irvan's determined lap was enough to sandwich the Texaco Ford between the two Felix Sabates-owned Chevrolets, but not enough to move Nemechek from the pole. And Jarrett found his lap good enough to line up behind Irvan on the outside of the second row.

Dale Earnhardt and Gordon put their Chevrolets into the third row, while Ken Schrader and Jeff Green made it six Chevrolets in the first eight positions on the grid for the Sunday race. Mark Martin was ninth fastest with his Valvoline Ford, while Bobby Labonte was the fastest Pontiac driver, ousting Mike Skinner and Steve Grissom from the final position in the top 10 following the first round of qualifying.

131

One of the most disappointed drivers in the field was Sterling Marlin, who was the victim of a practice crash earlier in the day, forcing the Morgan-McClure team to pull the backup Kodak Chevrolet from the transporter for Sterling to qualify. He made the field during the first day, posting the 23rd-fastest lap — no small feat considering the circumstances. The final qualifier during the first day was Michael Waltrip, who was pleased to be part of an announcement that he would remain with the Wood Brothers and with CITGO for the 1998 season.

The second round of qualifying brought cooler temperatures and lower humidity — and sent all but one team scurrying to run in the second round in hopes of getting the best possible starting position for the Pennsylvania 500. Jerry Nadeau was the only driver not to run, after barely missing the field during the first day. He stood on his time, but the temperatures made a big difference, and he fell from 26th to 35th in the starting lineup. Rick Mast set the pace in the second session with a lap that would have earned him the 16th starting position had it come in the first round.

With the second round complete, Ricky Craven and Geoff Bodine found themselves the final qualifiers. Rusty Wallace, Johnny Benson, Dave Marcis (with a blown engine prior to the second qualifying round) and David Green were forced to use provisionals to make the Pocono field. Hillin and Sacks had to watch their cars being loaded on the transporters, as did Park, who was exceedingly disappointed in not making the field with the Burger King Monte Carlo.

It took just 30 laps of the Pennsylvania 500 to see that the two best cars in the field belonged to Jarrett and Gordon. If neither of the two had any problems during the remainder of the event, the capacity crowd knew one driver or the other would wheel into victory lane.

Although there would be 23 lead changes throughout the event, Jarrett clearly established the fact that he had the horse for the course this Sunday afternoon. His team cranked him off pit road with mid-18-second, four-tire pit stops, and when Jarrett needed the Yates horsepower on the long straights at Pocono, he merely buried his right foot. There was plenty there for his use, and he cruised to the victory, leading more than half the laps on his way to his third win of the season.

Gordon was nearly three seconds behind, and when the race was over, he grudgingly said that nothing the DuPont team did could match the supremacy of Jarrett's Quality Care Thunderbird that afternoon. "There was really only one good car out there today," Gordon said. "That was about as perfect as we've had our car here. Our setup was great. We just couldn't compete. We were in a different class."

Jarrett was delighted with his second Pocono victory, and credited his crew with their magnificent stops and the tweaks that had been

Ted Musgrave pilots his Family Channel/PRIMESTAR Ford behind Jeff Gordon, while Jeff Burton challenges Musgrave in his Exide Thunderbird, all on the inside of Dale Jarrett. Burton would eventually get past Musgrave in their battle for third place.

The Todd Parrott-led crew cranks off another outstanding pit stop, as they had all afternoon, keeping Jarrett in position to claim his third win of the season.

made to the Thunderbird during the course of the event that enabled him to run — and stay — at the front of the field.

"The engine I had in there today was perhaps the best I've ever had in a race car," Jarrett said after his 11th career triumph. "Even when I'd mess up a little bit, or my car was a little tight, I could still get down the straightaway. This was just an awesome piece and an awesome victory."

Behind the two, Jeff Burton battled his way to a solid third place in a backup car after a practice crash eliminated his primary Exide Ford. He came in ahead of Ted Musgrave, who also had a fine afternoon in the Family Channel/PRIMESTAR Ford. Martin completed a Roush Racing 3-4-5 finish, ahead of Skinner, who took sixth, the best finish of his brief NASCAR Winston Cup career.

Jimmy Spencer raced to seventh place, ahead of Kyle Petty, while Jeremy Mayfield and Bill Elliott rounded out the top 10, with Elliott winning a battle with Bobby Labonte for 10th place. Elliott appeared headed for a better finish, but lost time and track position early in the race, when the hood pins worked themselves loose on the right side of his car.

Dallenbach and Nemechek both hoped for good luck in the race, but didn't find it. Wally had a strong run, until the engine went south three-quarters of the way through the race, and Nemechek was involved in a multi-car accident in the second turn.

Where was series point leader Terry Labonte? He was classified 35th in the final rundown, struggling to the finish seven laps behind after he was nudged by brother Bobby and ended up in the grass just past half-distance. The incident also included Earnhardt, who fought his way back to 12th place by the conclusion of the race.

The off-track excursion cost Terry the lead he had fought so hard to get, and when the points were counted at the conclusion of the Pennsylvania 500, Gordon was back on top. Terry had fallen all the way to third place, 114 points behind Gordon, with Martin moving to second, 64 points back.

Pennsylvania 500

Fin. Pos.	Start Pos.	Car #	Driver	Team
1	4	88	Dale Jarrett	Quality Care/Ford Credit Ford
2	6	24	Jeff Gordon	DuPont Refinishes Chevrolet
3	20	99	Jeff Burton	Exide Batteries Ford
4	22	16	Ted Musgrave	Family Channel/PRIMESTAR Ford
5	9	6	Mark Martin	Valvoline Ford
6	11	31	Mike Skinner	Lowe's Chevrolet
7	14	23	Jimmy Spencer	Camel Cigarettes Ford
8	34	44	Kyle Petty	Hot Wheels Pontiac
9	17	37	Jeremy Mayfield	Kmart/RC Cola Ford
10	15	94	Bill Elliott	McDonald's Ford
11	10	18	Bobby Labonte	Interstate Batteries Pontiac
12	5	3	Dale Earnhardt	GM Goodwrench Service Plus Chevrolet
13	40	30	Johnny Benson	Pennzoil Pontiac
14	7	33	Ken Schrader	Skoal Bandit Chevrolet
15	32	22	Ward Burton	MBNA America Pontiac
16	29	36	Derrike Cope	Skittles Pontiac
17	38	7	Geoff Bodine	QVC Ford
18	37	25	Ricky Craven	Budweiser Chevrolet
19	27	90	Dick Trickle	Heilig-Meyers/Simmons Ford
20	23	4	Sterling Marlin	Kodak Film Chevrolet
21	1	42	Joe Nemechek	BellSouth Chevrolet
22	25	21	Michael Waltrip	CITGO Ford
23	24	8	Hut Stricklin	Circuit City Ford
24	13	98	John Andretti	RCA Ford
25	26	75	Rick Mast	Remington Arms Ford
26	16	17	Darrell Waltrip	Parts America Chevrolet
27	33	77	Morgan Shepherd	Jasper Engines/Federal-Mogul Ford
28	36	97	Chad Little	John Deere Pontiac
29	31	11	Brett Bodine	Close Call Phone Card Ford
30	12	41	Steve Grissom	Kodiak Chevrolet
31	8	29	Jeff Green	Cartoon Network Chevrolet
32	28	43	Bobby Hamilton	STP Pontiac
33	35	1	Jerry Nadeau	R&L Carriers/Cruisin' America Pontiac
34	18	81	Kenny Wallace	Square D Ford
35	21	5	Terry Labonte	Kellogg's Corn Flakes Chevrolet
36	19	10	Ricky Rudd	Tide Ford
37	39	2	Rusty Wallace	Miller Lite Ford
38	3	46	Wally Dallenbach	First Union Chevrolet
39	42	96	David Green	Caterpillar Chevrolet
40	2	28	Ernie Irvan	Texaco Havoline Ford
41	41	71	Dave Marcis	Realtree Camouflage Chevrolet
42	30	40	Robby Gordon	Coors Light Chevrolet

NASCAR WINSTON CUP SERIES 1997

Brickyard 400

(Indianapolis Motor Speedway • August 2, 1997)

With a weekend off between Pocono and Indianapolis, Jeff Gordon had a few days to relish being back at the top of the point table — and a few hours to relax before the stress of the Brickyard 400.

Since the inaugural race at the 2.5-mile oval in 1994, the Brickyard 400 has been one of the biggest races of the season. Once the teams arrived at the world's most famous race track, the lid was clamped on the pressure cooker, and the flame was turned up to high. The richest race of the season also marked the beginning of the stretch run to the championship, and, this year, the string was 11 consecutive races from early August until the middle of October.

Without question, this stretch of races would separate the men from the boys, the unprepared from the prepared, the contenders from the pretenders. The 11 consecutive races would test the preparation of the teams, the strategy of the crew chiefs, the chemistry of the crew members, and the skill and stamina of the drivers. Only the finest would emerge after the DieHard 500 at Talladega — 11 races from now — as bona fide challengers for the NASCAR Winston Cup.

(Right) Ricky Rudd pays homage to hollowed ground – a strip of bricks from the Speedway's original surface that form the start-finish line – after he drove to the biggest win of his racing career. A delighted Linda Rudd looks on.

(Below) NASCAR President Bill France (left) and IMS President Tony George (right) flank IMS Chairman Mari George during pre-race ceremonies for the Brickyard 400.

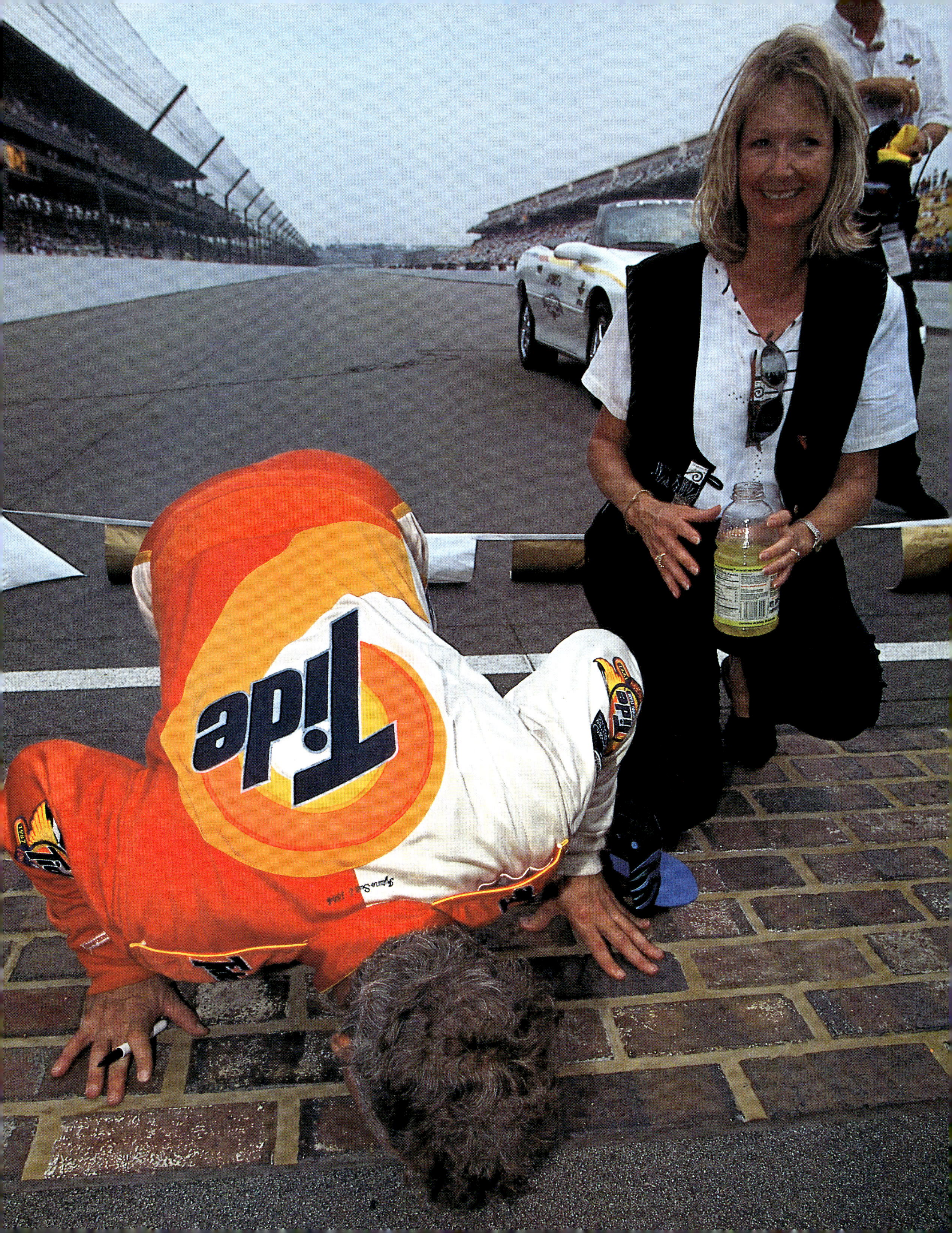
Tide

It is the fury of this week-to-week struggle that is the forge where championships are won or lost — every contender knows it. To have the brutal stretch run begin with the highest paying and one of the most prestigious races of the season was almost more than some teams could grasp. Winning the Brickyard 400 was a primary goal of every team in the garage area all year.

Gordon's solid second place at Pocono, coupled with Terry Labonte's struggle to finish that race after his off-course excursion, put Jeff back at the top of the standings. He led Mark Martin by 64 markers, with Terry 114 behind. Jarrett's overpowering victory moved him to 152 behind Gordon, while Jeff Burton, perhaps the surprise of the season, and Dale Earnhardt were 53 points apart in their personal battle for fifth place. Behind them, the battle for eighth, ninth and 10th was torrid. Just over 100 points separated Ricky Rudd, Jeremy Mayfield, Ted Musgrave and Bill Elliott in their battle for the 8-9-10-11 positions. Terry Labonte found out the previous race just how easy it was to lose more than 100 points in a single Sunday afternoon.

When the teams arrived at The Brickyard, several changes had occurred within the sport. Penske Motorsports Inc. and International Speedway Corporation had made the announcement that they had each purchased 40 percent of the Homestead track just outside of Miami at a cost of $11.8 million each. The Homestead announcement followed on the heels of ISC's purchase of Phoenix.

Within the teams, Mike Wallace had been named the driver for Richard Jackson's R&L Carriers Pontiac for the Brickyard event, after Jerry Nadeau was released following his fifth race of the season. Jimmy Martin, one of the most popular and well-known men in the garage area, decided to leave Petty Enterprises after 28 years to become the

Ford unveils the racing version of its popular Taurus model, the designated replacement for the Thunderbirds in 1998, at a press conference in Indianapolis. All of the current Ford drivers were on hand to help celebrate the occasion.

136

(Above) In a special promotion sponsored by Kentucky Fried Chicken, "Team Twister," with driver Rich Bickle, entered this Chevrolet from the shops of Darrell Waltrip Motorsports. (Right) Joining the unique entries at The Brickyard was this Indianapolis Colts-sponsored car from David Blair Motorsports with Rick Wilson behind the wheel.

general manager of the new Washington/Erving Motorsports team for the coming season. Todd Bodine was introduced as the driver for a new team owned by ISM Motorsports and carrying Tabasco as the primary sponsor, beginning in the 1998 season.

Dave Charpentier, who had worked with both Ricky Rudd and the SABCO team as an engineer, joined Butch Mock's Remington effort for driver Rick Mast as the team's new crew chief. At Diamond Ridge racing, Wes Ward was named the team's new director of operations, with Bill Ingle apparently being relieved of his duties. In yet another story, an appeals board had turned down the appeal from Cale Yarborough's team regarding the offset carburetor bolts found prior to the Pepsi 400, and the $50,000 fine was upheld.

(Above) Bobby Labonte (18) follows Ricky Rudd in preparation for a single file restart with just three laps remaining in the race. Labonte was unable to catch Rudd after the green flag flew, but did manage to protect his position and finish second.
(Left) Darrell Waltrip and Dale Earnhardt, who would start fourth and fifth, respectively, trade psyche jobs before climbing aboard their mounts. Waltrip, who mastered the technique early in his career, came out on top; he finished 15 spots ahead of Earnhardt.

Robert Yates announced his driver for the Texaco team for the 1998 season. To no one's surprise, the choice was Kenny Irwin, who had turned in several strong performances in the NASCAR Craftsman Truck Series during the summer. It was obvious Ford was not about to let this horse out of its stable, after losing several others, including Jeff Gordon, who had been groomed in the Ford pipeline before they headed for General Motors teams.

During the weekend, the new Ford Taurus race car was shown for the first time, with the four-door passenger sedan stretched and fitted here and there to help turn it into a race car. Ford had previously announced it would stop producing Thunderbirds, and the Taurus had become the car of choice for the 1998 season. It meant that every team would have to change the sheet metal of its Fords for the coming season, and it also meant that there would be untold hours and days of testing in the months to come to convert the sedan into a competitive racing machine.

As in the previous three runnings of the Brickyard 400, a stellar field entered the event. A total of 51 cars were on hand to run for the maximum 43-car field, and there would be no holds barred during either of the qualifying sessions. There was no doubt that tenths of a second — and perhaps even thousandths of a second — would mean the difference between making the field or watching the race on television.

When the first round was over, Ernie Irvan had turned the fastest lap to claim the rich Busch Pole for the event. His thoughts were still of his mother in a North Carolina hospital in critical condition after com-

Michael Waltrip, who was collected in a multi-car accident early in the race, actually finished the event in this somewhat modified version of the CITGO Ford.

139

plications from emergency surgery for a perforated ulcer, but he had a little smile after his accomplishment. He knew he had stolen the headlines the day before his team owner would make the announcement of the new driver for the "28" car. Joe Nemechek ripped to his fourth front-row start in six events by turning the second-fastest lap of the session, just nipping Dale Jarrett and preventing a Robert Yates Racing sweep of the front row.

Chevrolet to claim the Busch "wild card" entry for the Brickyard event. Terry Labonte was the surprise of the qualifying sessions, only able to get a lap fast enough to earn the final position in the field based on speed, leaving Kyle Petty, Jimmy Spencer, Ricky Craven and Brett Bodine to use provisionals to make the race. Rusty Wallace was forced to use a former champion's provisional, putting the starting grid at the maximum 43

Ricky Rudd has every reason to smile. The independent owner/driver had just beaten the biggest teams in the sport, in the richest race of the year.

Irvan, Nemechek and Jarrett may have been grinning, but, clearly, the most delighted driver was Darrell Waltrip, who, for a moment, flashed some of the brilliance that seemed lost in the last couple of years when he flogged the "Chromemobile" to the fourth-fastest lap of the session. For a few moments, he had actually claimed the pole, and a face-splitting grin was pasted on the three-time champion's face.

Lined up in the third row were Dale Earnhardt and Mike Skinner, who many will remember shared the driving duties of the Goodwrench Chevrolet last year at The Brickyard when Earnhardt was too battered to race. Their fifth and sixth positions put the Richard Childress-owned Monte Carlos ahead of Ricky Rudd and Ken Schrader. David Green and Rich Bickle, driving in a one-off Kentucky Fried Chicken-sponsored Chevrolet for Waltrip's team, made up the fifth row.

With 18 drivers making second-round runs in hopes of getting into the field, the fastest lap was turned by Jeff Green in the Cartoon Network

cars, and sending Mike Wallace, Dick Trickle, Bobby Hillin, Tim Steele, Morgan Shepherd, Dave Marcis and Hut Stricklin home. The other driver who failed to make the field was Geoff Bodine, who missed his second race in the last four events.

For the first two-thirds of the fourth annual Brickyard 400, it seemed that the event was headed for its first double winner. Jeff Gordon, who had been the recipient of the Indiana March of Dimes Professional Sports Achievement Award for his 1996 performances, appeared to have one of the strongest cars in the field, and Dale Jarrett, last year's victor, was right in his tire tracks. The two were either leading or in the battle for the lead, along with others like Jeff Burton and pole-sitter Irvan.

As the event rolled into the final third, however, Ricky Rudd decided to play a fuel mileage game, knowing it was his only hope of winning. His Tide Ford was good — perhaps good enough for a top-five finish — but the Virginian knew that without some luck, he had little chance of bat-

Terry Labonte pulls his Chevrolet off the track and heads for the garage with a broken motor. His second straight finish of 35th or worse dropped the defending champion from third to fourth in the point standings.

tling with the likes of Gordon, Jarrett and Mark Martin for the win.

The fuel window was in the 38-42-lap range for all the teams, but with 46 laps to go and a full load of fuel on board, Rudd decided to roll the dice. He began conserving right from the beginning of those 46 laps. His team knew he would need a little luck somewhere, or he would run out of gas on the final tour of the 2.5-mile oval.

With other teams planning to make their final stops with less than 10 laps to go, Rudd maintained his conservative pace. Then, with 14 laps remaining in the race, the yellow flew after Robby Gordon slapped the wall between the first and second turns. Most teams headed for pit road, but Rudd and other gamblers Bobby Labonte and Johnny Benson remained on the track and gained the front of the field for the restart. The race restarted on lap 151, and, for Rudd, the worry was gone. The caution laps meant he would have just enough fuel to go the distance, and when the green dropped, he began to pull away from the field.

His lead was erased, however, when Bickle hit the third turn wall on lap 154 of the 160-lap race. Rudd was still at the point, but now he had to be concerned with a furious dash to the checkered flag if the green waved again. The cleanup was speedy, and with three laps left in the event, the green flag flew. Because the restart came with less than 10 laps to go, it was a single-file start, eliminating any problem for Rudd with lapped cars on his left, and he was able to burst away to a small lead. With a 10 car-length margin, Ricky was able to see the battle for the second place scraps behind him — and the clear track in front of him.

He motored to a .183-second victory, becoming the fourth different driver to win the Brickyard 400. But behind him, the dicing was furious. Bobby Labonte maintained his second place, while Benson was banged from side to side like a billiard ball in the final laps, falling to a seventh-place finish. Jarrett rocketed to third, ahead of Gordon and Jeremy Mayfield, while Martin, who had clinched his second IROC championship the previous weekend at Michigan, came home sixth. Bill Elliott claimed eighth, ahead of Mike Skinner in his backup Lowe's Chevrolet, and Irvan came home 10th.

Brickyard 400

Fin. Pos.	Start Pos.	Car #	Driver	Team
1	7	10	Ricky Rudd	Tide Ford
2	25	18	Bobby Labonte	Interstate Batteries Pontiac
3	3	88	Dale Jarrett	Quality Care/Ford Credit Ford
4	24	24	Jeff Gordon	DuPont Refinishes Chevrolet
5	16	37	Jeremy Mayfield	Kmart/RC Cola Ford
6	31	6	Mark Martin	Valvoline Ford
7	20	30	Johnny Benson	Pennzoil Pontiac
8	15	94	Bill Elliott	McDonald's Ford
9	6	31	Mike Skinner	Lowe's Chevrolet
10	1	28	Ernie Irvan	Texaco Havoline Ford
11	8	33	Ken Schrader	Skoal Bandit Chevrolet
12	27	9	Lake Speed	Melling Engine Parts Ford
13	39	44	Kyle Petty	Hot Wheels Pontiac
14	4	17	Darrell Waltrip	Parts America Chevrolet
15	33	99	Jeff Burton	Exide Batteries Ford
16	41	25	Ricky Craven	Budweiser Chevrolet
17	35	98	John Andretti	RCA Ford
18	42	11	Brett Bodine	Close Call Phone Card Ford
19	36	22	Ward Burton	MBNA America Pontiac
20	12	43	Bobby Hamilton	STP Pontiac
21	34	27	Rick Wilson	Indianapolis Colts Ford
22	23	92	Ron Barfield	New Holland Ford
23	17	75	Rick Mast	Remington Arms Ford
24	40	23	Jimmy Spencer	Camel Cigarettes Ford
25	26	29	Jeff Green	Cartoon Network Chevrolet
26	19	41	Steve Grissom	Kodiak Chevrolet
27	30	95	Ed Berrier	Realtree Camouflage Chevrolet
28	11	40	Robby Gordon	Coors Light Chevrolet
29	5	3	Dale Earnhardt	GM Goodwrench Service Plus Chevrolet
30	29	81	Kenny Wallace	Square D Ford
31	37	91	Greg Sacks	Kruse International Chevrolet
32	2	42	Joe Nemechek	BellSouth Chevrolet
33	22	16	Ted Musgrave	Family Channel/PRIMESTAR Ford
34	10	26	Rich Bickle	KFC Team Twister Chevrolet
35	9	96	David Green	Caterpillar Chevrolet
36	14	46	Wally Dallenbach	First Union Chevrolet
37	28	12	Jeff Purvis	Gazelle/QVC Chevrolet
38	43	2	Rusty Wallace	Miller Lite Ford
39	18	21	Michael Waltrip	CITGO Ford
40	38	5	Terry Labonte	Kellogg's Corn Flakes Chevrolet
41	32	36	Derrike Cope	Skittles Pontiac
42	21	97	Chad Little	John Deere Pontiac
43	13	4	Sterling Marlin	Kodak Film Chevrolet

NASCAR WINSTON CUP SERIES 1997

The Bud at the Glen

(Watkins Glen International • August 10, 1997)

For Ricky Rudd and the entire Tide team, there was simply too little time to savor their victory at The Brickyard.

Without question, it was the biggest win of Rudd's long and solid NASCAR Winston Cup career. After winning an event like the Brickyard 400 and establishing his team as one of the best "Davids" against the "Goliath" multicar efforts in NASCAR Winston Cup racing today, a one- or two-week break in the schedule for his hard-working group to enjoy the strategic victory would have seemed more appropriate.

Instead, the fact that Rudd had won two races in a single season for the first time since 1987, when he drove Bud Moore's cars, was simply another fact for the record book. His $571,000 payday was the biggest of his career by far — but it was just another line of type in a story.

This huge win and his sharing of the silver brick trophy with wife Linda in victory lane at Indianapolis were fresh in his memory when the teams arrived at Watkins Glen just days later for The Bud at the Glen. But, in the cauldron of the NASCAR Winston Cup championship chase, the glorious weekend at Indianapolis was pushed back into the recesses of the storage area.

The Glen was here, and it was time to focus the team's total concentration and energy on the 2.45-mile road course, as well as the championship chase.

(Right) Todd Bodine (34) whips his Chevrolet through the turns in front of Bobby Labonte. Bodine, in a one-off effort with local sponsorship from Hardinge, shocked fans and competitors by capturing the pole at the track near his hometown of Chemung, N.Y.

(Below) Adding yet another page to his already impressive resume, Jeff Gordon christens his first NASCAR Winston Cup career victory on a road course by spraying onlookers from the podium at Watkins Glen.

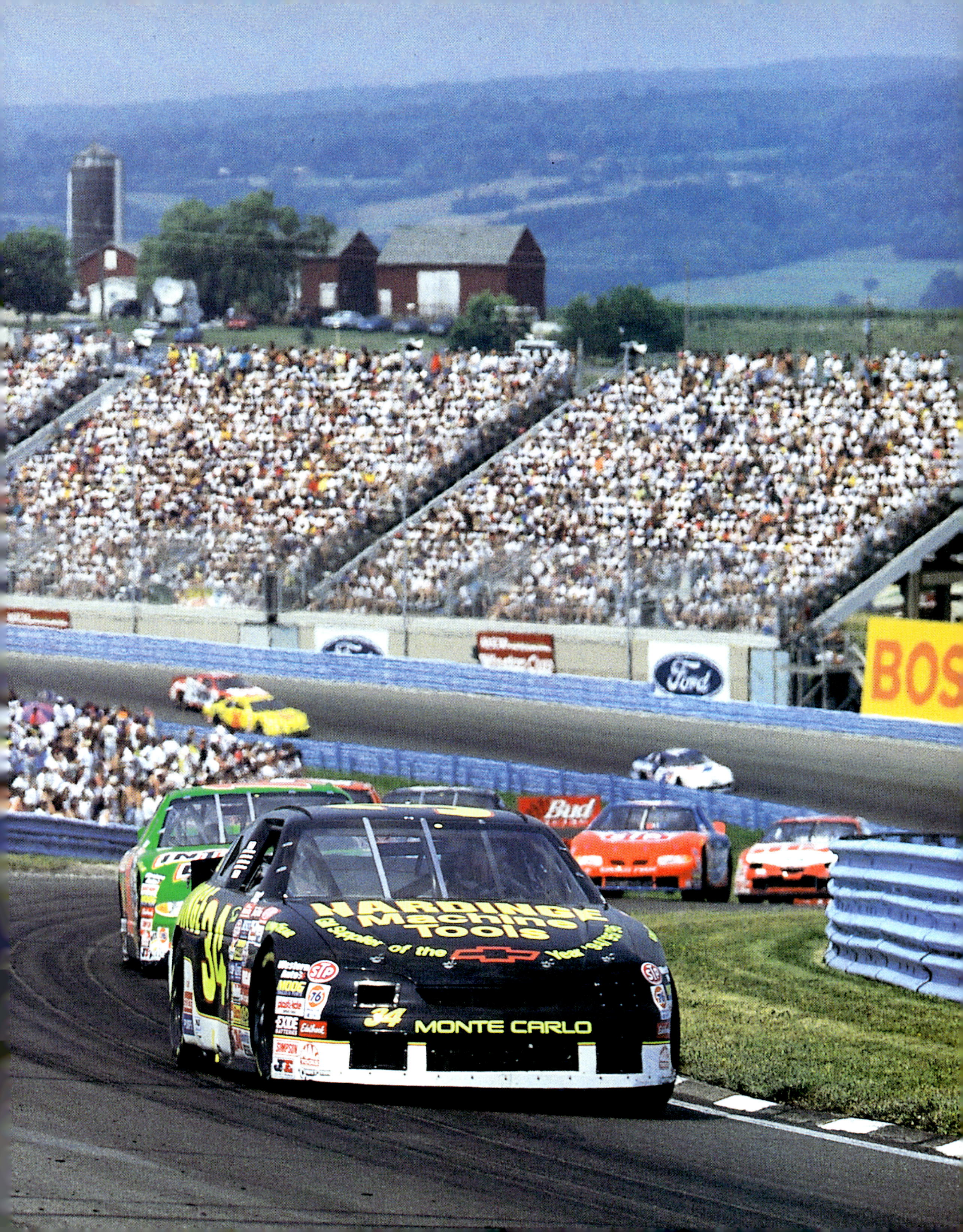
Machine Tools
34
MONTE CARLO
Ford
Bud
STP

(Above) Driving in his NASCAR Winston Cup debut, Steve Park (14) feels the heat of seasoned road-course veterans Ernie Irvan (28) and Terry Labonte (5) at the entrance to the second turn. After two previously unsuccessful attempts, Park qualified the Burger King Chevrolet in 12th for car owners Dale and Teresa Earnhardt. *(Right)* Dale Earnhardt is swamped by reporters seeking his comments, first, as a car owner, and second, as the driver who qualified an impressive third for the race.

The combination of finishes at Indy kept Jeff Gordon at the top of the point ladder, with Mark Martin now 79 points behind and Dale Jarrett 147 in arrears. Defending NASCAR Winston Cup Champion Terry Labonte was still well within striking range, trailing by 234, while Jeff Burton had moved to within 12 points of Terry. Dale Earnhardt now trailed Burton by an even 100 points, with Bobby Labonte 80 points behind the Goodwrench driver. Rudd's victory put him within 102 points of Bobby, while Jeremy Mayfield had eased out to a 76-point lead over Bill Elliott.

In the days prior to The Bud at the Glen, Anheuser Busch and NASCAR staged a press conference at the famed Tavern on The Green in New York to announce that Budweiser would become the Official Beer of NASCAR, and that, beginning in

(Right) Ricky Rudd's jubilation from his win at The Brickyard just one week before, ended abruptly at The Glen when he wadded up his Tide Ford during practice. Rudd pulled out his backup car for the race, but his bad luck continued when it suffered transmission problems, sending Ricky to the garage after only 24 laps.

February at Daytona Beach, the Busch Clash would be renamed the Bud Shootout. The race would have a new format as well, with the 25-lap race featuring the 1997 pole winners. In addition, there would be a 25-lap event for the 1997 second-round fastest qualifiers, with the winner advancing to the Bud Shootout. The Busch Pole Award, given at every event to the pole winner, would become the Bud Pole Award in 1998.

On the race-track acquisition front, International Speedway Corporation and Penske Motorsports had each purchased a seven percent stake in the Grand Prix Association of Long Beach, the company that owns Gateway International Raceway near St. Louis. This gave GPLB president Chris Pook some working capital to continue improvements at Gateway. ISC also announced it had entered into a 60-day, exclusive negotiating period with the city of Kansas City, Kan., to develop a 75,000-seat superspeedway for a scheduled opening in 1999. On the Rockingham front, O. Bruton Smith and Roger Penske were still vying for control of North Carolina Motor Speedway.

From a team standpoint, there were several items of note at The Glen. Brett Bodine announced that he had sold a half-interest in his team to Andy Evans and Team Scandia, giving Brett a needed influx of capital while he worked with sponsor Close Call to shore up the financial status of his team. Diamond Ridge and the Cartoon Network announced they would split at the end of the season, with Diamond Ridge looking for another sponsor and the Cartoon Network beginning the search for a new team for the coming season.

The Stavola Brothers' Circuit City-backed team and crew chief Richard Broome parted company four days after driver Hut Stricklin failed to qualify for the Brickyard 400. At Geoff Bodine's team, Lee Morse, the team manager, found himself out of a job as Geoff's investors began making changes within the structure of the effort.

In the garage area, rookie NASCAR Busch Series standout Steve Park was on hand in hopes of qualifying for his first NASCAR Winston Cup race in Dale and Teresa Earnhardt's Burger King-backed Chevrolet, and the Heilig-Meyers team owned by Junie Donlavey found itself working with road-racing star Dorsey Schroeder for the weekend. Regular driver Dick Trickle, who would be the first to admit that the winding, twisting road courses are not

The back of the starting field rounds turn 11 as the leaders thunder under the flagstand to begin the first of 90 laps in scenic New York State.

his forte, graciously stepped aside for Schroeder. Trickle felt that the team's goal of finishing in the top 25 in car owner points at the end of the season was more important than letting him drive and perhaps hold the effort back by his struggling around the course.

If Rudd had been "David" at The Brickyard, the slingshot he used had moved to the hands of another during Busch Pole qualifying at The Glen. The driver holding it this week was an even more unlikely candidate than Ricky had been at Indianapolis.

Team 34, a power in the NASCAR Busch Series, annually makes a one-off showing at The Glen in the NASCAR Winston Cup garage. The team owners, Frank Cicci and Scott Welliver, are from the Elmira-Corning area, and they had a machine tool company in Elmira Heights by the name of Hardinge as the sponsor for its effort this year. With practice completed, driver Todd Bodine found himself 25th on the speed list, and although it looked like he would be able to make the race, few expected a front-running performance. But with a change in front shock absorbers, Todd found himself flying through the corners at The Glen during his timed lap. When it was completed, the Hardinge Chevrolet shot to the top of the qualifying list.

Todd was amazed. When the session was complete, the local effort had stolen the headlines for the next day's papers. Against all odds, Todd had won the first Busch Pole Award of his NASCAR Winston Cup career.

His lap was more than good enough to keep Dale Jarrett off the pole, and the Quality Care Thunderbird driver was forced to settle for the outside of the front row. Dale Earnhardt and Bill Elliott shared the second row in strong runs for both, while Wally Dallenbach and Sterling Marlin made up the third row for The Bud at the Glen. Geoff Bodine, after failing to make the field at The Brickyard, surged to the seventh-fastest lap in hopes of defending the title he won here last year, and Joe Nemechek plunked the BellSouth Chevrolet on the outside of the fourth row. Mark Martin and Robby Gordon barely beat Jeff Gordon for the final positions in the top 10, and Park found himself ready to make his NASCAR Winston Cup debut by qualifying 12th.

(Right) Defending Bud at the Glen champion Geoff Bodine (7) holds off road-racing ace Rusty Wallace in the closing laps in their battle for second place. Geoff succeeded, forcing Rusty to settle for third. (Below) Lance Hooper spins the R&L Carriers Pontiac in front of Dorsey Schroeder (90) in turn one, with Steve Grissom anxiously looking for a hole large enough for his Kodiak Chevrolet to get through.

The DuPont Chevrolet seemingly gets wider through turn 11 as Jeff Gordon protects his position from Dale Earnhardt, who fights to keep the Goodwrench Monte Carlo on course. Earnhardt was unable to take the lead in the race, and eventually was shuffled back to a 16th-place finish.

Most expected to see one of the sport's established "road-racing experts" take command of the event, but when The Bud at the Glen was over, a familiar face had emerged in victory lane. The fact that several contenders had problems didn't mar Jeff Gordon's first career road-course victory.

He put the DuPont Chevrolet in the wind in the final third of the race and was untouchable as he rolled to his eighth victory of the season. His way was made easier by problems suffered by others, but there was no denying that it was a convincing victory for the Rainbow Warriors, who contributed greatly to putting Gordon at the point when he needed to be there.

For several of the championship contenders, The Bud at the Glen turned out to be a nightmare. Jarrett, with high hopes of closing ground in the point battle, eventually went out with a smoking transmission. Jeff Burton, the surprise of the season, was punted off course by Lance Hooper, who was making his debut in Richard Jackson's R&L Carriers Pontiac. Earnhardt ran over an air hose, forcing him into a stop-and-go penalty on pit road that cost him dearly in track position. Rudd lost the transmission in his Tide Ford, after destroying his primary car in a practice shunt, and Martin fought handling problems all day in his Valvoline Ford.

In the end, Geoff Bodine and Rusty Wallace were second and third behind Gordon's rainbow-hued Chevrolet, but neither could muster the juice needed to dislodge the Series' point-leader from his hold at the front of the field. Despite losing, the second place put a big smile on Geoff's face — sweet retribution for his failure to make the field the previous race.

Robby Gordon, forced to make a stop-and-go on pit road when he was black-flagged for jumping a restart, lost his chance to score his first career NASCAR Winston Cup victory. He finished fourth, ahead of Roush Racing teammates Mark Martin and Ted Musgrave. Bill Elliott was seventh, while Terry Labonte claimed eighth ahead of Steve Grissom and Wally Dallenbach.

The Bud at the Glen

Fin. Pos.	Start Pos.	Car #	Driver	Team
1	11	24	Jeff Gordon	DuPont Refinishes Chevrolet
2	7	7	Geoff Bodine	QVC Ford
3	13	2	Rusty Wallace	Miller Lite Ford
4	10	40	Robby Gordon	Coors Light Chevrolet
5	9	6	Mark Martin	Valvoline Ford
6	29	16	Ted Musgrave	Family Channel/PRIMESTAR Ford
7	4	94	Bill Elliott	McDonald's Ford
8	16	5	Terry Labonte	Kellogg's Corn Flakes Chevrolet
9	33	41	Steve Grissom	Kodiak Chevrolet
10	5	46	Wally Dallenbach	First Union Chevrolet
11	25	30	Johnny Benson	Pennzoil Pontiac
12	8	42	Joe Nemechek	BellSouth Chevrolet
13	6	4	Sterling Marlin	Kodak Film Chevrolet
14	15	33	Ken Schrader	Skoal Bandit Chevrolet
15	28	37	Jeremy Mayfield	Kmart/RC Cola Ford
16	3	3	Dale Earnhardt	GM Goodwrench Service Plus Chevrolet
17	39	25	Ricky Craven	Budweiser Chevrolet
18	32	17	Darrell Waltrip	Parts America Chevrolet
19	26	31	Mike Skinner	Lowe's Chevrolet
20	30	98	John Andretti	RCA Ford
21	22	28	Ernie Irvan	Texaco Havoline Ford
22	38	96	David Green	Caterpillar Chevrolet
23	40	75	Rick Mast	Remington Arms Ford
24	34	1	Lance Hooper	R&L Carriers Pontiac
25	17	21	Michael Waltrip	CITGO Ford
26	35	44	Kyle Petty	Hot Wheels Pontiac
27	23	81	Kenny Wallace	Square D Ford
28	24	43	Bobby Hamilton	STP Pontiac
29	36	99	Jeff Burton	Exide Batteries Ford
30	42	29	Jeff Green	Cartoon Network Chevrolet
31	19	90	Dorsey Schroeder	Heilig-Meyers/Simmons Ford
32	2	88	Dale Jarrett	Quality Care/Ford Credit Ford
33	12	14	Steve Park	Burger King Chevrolet
34	21	23	Jimmy Spencer	Camel Cigarettes Ford
35	1	34	Todd Bodine	Hardinge Chevrolet
36	41	8	Hut Stricklin	Circuit City Ford
37	14	18	Bobby Labonte	Interstate Batteries Pontiac
38	37	36	Derrike Cope	Skittles Pontiac
39	20	11	Brett Bodine	Close Call Phone Card Ford
40	31	10	Ricky Rudd	Tide Ford
41	18	22	Ward Burton	MBNA America Pontiac
42	27	97	Chad Little	John Deere Pontiac

NASCAR WINSTON CUP SERIES 1997

DeVilbiss 400

(Michigan Speedway • August 17, 1997)

Jeff Gordon's first career NASCAR Winston Cup victory on a road circuit, coupled with the finishes of those behind him in the point standings, boosted him to a 109-point margin following The Glen, and when the Rainbow Warriors rolled into the Irish Hills of Michigan for their second visit of the season, Jeff found himself with some breathing room at the top of the ladder.

Mark Martin had lost 30 points to Gordon at The Glen, where he had hoped to close the margin based on his past performances at the winding road course high above majestic Seneca Lake. But the big loser had been Dale Jarrett, when transmission problems in the Quality Care Ford dropped him to 260 behind. After losing 113 points in a single race, Jarrett now faced a huge uphill battle to once again draw within striking distance of the DuPont Chevrolet driver.

Terry Labonte, still looking for his first victory of the season as he tried to defend his NASCAR Winston Cup championship, lost 37 points to Gordon and now trailed by 269.

(Right) Johnny Benson climbs aboard his Pennzoil Pontiac, preparing to lead the field off the line from the pole, his first of the 1997 season.

(Below) The Exide crew puts the final touches on a green-flag stop for tires and fuel for their driver Jeff Burton, one of three Roush teammates who combined to lead 88 percent of the 200 laps at Michigan.

148

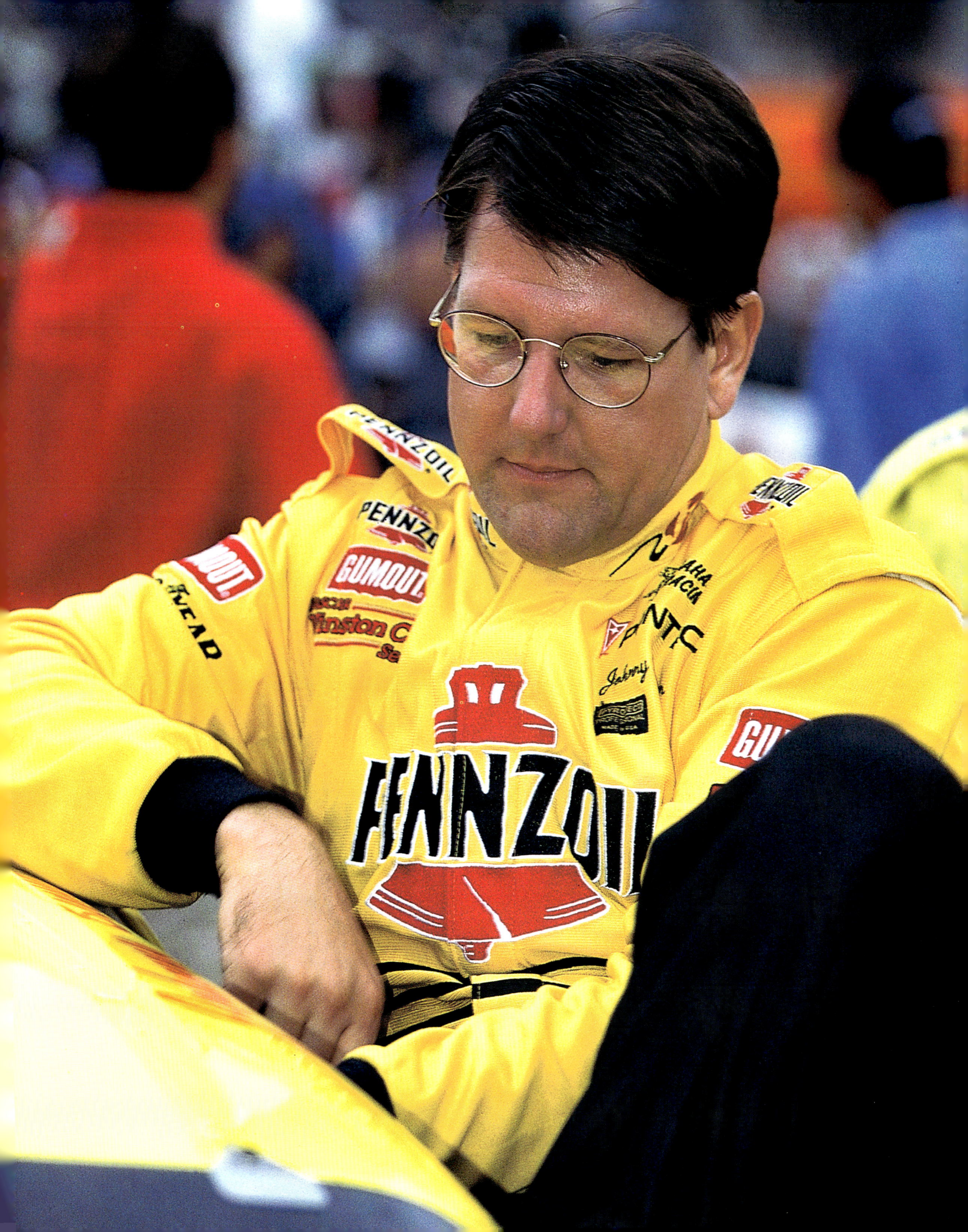
PENNZOIL
GUMOUT
PENNZOIL

Jeff Burton lost 99 points at The Glen after being punted by Lance Hooper, and now trailed Gordon by 352. For Dale Earnhardt, it was clear that his chase for an eighth championship was all but over this year. Winless this season, he was 61 points behind Burton and 413 behind Gordon, and the Goodwrench team was in the position of trying to gather some momentum that might carry it to a championship run, but not until the 1998 season.

The Michigan weekend brought plenty for media and crew members to talk about in the garage area. A glitzy announcement had been made in Las Vegas that the newly built race track there would be the site of a March 1 NASCAR Winston Cup race in 1998, taking the

Much more had changed for Geoff Bodine at Michigan than his usual black driver's suit. Geoff had finally sealed his partnership with two majority investors, and had added Tim Brewer to his staff in hopes of turning his season around.

Richmond date, and allowing Richmond to move its first event further into the season, providing much better weather for competitors in the Capital City.

Geoff Bodine was pleased to introduce his new partners, Jim Mattei and John Porter, to the NASCAR Winston Cup family and also announced that Tim Brewer had joined the team as its new team manager. Jack Roush was delighted to share the news that he had purchased an interest in Chad Little's John Deere-sponsored Pontiac team. It was unclear whether the team would continue to field Pontiacs in 1998, or switch to the Ford Tauruses the other Roush teams would field for the coming season.

Rick Hendrick, owner of the 1996 NASCAR Winston Cup championship team as well as the point-leading Jeff Gordon effort, was, once again, not at Michigan Speedway for the running of the DeVilbiss 400, as had been the case for the entire first half of the season. Hendrick remained at his home in North Carolina, turning his attention to his battle with leukemia.

150

On the race track front, word was received that Penske Motorsports was preparing to build a new two-mile oval superspeedway on the south edge of Denver International Airport, adding yet another potential venue for future NASCAR Winston Cup racing.

In the garage area, it became obvious during practice that there was some home cooking going on. Although he wasn't at the top of the speed charts, Johnny Benson and the Pennzoil Pontiac were in the hunt. And when the first round of qualifying was completed, Benson had found the right combination to put the bright yellow Grand Prix at the top of the scoring pylon and grab his first Busch Pole of the season — and become the 15th different pole-winner in the season's first 21 events.

It marked the second straight week that a "hometowner" had claimed the pole, with the Grand Rapids, Mich., native joining Todd Bodine in the 1998 Bud Shootout. Benson's lap barely beat the time turned by Martin, while Ricky Craven and Dale Jarrett earned positions in the second row, ahead of Jeff Burton and Bobby Labonte. The fourth row was comprised of Ted Musgrave and Ken Schrader, while

(Left) Johnny Benson (30) brings the field of 43 cars to the line with Mark Martin (6) starting on his right. Benson would lead the first five laps before giving way to third-place starter Ricky Craven (25).
(Below) Dale Earnhardt (3) sneaks up on the inside of Ken Schrader (33), while Bill Elliott waits for an opening for his McDonald's Ford. Elliott and Earnhardt, after starting 24th and 28th, respectively, worked their way up to the top 10 by the end of the day.

the final top-10 starting positions were earned by Dick Trickle and Geoff Bodine.

With the second round of qualifying rained out, provisionals were taken by Jimmy Spencer, Ward Burton, Kenny Wallace and Lake Speed, while Rusty Wallace took a former champion's provisional to make the field at team owner Roger Penske's track. The only driver to miss the field was Dave Marcis. One of the happiest drivers in the field was Gary Bradberry, who had replaced Bobby Hillin behind the wheel of the Hanes Ford for the Michigan race. Hillin, who had failed to qualify for a race since taking over the seat from Billy Standridge, found himself on the outside looking in while Bradberry claimed the 36th starting position.

Sunday's DeVilbiss 400 began under the threat of rain from the grey clouds overhead, and it became clear from the outset that the Jack Roush stable of three Ford Thunderbirds had the measure of the field. When the day was over, the three Fords would have led 176 of the 200 laps. Martin's Valvoline Thunderbird seemed to lead at will, and many in the crowd of more than 140,000 began wagering how large his margin of victory would be at the end of the 400-miler.

The race ran under green for the first half of the event, and as it did, Martin's luck turned sour when he cut a tire and was forced to head for pit road for a replacement. When he stopped, the Valvoline Thunderbird team fell to work, but had problems with the shredded left rear, with some of the tire rubber winding itself around the spindle. By the time the crew finished and Mark returned, he was two laps behind and it looked like his chances for his third win of the season were over.

He made up one of the laps when the field pitted under green for fuel and tires, and on lap 106, he received some help from teammate Jeff Burton to get back onto the tail end of the lead lap. Burton was

(Right) Apparent disaster strikes Mark Martin, who limps toward his pit after shredding the left-rear tire while leading the race. Martin fell two laps behind the leaders as a result, and would be forced to rely on a little luck and a helping hand to cancel the deficit and return to the front.
(Below) Bobby Labonte works his Interstate Batteries Pontiac to the inside of Dick Trickle, while trying to keep pace with Ford driving Jeff Burton and Mark Martin (6). Labonte was able to log another strong performance at Michigan, leading all Pontiacs with a sixth-place finish.

leading the race, and when the caution flag flew on lap 106 for a light rain shower, Burton slowed and allowed Martin to catch and pass him before the two team cars flashed under the waving yellow flag.

Mark still had plenty of work to do, and after a second, longer yellow for another rain shower, Martin finally went to the point for the final time on lap 169 and steadily pulled away from the field to score a two-second victory. He led more than half the race on his way to the win — but he could only make up 10 points on point-leader Jeff Gordon. Gordon fought his way to a strong second place, ahead of Ted Musgrave and the Robert Yates Racing Fords of Ernie Irvan and Dale Jarrett.

Bobby Labonte finished sixth, ahead of Bill Elliott and Jeff Burton, while Dale Earnhardt and Terry Labonte claimed ninth and 10th place.

Burton, who allowed his teammate back on the lead lap and gave him the chance to win the race, defended his actions by saying that if the shoe were on the other foot, Martin would have given him the same break. "If it had been late in the race and the two of us were fighting for the victory, that would

Dale Earnhardt (3) and Kyle Petty (44) try the frontstretch side by side, as Terry Labonte (5) and Ward Burton (22) go nose to tail in a two-car draft. Earnhardt and Labonte would eventually hook up and finish together in the top 10, while the two Pontiac drivers would fall from the top 20 by day's end.

be another story, entirely," Burton said after the race. "But at the time of the race that it occurred, it was the right thing to do. He wasn't the only one I let back on the lead lap, several other cars passed me, too. But the important thing is that Mark is fighting for the championship and I'm not. And we, as a team, will help our teammates in that situation."

Had Martin not made it back onto the lead lap, the best he would have finished was 18th, with 17 cars on the lead lap at the end of the race. Instead of gaining 10 points on Gordon, he would have lost another pile, and might have seen his title hopes evaporate.

Jeff Gordon (24) and Ted Musgrave (16) scratch and claw for second place. Gordon finally sandwiched himself between the two Roush Fords, dropping Musgrave to third in the final rundown.

DeVilbiss 400

Fin. Pos.	Start Pos.	Car #	Driver	Team
1	2	6	Mark Martin	Valvoline Ford
2	17	24	Jeff Gordon	DuPont Refinishes Chevrolet
3	7	16	Ted Musgrave	Family Channel/PRIMESTAR Ford
4	20	28	Ernie Irvan	Texaco Havoline Ford
5	4	88	Dale Jarrett	Quality Care/Ford Credit Ford
6	6	18	Bobby Labonte	Interstate Batteries Pontiac
7	24	94	Bill Elliott	McDonald's Ford
8	5	99	Jeff Burton	Exide Batteries Ford
9	28	3	Dale Earnhardt	GM Goodwrench Service Plus Chevrolet
10	14	5	Terry Labonte	Kellogg's Corn Flakes Chevrolet
11	10	7	Geoff Bodine	QVC Ford
12	3	25	Ricky Craven	Budweiser Chevrolet
13	43	2	Rusty Wallace	Miller Lite Ford
14	8	33	Ken Schrader	Skoal Bandit Chevrolet
15	26	17	Darrell Waltrip	Parts America Chevrolet
16	16	36	Derrike Cope	Skittles Pontiac
17	29	40	Robby Gordon	Coors Light Chevrolet
18	13	29	Jeff Green	Cartoon Network Chevrolet
19	39	23	Jimmy Spencer	Camel Cigarettes Ford
20	23	96	David Green	Caterpillar Chevrolet
21	42	9	Lake Speed	Melling Engine Parts Ford
22	31	21	Michael Waltrip	CITGO Ford
23	33	44	Kyle Petty	Hot Wheels Pontiac
24	1	30	Johnny Benson	Pennzoil Pontiac
25	22	41	Steve Grissom	Kodiak Chevrolet
26	35	43	Bobby Hamilton	STP Pontiac
27	30	42	Joe Nemechek	BellSouth Chevrolet
28	40	22	Ward Burton	MBNA America Pontiac
29	27	10	Ricky Rudd	Tide Ford
30	34	31	Mike Skinner	Lowe's Chevrolet
31	37	11	Brett Bodine	Close Call Phone Card Ford
32	41	81	Kenny Wallace	Square D Ford
33	12	37	Jeremy Mayfield	Kmart/RC Cola Ford
34	32	1	Lance Hooper	R&L Carriers Pontiac
35	25	98	John Andretti	RCA Ford
36	38	8	Hut Stricklin	Circuit City Ford
37	36	78	Gary Bradberry	Hanes Ford
38	21	75	Rick Mast	Remington Arms Ford
39	9	90	Dick Trickle	Heilig-Meyers/Simmons Ford
40	15	77	Morgan Shepherd	Jasper Engines/Federal-Mogul Ford
41	11	46	Wally Dallenbach	First Union Chevrolet
42	18	97	Chad Little	John Deere Pontiac
43	19	4	Sterling Marlin	Kodak Film Chevrolet

NASCAR WINSTON CUP SERIES 1997

Goody's Headache Powder 500

(Bristol Motor Speedway • August 23, 1997)

All the fuss and flutter about Jeff Burton's decision to let Roush Racing teammate Mark Martin back onto the lead lap at Michigan — a move that ultimately led to Mark's third victory of the season — had, for the most part, ended by the time the teams rolled into Jeff Byrd's half-mile oval just five days later.

Bristol Motor Speedway's races, particularly the August night race, have long been among the most popular on the entire season's calendar. Since Bruton Smith's purchase of the track, and under the expert guidance of Byrd and the hard-working group of promotion specialists led by Wayne Estes and Logan McCabe, the track has become established as a premier outing on the schedule. With 140,000 seats circling the half mile, Bristol is one of racing's most spectacular venues — and it continues to be one of the biggest challenges for drivers.

The steep banks push speeds higher each weekend, and with just a couple of seconds on the straights, drivers barely have time to straighten out their mounts from the previous corner before pitching the car into the next. The field is tightly packed, and a single mistake by a driver, a single slip on the concrete surface, can spell disaster, with multi-car accidents the rule rather than the exception.

(Right) Dale Jarrett's smile in victory lane is telling of his emotions following a milestone win. After 10 full seasons on the tour, Jarrett had finally conquered Bristol and picked up his first career victory on a NASCAR Winston Cup short track.

(Below) Behind the wheel of the R&L Carriers Pontiac for the third straight race, Lance Hooper challenges the Skittles Pontiac of Derrike Cope after slipping past the Hanes Ford of Gary Bradberry.

NASCAR
Red Carpet Lease
Ford
Ford Credit
NASCAR Winston Cup Series
Quality Care
QC Quality Care
SIMPSON
MOOG
white rain

Few feared the evening at Bristol more than point-leader Jeff Gordon. He knew that his 99-point lead over Mark Martin could be wiped out in an instant, if he was collected in an accident on the high banks, or if he made any error at all. With less than a third of the season remaining, he had fought his way through the year to hold the point lead in the stretch run to the title, and with many of his best tracks coming, Bristol loomed as perhaps the biggest problem he would face.

For Dale Jarrett, Terry Labonte, Jeff Burton and sixth place Dale Earnhardt, the opportunities to catch Gordon and Martin, and turn the point battle into more than a two-driver race, were beginning to wind down. All needed some help from the Racing Gods if they were to close on the front-runners.

When the McDonald's Ford was unloaded from the Elliott Racing trailer, it drew surprised glances from crew members throughout the garage area. The usual red paint scheme had been replaced by midnight blue colors, complete with stars, as part of a Mac Tonight promotion. In other team-related activities, Jimmy Spencer signed to drive Travis Carter's Fords for the 1998 season, and Doug Richert returned to the LJ Racing Ford as an interim crew chief while the team continued to try to find the right combination. John Deere had made the decision to remain with Chad Little and his

(Left) For the popular Saturday night event at Bristol, Bill Elliott showed up with this Mac Tonight paint scheme. Bill wouldn't turn out to be the star of the show, however, as he struggled to a 16th-place finish, three laps off the pace. *(Below)* Under the lights in Thunder Valley. New grandstands and luxury suites that surround the facility will ensure that tickets for the popular speed bowl will remain some of the most difficult to obtain all year.

(Top) NASCAR officials stop the action on the track when a seven-car accident wound up blocking the frontstretch midway through the event. Cleanup crews hurriedly cleared the racing surface, limiting the red-flag delay to only 18 minutes. *(Right)* Rick Mast (75) slides up the 36-degree banking to allow Jeff Gordon (24) and Dale Jarrett to continue their struggle for the point as the race reaches mid-distance.

team for at least two years, with Jack Roush's influence in the team one of the key factors in the decision. Circuit City and Hut Stricklin would return in 1998 to the Stavola Brothers team. The Stavolas had closed their engine shop, and planned to contract with Ernie Elliott for motors for the remainder of the season.

One of the most important announcements regarding the future of the sport was made by NASCAR on August 19, when teams were informed that engines for the coming season would be changed from 14:1 compression to 12:1, slightly lowering the horsepower numbers

(Above) The Caterpillar Monte Carlo, driven by David Green, lands on all fours after sliding down the frontstretch on its side in the accident that brought out the red flag. *(Left)* The DuPont crew works on their Chevrolet behind the wall. Bringing his nightmares to life, Gordon tangled with Jeremy Mayfield just before the halfway point, and lost 50 laps — and the point lead — while repairs were being made. *(Below)* Hut Stricklin stands on the binders of his Circuit City Ford, hoping that a hole will open between the Chevrolets of Mike Skinner (31) and Wally Dallenbach after they were involved in a multi-car accident on lap 425.

for the motors. And the General Motors teams were delighted to learn that the proposed new cylinder heads for the all-new short-block motor had been approved for 1998. One leading GM engine builder said the combination of new engine and cylinder heads should mean an increase of horsepower for the Chevrolet teams, but he noted that it was too early to tell how much.

While the point-leaders were eyeing each other, keeping track of the lap times turned in practice, the Square D Ford team was in its garage slot, with crew members quietly going about their business. The blue-and-yellow Thunderbird was fast, and when

After slipping past Mark Martin on the way to a late-race caution flag, Dale Jarrett (88) holds the Valvoline Ford driver at bay in the closing laps to secure the victory. Martin came home second in the race, but moved to the top of the point ladder after the results were tallied.

Kenny Wallace rolled onto the race track late in the qualifying session, he benefited from some cloud cover that cooled the surface slightly. It was just enough to allow him to unseat Gordon for the Busch Pole. Dale Jarrett and Dick Trickle claimed the second-row positions, ahead of Martin and Ken Schrader, while Sterling Marlin and David Green locked up the fourth row. Behind them, Derrike Cope and Ward Burton completed the top 10, just ahead of Wally Dallenbach and Ted Musgrave. Gary Bradberry appeared to have earned the ride in the Hanes Ford for the remainder of the season and was the fastest second-round qualifier. Ricky Rudd, Brett Bodine, Rick Mast and Hut Stricklin used provisionals to get into the race, while Morgan Shepherd, Robby Gordon and Dave Marcis all failed to make the field.

Celebrating the 20th anniversary of racing at night at Bristol, Jeff Gordon appeared to be headed for another conquest of the half-mile oval. For the first half of the race, he led handily, appearing poised to take his ninth victory of the season. Then, the thing he had dreaded most happened. Geoff Bodine, trying to get a lap back, gouged Gordon out of the low groove, and on the backstretch, Gordon and Jeremy Mayfield tangled, with both smacking the inside wall. Gordon spent more than 50 laps in the pits and struggled for the remainder of the race, finally finishing 135 laps behind, in 35th place.

It opened the door for Martin and Jarrett, and the two diced furiously as the race wound down. Mark had the point, looking for a green-flag run to the finish, but slowed slightly when his spotter told him there was oil on the track with just 30 laps left in the race. Jarrett found the opening and flashed to the lead — and was greeted by the yellow flag when he arrived at the flagstand. The yellow gave him the chance to gather up his Quality Care Ford, and when the green dropped again on lap 479, he was in command of the race. Martin did all he could, but didn't have enough for Jarrett at the end, losing by a tenth of a second.

The victory, Jarrett's first on a short track in his NASCAR Winston Cup career, moved him to within 171 points of Gordon, while Martin's second place, coupled with Gordon's 35th, put the Valvoline Ford driver at the head of the point table for the first time since October 1990. Dick Trickle claimed third place — the best finish for a Junie Donlavey car since 1984, and Jeff Burton finished fourth, ahead of Steve Grissom and Schrader. Terry and Bobby Labonte were seventh and eighth, while Geoff Bodine was the final car on the lead lap and Marlin led the lap-down cars.

David Green was involved in a multi-car accident just past half-distance that also included Cope, Earnhardt, Michael Waltrip, John Andretti, Brett Bodine, Bobby Hamilton and Jeff Green. And for Darrell Waltrip, who had a 38,000-seat grandstand named in his honor before the start of the race, the night ended early. He was classified last after being involved in an accident that also included pole-winner Kenny Wallace less than one-quarter of the way through the race.

Goody's Headache Power 500

Fin. Pos.	Start Pos.	Car #	Driver	Team
1	3	88	Dale Jarrett	Quality Care/Ford Credit Ford
2	5	6	Mark Martin	Valvoline Ford
3	4	90	Dick Trickle	Heilig-Meyers/Simmons Ford
4	13	99	Jeff Burton	Exide Batteries Ford
5	35	41	Steve Grissom	Kodiak Chevrolet
6	6	33	Ken Schrader	Skoal Bandit Chevrolet
7	19	5	Terry Labonte	Kellogg's Corn Flakes Chevrolet
8	38	18	Bobby Labonte	Interstate Batteries Pontiac
9	15	7	Geoff Bodine	QVC Ford
10	7	4	Sterling Marlin	Kodak Film Chevrolet
11	20	98	John Andretti	RCA Ford
12	16	2	Rusty Wallace	Miller Lite Ford
13	14	25	Ricky Craven	Budweiser Chevrolet
14	34	3	Dale Earnhardt	GM Goodwrench Service Plus Chevrolet
15	12	16	Ted Musgrave	Family Channel/PRIMESTAR Ford
16	36	94	Bill Elliott	McDonald's Ford
17	10	22	Ward Burton	MBNA America Pontiac
18	22	30	Johnny Benson	Pennzoil Pontiac
19	39	10	Ricky Rudd	Tide Ford
20	37	97	Chad Little	John Deere Pontiac
21	30	29	Jeff Green	Cartoon Network Chevrolet
22	29	43	Bobby Hamilton	STP Pontiac
23	42	8	Hut Stricklin	Circuit City Ford
24	28	1	Lance Hooper	R&L Carriers Pontiac
25	33	21	Michael Waltrip	CITGO Ford
26	11	46	Wally Dallenbach	First Union Chevrolet
27	17	23	Jimmy Spencer	Camel Cigarettes Ford
28	21	95	Ed Berrier	Feed The Children Chevrolet
29	25	9	Lake Speed	Melling Engine Parts Ford
30	18	37	Jeremy Mayfield	Kmart/RC Cola Ford
31	40	11	Brett Bodine	Close Call Phone Card Ford
32	9	36	Derrike Cope	Skittles Pontiac
33	41	75	Rick Mast	Remington Arms Ford
34	31	31	Mike Skinner	Lowe's Chevrolet
35	2	24	Jeff Gordon	DuPont Refinishes Chevrolet
36	24	44	Kyle Petty	Hot Wheels Pontiac
37	26	78	Gary Bradberry	Hanes Ford
38	27	42	Joe Nemechek	BellSouth Chevrolet
39	1	81	Kenny Wallace	Square D Ford
40	8	96	David Green	Caterpillar Chevrolet
41	32	28	Ernie Irvan	Texaco Havoline Ford
42	23	17	Darrell Waltrip	Parts America Chevrolet

NASCAR WINSTON CUP SERIES 1997

Mountain Dew Southern 500

(Darlington Raceway • August 31, 1997)

Since 1985, when the program was initiated by R.J. Reynolds, Darlington's Mountain Dew Southern 500 has been the final event in the Winston Million program. The Winston Million pays a $1 million bonus to a driver who is able to win three of four selected races during the season, and since the beginning of the program, only one driver has been able to score the three victories in a single year to claim the award.

Bill Elliott, in the magnificent season that marked his emergence as one of the biggest superstars of the sport, claimed the Winston Million that first year, and since then has been the president, secretary-treasurer and membership of the elite club of one. Others have had the chance to claim the bonus — Darrell Waltrip in 1989, Davey Allison in 1992, and last year, Dale Jarrett. All have failed.

This year, Jeff Gordon rolled into Darlington with a chance to join Elliott in the prestigious circle of Winston Million winners, after his triumphs in the Daytona 500 and the Coca-Cola 600 at Charlotte put him within striking distance. A win at Darlington, where he was going for a three-peat in the Mountain Dew Southern 500 would make him the second winner of the Winston Million.

Few thought Gordon had a real chance of scoring the victory. If for no other reason than no driver had ever won three consecutive Southern 500s in the long and storied history of the pioneer superspeedway. Several had won twice in succession — Cale Yarborough, David Pearson, Dale Earnhardt, Bobby Allison and, way back in 1954-'55, Herb Thomas.

(Right) President of R.J. Reynolds' Sports Marketing Enterprises, T. Wayne Robertson, stands aside as Jeff Gordon emerges from his DuPont Chevrolet in victory lane. In a few moments, Mr. Robertson would present Gordon with a check for $1 million for his combined wins at Daytona, Charlotte and Darlington.

(Below) Bill Elliott (94), the only driver ever to have won the Winston Million in the history of the program, challenges Jeff Gordon (24), in an effort to remain the sole winner of the rich prize. Elliott had qualified on the front row and would lead the most laps in the race, but, ultimately, could not change destiny.

160

Winston Million
GMAC
PEPSI
ACDelco
GOODYEAR
CHARLOTTE DARLINGTON
24
HAAS CNC
Pedigree

The odds were long that tough old Darlington would hand three straight Southern 500 titles to Gordon.

Many also wondered if Gordon's good luck — perhaps the most vital link to a championship quest — had ended with the accident at Bristol just days before the Darlington event. Gordon had fallen from the point lead with his 35th-place finish, and had come to South Carolina 13 markers behind Mark Martin. Gordon's finish had also allowed Jarrett to move to within 158 of the DuPont Chevrolet driver, and Terry Labonte, doggedly determined to defend his title, had also closed on Gordon, now trailing by 240.

Each year, many teams use the Southern 500 weekend as the arena for announcements relating to the coming season, and there was a flurry of statements by several teams this year. Harry Melling and Lake Speed had linked up with the Cartoon Network for the '98 season, and Mike Skinner and Richard Childress said they had inked a renewal of their contract for the next two years. With Derrike Cope out of the Skittles car for '98, Ernie Irvan was introduced as the new driver for the candy-backed team. Bobby Hamilton was named the driver for the Kodak-sponsored Morgan-McClure team for '98, with Sterling Marlin headed for another ride. Pennzoil and Steve Park were also announced as a new effort in Dale Earnhardt's new NASCAR Winston Cup team. The oil company would also honor its commitment to Chuck Rider and Lowrance Harry's Bahari team in the coming year.

(Top) Dale Earnhardt and Terry Labonte chat prior to entering their cars for the Mountain Dew Southern 500. Immediately after the green flag flew, Earnhardt would hit the second turn wall in a bizarre incident that would necessitate him being relieved by rookie Mike Dillon. (Middle) Kyle Petty (left) and Bobby Hamilton discuss the setups on their Pontiacs before the start of the race. Both drivers were forced to use provisionals to make the Southern 500 field, and would start side by side from the 20th row. (Left) Never one to miss a date with big money on the line, Jeff Gordon needed no reminder of what this day meant should he achieve his ninth win of the season.

(Right) In front of the newly erected grandstands on what is now Darlington's frontstretch, the Bahari Racing team changes left-side tires and adds fuel to the Pennzoil Pontiac for driver Johnny Benson during a green-flag pit stop. (Below) Pole-winner Bobby Labonte paces the starting field through turn two, err, turn four, on the way to the backstretch, err, frontstretch, to take the initial green flag. Labonte jumped out to lead the first two laps, before being passed by Elliott, who would dominate the first two-thirds of the event.

In other news on the team front, Bill Ingle was in a Circuit City uniform, working with the Stavola Brothers as the crew chief on Hut Stricklin's team on a "try-out" basis. After a disappointing weekend at Bristol in the Budweiser colors of the past, Darrell Waltrip brought his Monte Carlo to Darlington dressed in the Mountain Dew colors that brought him successive NASCAR Winston Cup championships in 1981 and 1982. It was part of his "Silver Anniversary Celebration," using paint schemes that had become famous with his past driving successes. Banjo Matthews' Performance Center, the Mecca for chassis building over the last two decades, closed its doors during the week prior to the Southern 500, and Tim Brewer moved into the full-time crew chief's role at Mattei Motorsports for Geoff Bodine. Pat Tryson

(Top) Jeff Burton (99) brings the crowd to their feet as he lays a fender into Jeff Gordon's Chevrolet while taking the white flag. The victory — and one million dollars — hangs in the balance. *(Left)* One lap later, Gordon flashes under the flagstand, this time showing checkers, to claim the win and become only the second driver in history to score the lucrative trifecta.

had left that team in mid-race at Bristol when there were obviously two many cooks in the kitchen during the running of the Goody's 500. Pat immediately found work as the crew chief for the new Tabasco-sponsored effort and driver Todd Bodine.

The Mountain Dew Southern 500 may have been the oldest race on the schedule, but the venerable egg-shaped track had a new look in store for competitors. Since the spring race, the track had been "flopped," with the start/finish line moved to the old backstretch, bringing an entirely different feeling to the track for competitors — and for fans. It meant intensive testing by almost every team at the track in preparation for the event.

When the first round of Busch Pole qualifying was completed, Bobby Labonte had zipped to the fastest lap of the session and his second pole of the season — and he had to be perfect to beat a sizzling lap posted by Elliott. The difference between the two drivers was .025 seconds.

Jarrett was crackling and beat Martin for the inside of the second row, ahead of Ken Schrader and a hot-running Stricklin. Gordon was inside the fourth row, and Dick Trickle was on his right with a second straight strong qualifying effort. Marlin and Irvan were in the fifth row, just ahead of brothers Brett and Geoff Bodine. In the second round of qualifying, every driver who ran failed to make the field. Dave Marcis, who missed his fifth straight race, ended his string of 23 consecutive Southern 500 starts. Provisionals went to Kyle Petty and Hamilton, along with Lance Hooper and Jeff Green. Rusty Wallace was forced to use a former champion's provisional to make the field.

Over the years, the Southern 500 has been the scene of bizarre happenings, and when the race began, yet another chapter was written in the track's history book. On the first two laps of the race, Dale Earnhardt found the wall. He finally made it to pit road, where he was helped from his car and then rushed to the infield medical center. Eventually, NASCAR Busch Series driver Mike Dillon returned the Goodwrench Chevrolet to the fray, finishing 30th.

Typically strong at Darlington, Michael Waltrip looks to push the CITGO Ford even with Jeremy Mayfield (37) on the outside, although both drivers stay well below Darlington's concrete wall, already showing it's knack for collecting tire marks. Waltrip was able to score his sixth top-10 finish of the year by finishing ninth on the day.

While the Goodwrench team frantically tried to find out what had happened to its driver, Elliott rolled to a handsome lead in the early stages of the Mountain Dew Southern 500. For the first two-thirds of the race, he was the dominant force, and it appeared his winless string would end with a fourth career Southern 500 victory. When the sun went under the clouds later in the race, however, the handling disappeared from The Redhead's McDonald's Ford, and he ended up fourth. Jarrett saw his chance and moved past Elliott in that interval and it looked as though the Quality Care driver was headed for victory.

The yellow came out when a brief shower splattered the track on lap 303, and Jarrett at first planned to stay on the track. But a hasty, last-second decision to head for pit road caused him to lose the lead while in the pits, and Gordon emerged at the point. Try as he did, Jarrett could not pass the DuPont driver, and eventually yielded second place to Jeff Burton. Burton ripped and chased and wheeled and stomped and finally got into position to challenge Gordon for the lead in the closing laps of the race. If he could get the nose of the Exide Ford ahead, he could prevent Gordon from winning the Winston Million — plus, he could chalk up his own initial Southern 500 victory.

Gordon was having none of it. On the final lap, the two drivers slapped sides more than once, sheet metal screeched and Bondo dust flew as the two youngsters fought door handle-to-door handle for the victory. It was wonderful stuff — the way Southern 500s and Winston Millions should be won or lost — and when the race to the flag was over, Gordon had triumphed.

He had won his third consecutive Southern 500, for his own page in Darlington's record book, and also claimed the Winston Million. All of that was important to him, but the fact that Martin had finished eighth, behind Ricky Rudd, Terry and Bobby Labonte, meant that the Rainbow Warriors were once again at the top of the point heap. Ninth and 10th places went to Michael Waltrip and Schrader.

Mountain Dew Southern 500

Fin. Pos.	Start Pos.	Car #	Driver	Team
1	7	24	Jeff Gordon	DuPont Refinishes Chevrolet
2	16	99	Jeff Burton	Exide Batteries Ford
3	3	88	Dale Jarrett	Quality Care/Ford Credit Ford
4	2	94	Bill Elliott	McDonald's Ford
5	21	10	Ricky Rudd	Tide Ford
6	17	5	Terry Labonte	Kellogg's Corn Flakes Chevrolet
7	1	18	Bobby Labonte	Interstate Batteries Pontiac
8	4	6	Mark Martin	Valvoline Ford
9	14	21	Michael Waltrip	CITGO Ford
10	5	33	Ken Schrader	Skoal Bandit Chevrolet
11	37	97	Chad Little	John Deere Pontiac
12	12	7	Geoff Bodine	QVC Ford
13	8	90	Dick Trickle	Heilig-Meyers/Simmons Ford
14	24	36	Derrike Cope	Skittles Pontiac
15	11	11	Brett Bodine	Close Call Phone Card Ford
16	19	37	Jeremy Mayfield	Kmart/RC Cola Ford
17	6	8	Hut Stricklin	Circuit City Ford
18	23	9	Lake Speed	Melling Engine Parts Ford
19	18	30	Johnny Benson	Pennzoil Pontiac
20	40	43	Bobby Hamilton	STP Pontiac
21	29	41	Steve Grissom	Kodiak Chevrolet
22	34	40	Robby Gordon	Coors Light Chevrolet
23	20	42	Joe Nemechek	BellSouth Chevrolet
24	25	81	Kenny Wallace	Square D Ford
25	27	78	Gary Bradberry	Hanes Ford
26	38	17	Darrell Waltrip	Parts America Chevrolet
27	13	22	Ward Burton	MBNA America Pontiac
28	30	23	Jimmy Spencer	Camel Cigarettes Ford
29	15	16	Ted Musgrave	Family Channel/PRIMESTAR Ford
30	36	3	Dale Earnhardt	GM Goodwrench Service Plus Chevrolet
31	31	25	Ricky Craven	Budweiser Chevrolet
32	39	44	Kyle Petty	Hot Wheels Pontiac
33	10	28	Ernie Irvan	Texaco Havoline Ford
34	28	75	Rick Mast	Remington Arms Ford
35	41	1	Lance Hooper	R&L Carriers Pontiac
36	33	31	Mike Skinner	Lowe's Chevrolet
37	32	98	John Andretti	RCA Ford
38	22	12	Jeff Purvis	Opryland Chevrolet
39	42	29	Jeff Green	Cartoon Network Chevrolet
40	9	4	Sterling Marlin	Kodak Film Chevrolet
41	26	46	Wally Dallenbach	First Union Chevrolet
42	35	96	Todd Bodine	Caterpillar Chevrolet
43	43	2	Rusty Wallace	Miller Lite Ford

NASCAR WINSTON CUP SERIES 1997

Exide NASCAR Select Batteries 400

(Richmond International Raceway • September 6, 1997)

Nearly every competitor in the garage area at Paul Sawyer's Richmond International Raceway was delighted that there were no special events or bonus pools, other than the NASCAR Winston Cup point fund, left in the season to win. If there had been, it seemed Jeff Gordon would be the odds-on choice to claim them.

He had won the Busch Clash, and then grabbed The Winston all-star race at Charlotte. Now, with his victory in the Mountain Dew Southern 500 at Darlington, he had gobbled up the Winston Million. During the course of the season, his nine victories had helped him

(Right) Bill Elliott pushes his specially painted Mac Tonight Thunderbird to the line, preparing to race under the stars at Richmond. Bill would start from the pole and lead the first 43 laps of the event.

(Left) NASCAR Craftsman Truck Series rookie standout and future driver of the Texaco Havoline Ford for car owner Robert Yates, Kenny Irwin Jr., looks confident prior to the start of the race. In an outstanding effort, Irwin, who qualified on the front row next to Elliott, raced hard, leading at times, before finishing a very impressive eighth in his NASCAR Winston Cup debut.

McDonald's
SIMPSON
WE CARE
DEA
Coca-Cola CLASSIC
94
NASCAR RACE CAR
BUSCH
BEER
Pole Award
Gatorade
Goody's
HEADACHE POWDERS
SPICER
DANA
EAGLE
McDonald's

dad, Ralph Earnhardt, had died of a heart attack while working on a carburetor from his Late Model Sportsman car at the age of 45. Dale is 46. The doctors' opinions and reports were all forwarded to NASCAR officials in Daytona Beach, and, in the end, Dale was cleared to race at Richmond.

Friday at Richmond, Dale faced the media and discussed the situation, saying he felt better than he had in a long time, but admitting that he had thought about taking the weekend off. However, he explained, he felt so well, and there was a race, so ...

Earnhardt was admittedly out of the point hunt, but Gordon's Darlington victory, combined with Mark Martin's finish, had allowed him to gain 25 markers on the Valvoline Ford driver and to move back

(Left) Car owner and crew chief of the "33" Skoal Bandit Chevrolet, Andy Petree, watches his driver, Ken Schrader, during practice on the three-quarter-mile oval. (Below) Circuit City Ford driver Hut Stricklin (center) surveys what remains of a cut tire that forced him off the track during practice. Hut got back out and qualified 15th in the first round, but fell to 27th by the end of the race.

pocket $200,000 of the Winston Leader bonus, a $10,000 rollover that was paid to the winner of each event if the race winner was also the NASCAR Winston Cup point leader.

The Darlington duel between Gordon and Jeff Burton for the Southern 500 win had left the crowd standing and cheering both competitors. Now the scene shifted to Burton's home turf, where he hoped to avenge his close loss to Gordon. Following the Darlington race, the headlines had been Gordon, Gordon, Gordon, but that also changed during the week between his wonderful Darlington victory and the opening of the Richmond gates.

Dale Earnhardt's mysterious ailment remained just that. Although released from a Florence, S.C., hospital 24 hours after he was admitted Sunday afternoon, Dale had been poked, prodded, viewed and tested Monday, Tuesday and Wednesday, with the results read by some 25 different doctors. He had run the gamut of EEGs, EKGs, MRAs and MRIs. "They tested me for everything except to see if I was pregnant," he joked. The end result was that no one could explain what had happened at the start of the Southern 500.

Much to his relief, the findings were all negative, and Earnhardt was told he had the heart of a 30-year old man. Never far from his mind is the fact that his

(Top) Rusty Wallace (2) and Ernie Irvan (28) show the form that took them to wins in the previous two Saturday night events at Richmond, as Derrike Cope (36) and Dale Earnhardt try to hold their ground on the outside. (Right) Ward Burton puts his MBNA Pontiac on the yellow line to gain a spot on Dale Earnhardt. Burton would tie his best performance of the season with a seventh-place finish, giving his team much needed encouragement for the remainder of the season.

into the point lead. Dale Jarrett lost 10 points to Gordon, as well, and now trailed by 168. Terry Labonte, who was finding that his consistency wasn't working this year, fell another 30 points off the pace, and was 257 behind. His hopes for a successful defense of his title were beginning to fray around the edges. And Labonte had another worry. Just 26 points behind him was Burton, who was determined to move his Exide Ford into the fourth rung on the ladder.

The point battle, Earnhardt's strange Darlington situation, and Gordon's triumph in the Winston Million were all topics of conversation at Richmond, but so was the 1998 NASCAR Winston Cup schedule. Released much earlier than the usual December unveiling at the New York City banquet, the list of dates, not including the Bud Shootout and The Winston, had stretched to 33. Las Vegas received a March 1 date, the only new event added. The Vegas race would allow

169

Ernie Irvan's Texaco Thunderbird rides up the side of Mark Martin's Valvoline Ford in the second turn early in the race. Jeff Burton (99) and Hut Stricklin (8) are also involved, while David Green (96) and Ward Burton (22) try to weave their way through without incident.

For Ricky Craven and the Richard Jackson team, with Lance Hooper behind the wheel, as well as for Dave Marcis, Morgan Shepherd and Wally Dallenbach, qualifying took on added importance at Richmond. Craven, along with the R&L Carriers team, were out of provisionals, and the car owners for Marcis, Shepherd and Dallenbach had all fallen out of the top 40 in car owner points, so those drivers wouldn't be able to use provisionals. All had to race their way into the field.

Craven and Dallenbach responded, making the field with their times, and Hooper's qualifying attempt earned his team a provisional, which they were forced to use. However, Marcis and Shepherd went home, along with Mike Bliss, Ron Hornaday and Gary Bradberry.

At the top of the heap following qualifying was none other than Bill Elliott, who had barely missed the pole the previous weekend at Darlington. Elliott had the specially painted blue Mac Tonight car at Richmond, and the reflective stars on the car were ready to lead the

the first Richmond race to move to a better time frame. The Sawyers, after struggling with the February and March weather at Richmond for years, were grinning to see June 6 as their new date. The Richmond event would be run Saturday evening under the lights. The California 500 race moved to May 3, and Sears Point's date moved to June 28. The season would end earlier than usual on November 8 to allow for a pair of exhibition races in Japan after the season concluded.

Looking at the list, crew members groaned. This year's stretch run began at Indianapolis, with the Brickyard 400 triggering an 11-race string of consecutive weekends. In 1998, the schedule showed a 12-race string, beginning with the Pocono race. From July 26 until October 11 at Talladega, teams would race without a break.

In a defining moment near the end of the race, Dale Jarrett (88) slips past Jeff Burton (99) to take the lead when Jeff is forced to slow behind his brother Ward, running one lap down. The Exide Ford driver took the lap-leader bonus in the race, but could not catch Jarrett over the final 39 laps, settling for second place for the second straight week.

170

Dale Jarrett flashes a big smile from Richmond's winner's circle, having taken a recent liking to racing on short tracks under the lights, and bringing home his fifth win of the season.

field away. On Elliott's right was the surprise of the weekend — Kenny Irwin making his NASCAR Winston Cup debut. The Tonka Toys Ford he drove was entered by David Blair's team and carried the number 27, but it was a Robert Yates Thunderbird and engine under the paint scheme. Irwin was making the first of five races in the closing events of the season in preparation for his taking over the Texaco-sponsored Yates ride in 1998.

Bobby Hamilton had the flat-track STP Pontiac cranked, gaining the inside of the second row, with Robby Gordon alongside. Kenny Wallace had another good qualifying run to fifth fastest, and Dick Trickle gave Richmond fans reason to cheer with his sixth starting position (and his fourth straight top-10 start) for hometown owner Junie Donlavey and Richmond-based sponsor Heilig-Meyers. Behind them, Joe Nemechek and David Green lined up in the fourth row, with Ken Schrader and Jeff Gordon in the fifth row, just ahead of Virginians Jeff and Ward Burton.

Elliott's hopes for his first victory of the season dimmed after the first 43 laps, when the handling on his McDonald's Ford disappeared. Hamilton slashed past, but the handling began to fade on the STP Pontiac, and, eventually, a faulty rear end ended his chances for victory. That put Jeff Burton in command of the race, and he led 234 of the 400 laps — but not the one that counted. Making his way through lapped traffic, Burton was momentarily slowed while trying to lap his brother, Ward, and Jarrett found a way past the Exide Ford. Once the red-white-and-blue Thunderbird was at the point, Jarrett eased to the second short-track victory of his career.

Jeff Burton finished as the runner-up for the second straight event, while point-leader Jeff Gordon soldiered his way to a solid third place with a car he couldn't get to the front of the pack. Geoff Bodine was fourth, ahead of Rusty Wallace and Nemechek, the final driver on the lead lap. Ward Burton, Irwin, Musgrave and Jeremy Mayfield rounded out the top 10, all one lap behind.

Exide NASCAR Select Batteries 400

Fin. Pos.	Start Pos.	Car #	Driver	Team
1	23	88	Dale Jarrett	Quality Care/Ford Credit Ford
2	11	99	Jeff Burton	Exide Batteries Ford
3	10	24	Jeff Gordon	DuPont Refinishes Chevrolet
4	31	7	Geoff Bodine	QVC Ford
5	14	2	Rusty Wallace	Miller Lite Ford
6	7	42	Joe Nemechek	BellSouth Chevrolet
7	12	22	Ward Burton	MBNA America Pontiac
8	2	27	Kenny Irwin Jr.	Hasbro/Action Performance Ford
9	38	16	Ted Musgrave	Family Channel/PRIMESTAR Ford
10	16	37	Jeremy Mayfield	Kmart/RC Cola Ford
11	27	23	Jimmy Spencer	Camel Cigarettes Ford
12	33	41	Steve Grissom	Kodiak Chevrolet
13	37	30	Johnny Benson	Pennzoil Pontiac
14	9	33	Ken Schrader	Skoal Bandit Chevrolet
15	22	3	Dale Earnhardt	GM Goodwrench Service Plus Chevrolet
16	19	36	Derrike Cope	Skittles Pontiac
17	24	5	Terry Labonte	Kellogg's Corn Flakes Chevrolet
18	21	25	Ricky Craven	Budweiser Chevrolet
19	6	90	Dick Trickle	Heilig-Meyers/Simmons Ford
20	17	44	Kyle Petty	Hot Wheels Pontiac
21	39	11	Brett Bodine	Close Call Phone Card Ford
22	32	98	John Andretti	RCA Ford
23	20	28	Ernie Irvan	Texaco Havoline Ford
24	5	81	Kenny Wallace	Square D Ford
25	13	6	Mark Martin	Valvoline Ford
26	30	75	Rick Mast	Remington Arms Ford
27	15	8	Hut Stricklin	Circuit City Ford
28	35	10	Ricky Rudd	Tide Ford
29	40	31	Mike Skinner	Lowe's Chevrolet
30	1	94	Bill Elliott	McDonald's Ford
31	25	29	Jeff Green	Cartoon Network Chevrolet
32	18	17	Darrell Waltrip	Parts America Chevrolet
33	41	1	Lance Hooper	R&L Carriers Pontiac
34	34	18	Bobby Labonte	Interstate Batteries Pontiac
35	29	21	Michael Waltrip	CITGO Ford
36	26	9	Lake Speed	Melling Engine Parts Ford
37	8	96	David Green	Caterpillar Chevrolet
38	3	43	Bobby Hamilton	STP Pontiac
39	36	4	Sterling Marlin	Kodak Film Chevrolet
40	42	97	Chad Little	John Deere Pontiac
41	28	46	Wally Dallenbach	First Union Chevrolet
42	4	40	Robby Gordon	Coors Light Chevrolet

NASCAR WINSTON CUP SERIES 1997

CMT 300

(New Hampshire International Speedway • September 14, 1997)

Entering the Mountain Dew Southern 500 at Darlington, Mark Martin found himself in the point lead. Two events later, as the team transporters drove through the brilliantly-hued foliage of New England on the way to the first September NASCAR Winston Cup race at Bob and Gary Bahre's New Hampshire International Speedway, Martin was 97 points behind Jeff Gordon.

Martin had lost 72 points to Gordon at Richmond, and now was looking over his shoulder at a hard-charging Dale Jarrett, who had moved to within 56 points of Mark in their battle for Ford supremacy. Behind them, Jeff Burton's back-to-back second places had moved him past Terry Labonte into fourth place on the point table. Burton now trailed Gordon by 268 points, while Labonte continued to see his hopes for a second straight championship fade. He was 310 behind.

Burton arrived at New Hampshire unsure if he would be able to compete in the race. He had caught a cold at Richmond, and a resulting ear infection left him wanting in the balance department. Another doctor's opinion was that the inner ear problem might be the lingering result of his Michigan crash, and the services of Todd Bodine were enlisted as a precaution for Burton's team.

(Right) Ken Schrader wheels the Skoal Bandit Monte Carlo ahead of the pack, having swept the Busch Poles at New Hampshire in 1997. Schrader's hopes to deliver car owner Andy Petree his team's first win faded, however, as Ken dropped all the way to 37th by the end of the race.

(Below) Ernie Irvan stands with Ryan Pemberton, crew chief of the Skittles Pontiacs that Ernie is slated to drive in 1998. At New Hampshire, however, Ernie would be back behind the wheel of the Texaco Ford, and would have a tremendous run all the way from the 40th starting spot to finish second.

172

SKOAL
BANDIT
MONTE CARLO
STP
Western Auto
MOOG
76
EXIDE BATTERIES
plasti-kote
SIMPSON
CRAFTSMAN
Edelbrock
CRANE Cams
GOODYEAR

At New Hampshire, Jack Roush announced that he would field a fifth team next season, and that Johnny Benson would be the driver of the effort, expected to be sponsored by Cheerios. It meant that there was an opening in the Bahari seat, and it appeared that Derrike Cope would join that team. Roush's interest in Chad Little's team proved to be the controlling one, and Roush also said that in 1998, Little would compete in Ford Tauruses, not in Pontiacs.

Pontiac's forces were bolstered by the news that NASCAR had changed the front and rear spoiler heights on the Grand Prix in hopes of making them even more competitive, taking a quarter inch off the

(Left) It's thumbs up for a smiling Dale Earnhardt as he prepares to run 300 laps on New Hampshire's one-mile oval. Assured of his health after having undergone intensive examinations following his mysterious illness at Darlington, Earnhardt was looking – and running – like the Dale of old. *(Below)* Drivers gather backstage, waiting for their grand entrance in front of the enormous New Hampshire crowd before the first NASCAR Winston Cup event to be run there in the fall.

Bill Ingle's "try-out" as crew chief for the Stavola Brothers had been satisfactory, with Stricklin qualifying sixth at Darlington and 15th at Richmond. Ingle signed on with the team for the remainder of this season and all of 1998, indicating with a wide grin that there might be some truth to the rumor that the team might switch from Fords to Chevrolets for the coming season.

front air dam and adding it at the rear spoiler.

As if that wasn't enough to keep the media types writing in their notebooks, Bruton Smith announced plans to build an oval track in the Atlantic City, N.J., area. Smith revealed nothing about the length of the track or other particulars, so details would remain sketchy until after the site for the track was chosen.

The action along pit road is furious after the first of eight cautions came out on lap 69, causing nearly the entire field to head for new tires, fuel and, in some cases, needed chassis adjustments.

With qualifying slated to begin at 4 p.m., most figured that a draw that put them late in the qualifying session would be the best number to pull. Overcast conditions were expected as the run for the Busch Pole Award continued, and the afternoon shadows from the frontstretch grandstands would help even more. Cooler race tracks mean higher speeds and more grip from the tires on the asphalt — and the later in the session one runs, the more comments the driver and crew chief hear from those who have already made their efforts.

Ken Schrader and car owner/crew chief Andy Petree had pulled the number 40 in the drawing for qualifying order, and the two paid close attention to drivers after they came back from their timed laps. The two consulted, and a half-pound of air pressure was changed in one tire on the Skoal Bandit before Schrader went out. He rocketed around the New Hampshire track, and when he returned to pit road, he had claimed his second Busch Pole of the season. The decision to change the air pres-

Local favorite Ricky Craven (25) leads outside pole-sitter Bobby Hamilton during the opening stages of the race. Craven jumped to the lead on lap four, then traded the point with Hamilton over the next 144 laps. Both drivers finished in the top five.

175

sure had worked — and he whipped the field by nearly two-tenths of a second, nearly a mile per hour faster than the lap turned by Bobby Hamilton in the STP Pontiac.

By current NASCAR Winston Cup standards, Schrader had smoked the competition, although the difference between the two cars is not measurable to the human eye. Brett Bodine had a superb run to claim the inside of the second row with his Close Call Ford, and Mike Skinner boosted the morale of his Lowe's Chevrolet team by grabbing the outside of the second row.

John Andretti and home-track favorite Ricky Craven were in the third row, while Rick Mast and

(Above) Chad Little spins the John Deere Pontiac in the middle of traffic, while Sterling Marlin (4) tries to squeeze through without becoming involved. Little had just learned that John Deere would remain on his cars in 1998 and '99, but they all would become Fords at the end of this season. *(Left)* Ernie Irvan pressures Jeff Gordon in the last 100 laps, trying to unnerve the point-leader and take his second win of the year. It was not to be, however, as Gordon hung on and forced Irvan to settle for second place. *(Below)* Jeff Gordon drops the window net on his Du Pont Chevrolet and disconnects his air hose during the cool-down lap, preparing to celebrate his 10th win of the 1997 season.

Wally Dallenbach were the seventh and eighth fastest in the first round of qualifying. Lake Speed and Bill Elliott grabbed the final top-10 positions, ahead of Kyle Petty and Bobby Labonte.

Where, then, were the championship contenders? Jeff Gordon qualified 13th, with Mark Martin 17th, and Dale Jarrett 19th. Burton, unable to drive because of the balance problem in his ear, watched as Todd Bodine was unable to qualify during the first day, and ultimately would need to use a provisional to make the field. Terry Labonte's difficult season continued, and he was forced to use a former champion's provisional to get into the race. Robby Gordon was the fastest driver in second-round qualifying, with Ernie Irvan, Sterling Marlin and Robert Pressley, driving the Jasper Ford, using provisionals. Lance Hooper, Steve Park and Kevin Lepage, in the LJ Racing Chevrolet, all went home, and Randy MacDonald was forced to withdraw his Chevrolet after a practice crash.

During the first half of the race, the standing-room crowd at New Hampshire had plenty of reason to stomp and cheer in the aluminum grandstands. Craven, with the bit in his teeth in front of the New

(Left) Former New Hampshire winner Ricky Rudd climbs from his Tide Ford after backing it into the wall and bringing out the fourth caution of the race on lap 236. (Below left) Despite a string of bad luck that began after his Brickyard 400 victory six races ago, Rudd gives his enthusiastic fans a smile and a wave as he makes his way back to garage.

Hamilton coming home third ahead of Steve Grissom and Craven. Jarrett was sixth, while Jimmy Spencer fought to seventh place ahead of Dale Earnhardt, Martin and Stricklin.

Gordon claimed his 10th victory of the season, the 29th of his brief career, and became the first driver to put together double-digit victories in back-to-back seasons since Darrell Waltrip did it in his consecutive championship seasons of 1981-82.

CMT 300

Fin. Pos.	Start Pos.	Car #	Driver	Team
1	13	24	Jeff Gordon	DuPont Refinishes Chevrolet
2	40	28	Ernie Irvan	Texaco Havoline Ford
3	2	43	Bobby Hamilton	STP Pontiac
4	23	41	Steve Grissom	Kodiak Chevrolet
5	6	25	Ricky Craven	Budweiser Chevrolet
6	19	88	Dale Jarrett	Quality Care/Ford Credit Ford
7	16	23	Jimmy Spencer	Camel Cigarettes Ford
8	30	3	Dale Earnhardt	GM Goodwrench Service Plus Chevrolet
9	17	6	Mark Martin	Valvoline Ford
10	25	8	Hut Stricklin	Circuit City Ford
11	10	94	Bill Elliott	McDonald's Ford
12	11	44	Kyle Petty	Hot Wheels Pontiac
13	29	42	Joe Nemechek	BellSouth Chevrolet
14	39	99	Jeff Burton	Exide Batteries Ford
15	12	18	Bobby Labonte	Interstate Batteries Pontiac
16	14	7	Geoff Bodine	QVC Ford
17	5	98	John Andretti	RCA Ford
18	9	9	Lake Speed	Melling Engine Parts Ford
19	20	30	Johnny Benson	Pennzoil Pontiac
20	7	75	Rick Mast	Remington Arms Ford
21	33	2	Rusty Wallace	Miller Lite Ford
22	28	90	Dick Trickle	Heilig-Meyers/Simmons Ford
23	35	22	Ward Burton	MBNA America Pontiac
24	26	40	Robby Gordon	Coors Light Chevrolet
25	27	37	Jeremy Mayfield	Kmart/RC Cola Ford
26	24	36	Derrike Cope	Skittles Pontiac
27	34	81	Kenny Wallace	Square D Ford
28	38	97	Chad Little	John Deere Pontiac
29	32	71	Dave Marcis	Realtree Camouflage Chevrolet
30	21	16	Ted Musgrave	Family Channel/PRIMESTAR Ford
31	8	46	Wally Dallenbach	First Union Chevrolet
32	15	17	Darrell Waltrip	Parts America Chevrolet
33	3	11	Brett Bodine	Close Call Phone Card Ford
34	31	78	Gary Bradberry	Hanes Ford
35	4	31	Mike Skinner	Lowe's Chevrolet
36	22	21	Michael Waltrip	CITGO Ford
37	1	33	Ken Schrader	Skoal Bandit Chevrolet
38	36	29	Jeff Green	Cartoon Network Chevrolet
39	41	4	Sterling Marlin	Kodak Film Chevrolet
40	18	96	David Green	Caterpillar Chevrolet
41	43	5	Terry Labonte	Kellogg's Corn Flakes Chevrolet
42	37	10	Ricky Rudd	Tide Ford
43	42	77	Robert Pressley	Jasper Engines/Federal-Mogul Ford

England-based crowd, had the red-and-white Budweiser Chevrolet in the wind, and appeared to have only Hamilton and the STP Pontiac to worry about. The duo traded the lead back and forth, and led all but two of the race's first 148 laps. Behind them, with little notice, Gordon was driving his usual race.

The point-leader worked his way up through the field. He figured out what his DuPont Chevrolet needed in the second half of the race, relayed the information to crew chief Ray Evernham, and the Rainbow Warriors began plotting the changes needed to turn the Monte Carlo into a race winner. By half-distance, he was at the point, and, thanks to some outstanding work by his crew during his second pit stop of the afternoon, stretched his lead to more than five seconds.

From there on, Gordon did what he does best when his car is working — lead and run the field into the ground. He was at the point without interruption in the second half of the race, leading 137 laps, fighting off every challenge Irvan could throw at him. He took the checkered flag two car-lengths ahead of the Havoline Ford driver, with

NASCAR WINSTON CUP SERIES 1997

MBNA 400

(Dover Downs International Speedway • September 21, 1997)

At the beginning of the 11-race string that comprised this year's stretch run to the title, Jeff Gordon had walked into the Indianapolis Motor Speedway garage area with a 64-point lead over Mark Martin, and with 114 points in hand over defending NASCAR Winston Cup champion Terry Labonte.

At that point, it looked like anyone's championship, with Dale Jarrett 152 points behind in fourth place and both Jeff Burton and Dale Earnhardt lurking around the edges, waiting to put together the run that would pull them within striking distance for the treasured Cup.

(Right) The bubbly flies in Dover's victory lane at the hands of Mark Martin, who celebrates a long-overdue win. Mark had knocked on the door three times before with strong runs at the Monster Mile only to finish second, but had finally outsmarted it to claim his fourth win of the season.

(Left) Kyle Petty puts the wheels near the apron after passing Dale Earnhardt to take his second lead of the race, just two laps before the halfway mark. Earnhardt, who started 33rd, had taken the lead for the first time just one lap prior.

NASCAR Winston Cup SERIES
Valvoline
BOSCH Spark Plugs
ROUSH RACING

The war had raged, and the rubber band had been pulled and released back and forth during the weeks between the Brickyard 400 and the opening of practice for the MBNA 400 at Denis McGlynn's "Monster Mile." Gordon had lost the point lead and then regained it during the roller coaster ride, and Martin had moved to the point for a single race before falling backward in the last three races. Labonte's hopes had been the biggest casualty. The accident at New Hampshire, when he tangled with Sterling Marlin and finished 41st, had all but ended his hopes for a second straight title.

With Labonte now trailing by 455, with Jeff Burton still struggling with the inner ear problem that had forced him to turn the wheel over to Todd Bodine at New Hampshire, and with Dale Earnhardt still in search of his first victory of the season, the stretch run had seen the battle for the championship culled to just Gordon, Martin and Jarrett.

Now Gordon arrived at Dover with a 139-point lead over Martin, and with Jarrett 188 in arrears. In reality, unless some bizarre circumstances intervened, the battle for this year's crown would be staged between the three — and Gordon clearly had the upper hand.

For Martin and Jarrett, the season was winding down. Wins and top-five finishes wouldn't get the job done for either. They needed to race well every single event for the remainder of the year and to hope that Gordon had some poor racing luck. There were few tomorrows left on the schedule.

Burton had stopped at Duke University's medical center between the New Hampshire race and the opening of Dover practice, hoping to receive a better picture of what was going on inside his ear. Tests determined he had a virus that attacked the message center between the inner ear and the brain, with the nerves that affect the message of balance inflamed between the two. There was no real treatment, other than waiting for things to return to normal. Burton arrived at Dover slightly better, but had Todd Bodine standing by for assistance if needed for the second week.

Morgan Shepherd, who had left Richard Jackson's team in the spring to replace Bobby Hillin in the Jasper car, had returned to the Jackson team at Dover. The experiment hadn't worked from either side, and while Morgan was away, R&L Carriers had stepped up to sponsor the Pontiac team. Shepherd was delighted to get back behind the wheel of the green-and-yellow car, and Jackson's team was just as pleased to have him back.

Of all the places to try to cut into Gordon's point lead, Dover would have been the last choice of either Martin or Jarrett. The Dover track is the "home" for sponsor DuPont, located just north of Delaware's capital city, and the Hendrick Motorsports team gets jacked

The pack fans out through the turns, using what has become a relatively wide groove on Dover's concrete surface since the track switched from asphalt between the 1994 and 1995 seasons.

even higher than usual when they have the chance to perform in front of the corporate executives who sign the sponsorship checks. Gordon had won three of the last four events at the one-mile concrete oval, and with the championship lead in hand, everyone knew the best mount in the stable would be under Jeff for the MBNA 400.

Still, Martin and Jarrett are racers, and knew that if they could find a way to beat Gordon in front of his corporate guests, it would underscore the fact that neither was giving up in the battle for the championship. For both Ford drivers, there was a slightly different glint in their eyes as qualifying for the event began. There would be no holding back. In Gordon's camp, the same steely determination was evident.

(Right) Michael Waltrip brought out the only caution of the 400-lap race on lap 89 when he slapped the first turn wall with his CITGO Ford. After coming to a stop, Michael signals for assistance (above) from the safety crew, who responds by helping him climb out of the car (below) on Dover's 24-degree banks. *(Below)* Taking care to get every possible drop of fuel into the Goodwrench Chevrolet, the Childress Racing crew services their driver, Dale Earnhardt, during a green-flag pit stop. Earnhardt, who would run with the leaders for most of the day, used fuel strategy to help him finish second, tying his best finish of the season.

When the first round of qualifying was completed, the three were the fastest of the 43 cars on hand for the race. Gordon had been the first of the three to make his run, and he put strong numbers on the board with a lap in excess of 151.7 miles per hour. He was forced to wait for almost the entire session before he found out what Martin had

Dick Trickle had yet another outstanding run to put Junie Donlavey's Ford on the outside of the second row, with Bobby Labonte and John Andretti posting the fifth- and sixth-fastest laps, ahead of Joe Nemechek and Hut Stricklin. Rick Mast and Ricky Craven were ninth and 10th, in front of David Green and Chad Little. Gary Bradberry's

(Above) Kyle Petty (44) slips past Mark Martin (6) to take the lead on lap 162, after working through the field from his 23rd starting position. Once he claimed the point, Petty was wicked fast, leading 191 of the remaining 239 laps. (Right) The Valvoline crew follows a carefully planned and perfectly executed pit strategy to allow Mark Martin to complete the 400 laps on just three pit stops, with just enough fuel left over to make it to victory lane.

up the sleeve of his Valvoline uniform. And when Mark played his cards, Jeff was relegated to the outside of the front row. Martin's lap was in excess of 152 miles per hour, while Jarrett took the inside of the second row. Fans wouldn't have to look very far to find the championship challengers!

Joe Nemechek gets a helpful push to pit road from SABCO teammate Robby Gordon, after the fuel cell in the BellSouth Chevrolet ran dry. Gordon dropped Nemechek off at the end of pit road, and by the time Joe had coasted to his pit, he had fallen several laps off the pace.

Hanes Ford was the fastest second-round qualifier. Todd Bodine used a provisional to get Burton's Exide Ford into the field, as did Ted Musgrave, Darrell Waltrip and Jeff Green. The only driver who failed to make the field was Steve Park in Dale Earnhardt's Burger King Chevrolet.

Sunday morning, in a brief conversation between Martin and team owner Jack Roush, the MBNA 400 was won. It would take hours after the quiet discussion for the checkered flag to fall, but the decision that turned the race into Martin's fourth victory of the season had been made. Roush asked Martin if a set of tires would last an entire fuel stop on the concrete surface. Mark said they would, so Jack went about tuning the engine in the Valvoline Thunderbird for mileage, rather than power. Had the tires not been able to withstand a full fuel run, the need would have been for power. Mark's quiet confidence made the difference.

And then the race played into Martin's hands. The first 88 laps were under green, and just after teams began pitting for fuel and tires, Michael Waltrip hammered the wall, bringing out what would be the only caution of the race.

Following that pit stop, the remainder of the event ran under green-flag conditions. Martin played his strategic game on the track, not worrying about the tremendous showing being put on by Kyle Petty at the front of the field. Kyle rocketed away from the pack, at one time building a lead in excess of 15 seconds. However, Martin's team knew that Kyle could only run about 90 laps on a full fuel stop, while Martin could stretch his fuel for 14 laps more. As the race rolled on, Mark stayed with his plan, eventually needing one less stop than Kyle did to make the end of the race. Petty was forced to dash to pit road for fuel with just 20 laps left to go — and it cost him the three-quarters of a lap he had built over the final half of the race. Mark merely motored on, positioning himself well clear (10 seconds) of Earnhardt, the only other driver who could match the Valvoline Ford for mileage.

The final laps were not without worry for Martin, despite his big lead over Earnhardt. At Richmond, a power steering belt had come off the car, knocking the oil pump belt off, and at Dover, Mark said the car and engine felt like the same thing was about to happen. It didn't, but the alternator light came on with less than two miles to go. It meant the alternator had failed, and Martin held his breath, hoping nothing would end his bid for his first career Dover victory.

Behind Earnhardt, Petty recovered to finish third, ahead of Bobby Labonte. Jarrett was fifth, ahead of spring Dover winner Ricky Rudd, while Gordon fought his car throughout the day and finished seventh, two laps behind. Bill Elliott, Ernie Irvan and Rick Mast claimed the final positions in the top 10, with relief driver Todd Bodine bringing Jeff Burton's Ford in at 11th place.

MBNA 400

Fin. Pos.	Start Pos.	Car #	Driver	Team
1	1	6	Mark Martin	Valvoline Ford
2	33	3	Dale Earnhardt	GM Goodwrench Service Plus Chevrolet
3	23	44	Kyle Petty	Hot Wheels Pontiac
4	5	18	Bobby Labonte	Interstate Batteries Pontiac
5	3	88	Dale Jarrett	Quality Care/Ford Credit Ford
6	16	10	Ricky Rudd	Tide Ford
7	2	24	Jeff Gordon	DuPont Refinishes Chevrolet
8	13	94	Bill Elliott	McDonald's Ford
9	31	28	Ernie Irvan	Texaco Havoline Ford
10	9	75	Rick Mast	Remington Arms Ford
11	39	99	Jeff Burton	Exide Batteries Ford
12	14	33	Ken Schrader	Skoal Bandit Chevrolet
13	34	43	Bobby Hamilton	STP Pontiac
14	25	7	Geoff Bodine	QVC Ford
15	6	98	John Andretti	RCA Ford
16	22	2	Rusty Wallace	Miller Lite Ford
17	8	8	Hut Stricklin	Circuit City Ford
18	4	90	Dick Trickle	Heilig-Meyers/Simmons Ford
19	30	31	Mike Skinner	Lowe's Chevrolet
20	7	42	Joe Nemechek	BellSouth Chevrolet
21	28	41	Steve Grissom	Kodiak Chevrolet
22	27	22	Ward Burton	MBNA America Pontiac
23	24	37	Jeremy Mayfield	Kmart/RC Cola Ford
24	40	16	Ted Musgrave	Family Channel/PRIMESTAR Ford
25	11	96	David Green	Caterpillar Chevrolet
26	17	11	Brett Bodine	Bodine Enterprises Ford
27	21	4	Sterling Marlin	Kodak Film Chevrolet
28	29	30	Johnny Benson	Pennzoil Pontiac
29	12	97	Chad Little	John Deere Pontiac
30	39	36	Derrike Cope	Skittles Pontiac
31	15	1	Morgan Shepherd	R&L Carriers Pontiac
32	41	17	Darrell Waltrip	Parts America Chevrolet
33	35	40	Robby Gordon	Coors Light Chevrolet
34	37	71	Dave Marcis	Realtree Camouflage Chevrolet
35	26	78	Gary Bradberry	Hanes Ford
36	18	23	Jimmy Spencer	Camel Cigarettes Ford
37	36	5	Terry Labonte	Kellogg's Corn Flakes Chevrolet
38	19	81	Kenny Wallace	Square D Ford
39	32	77	Robert Pressley	Jasper Engines/Federal-Mogul Ford
40	42	29	Jeff Green	Cartoon Network Chevrolet
41	10	25	Ricky Craven	Budweiser Chevrolet
42	20	21	Michael Waltrip	CITGO Ford

NASCAR WINSTON CUP SERIES 1997

Hanes 500

(Martinsville Speedway • September 29, 1997)

If there had been any question of whether or not the teams involved in the point battle had been prepared for the grueling stretch toward the NASCAR Winston Cup, a quick look at the results of the first eight events in the 11-race string told the story.

For the DuPont, Valvoline and Quality Care teams, the finishes were almost identical in those eight races. Perhaps that explained the tinge of frustration that hung around the Mark Martin and Dale Jarrett camps when the teams arrived at Martinsville for the 27th race of the season.

(Right) Jeff Gordon lays a bumper on Joe Nemechek, politely suggesting that Joe might move over to let him by – a common occurrence within the tight confines of Martinsville's half-mile oval.

(Left) Brothers Ward and Jeff Burton share a friendly moment while waiting to start the Hanes 500. The boys from nearby South Boston, Va., made their home state proud this day, with Ward leading the field off the pole, and with Jeff taking the victory, his third of the year.

184

Western Auto
MOOG
CHASSIS PARTS
76
OFFICIAL FUEL
NASCAR
plasti-kote
SPRAY PAINT
SIMPSON
COMPETITION CAMS
MAC TOOLS
Edelbrock

During practice earlier in the weekend, the Quality Care Ford erupts in flames while on the track, forcing Dale Jarrett to break out the backup car for the race.

Martin's gutsy Dover victory had been his second in the eight races. The Jack Roush team had stayed with its pre-race strategy, even though it appeared for the longest time that Mark would end up a distant second to Kyle Petty. The team had stumbled just once, at Richmond, when the power steering and oil pump belts came off the motor, forcing Mark to a 25th-place finish. Other than that single race, he had been in the top six in all the other races, except for an eighth and a ninth. His average finish for the eight races was 7.1, and there was little doubt his team had been prepared for the battle.

From Jarrett's standpoint, the eight races had been just as impressive. Like Martin, he had won twice, at Richmond and at Bristol, and had just a single event that had given him and the team trouble — the fried transmission in the late going at The Glen that had dropped him to a 32nd-place finish in the final rundown. With the exception of that race, he had been out of the top five just a single time — a sixth place at New Hampshire. At any other time, a run through eight races with the record he had posted would have moved him into a furious battle for the championship. His average finish was just a tick better than Mark's, at 7.0.

The frustration for Martin and Jarrett came from the string of results posted by Gordon in the heat of the battle.

(Top) Kenny Irwin (27) holds the inside line despite pressure from Hut Stricklin (8) and Ricky Rudd, while Kenny Wallace (81) tries the high line with Joe Nemechek on his tail. Irwin, in his second career NASCAR Winston Cup start, qualified an impressive third, but eventually retired from the event with a broken fuel pump. (Above) The Morgan-McClure crew gangs up on the Kodak Chevrolet to repair the damage sustained in a multi-car accident that brought out the sixth caution flag on lap 237. Despite their best efforts, the Chevrolet was not able to continue, dropping driver Sterling Marlin to 39th place in the final rundown. (Left) Under clear blue skies, the fans fill the stands on Monday, to watch Ward Burton and Mark Martin lead the field to the green flag for the rain-delayed Hanes 500.

Gordon's run had been brilliant, and every time Martin or Jarrett made a move at him, he met it nose-to-nose with unmatched pit strategy and the grit in the seat of his pants that makes the difference between winners and champions.

Like Martin and Jarrett, Gordon had struggled once in the eight races — the collision at Bristol that put the DuPont Chevrolet behind the wall for what seemed an interminable amount of time and left him 35th in the rundown. But it was the other seven races that made the difference in the point standings.

Gordon had won three events — The Glen, New Hampshire, and of course, the third consecutive Mountain Dew Southern 500 triumph

(Above) "Hey Rick, got any of that spicy mustard stuff?" *(Right)* Rusty Wallace gets the jump off pit road during one of the race's 11 caution periods to maintain his lead. Wallace was having his way with the rest of the field, leading 226 of the final 300 laps, before the black flag dropped him out of contention.

alongside Ted Musgrave's effort in the Liberty shops. The Stavolas made it clear they would switch from Ford to Chevrolet for the coming season, putting truth to the rumor that had floated for several weeks. However, the biggest surprise came in the announcement that the Stavolas would use Pro Motor for their engines. Peter Guild's company has been a contract supplier of Ford motors for a variety of teams, and now he would be building both Ford and Chevrolet powerplants. It was the first such undertaking veteran NASCAR garage denizens could recall.

that netted him the Winston Million. In the remainder, he had finished out of the top four just once, the seventh place at Dover. His average finish in the eight races explained why he was still at the top of the point heap. At 6.75, it was just slightly better than Martin's and Jarrett's. And at this stage of the season, just slightly better was plenty good enough.

Martin's Dover win had trimmed the margin to 105, while Jarrett moved to 188 behind in the three-way struggle for the title. Any hopes Terry Labonte had were drowned with a 37th-place finish. Jeff Burton, with the help of Todd Bodine for the past two races, was solidly in fourth place in points, a long way behind Jarrett, but now well clear of Labonte. With Burton's inner ear difficulty nearly cleared up, his good news was that he would be back in the car for the entire race at Martinsville.

In two surprise announcements, Jack Roush and the Stavola Brothers clarified plans for their 1998 programs. Roush was preparing to move Martin's team to the Mooresville, N.C., location that housed Burton's effort. The team's move from Liberty, N.C., where it had been since the inception of Roush's efforts in NASCAR Winston Cup, meant that the new "26" team for Johnny Benson would be built

Crew chief Buddy Parrot (left) and car owner Jack Roush (right) display their new shirts, proclaiming Ford as the 1997 manufacturer's champion. Jeff Burton's big smile shows his satisfaction in being able to seal the title for his marque.

It was clear throughout practice that Martin was aiming at a second straight victory in his quest to overtake point-leader Gordon. And, in qualifying, he ripped to a lap good enough to put the Valvoline Thunderbird on the pole — until Ward Burton rolled out in the MBNA Pontiac. Ward, who failed to qualify for this event last year, put together a sparkling lap that resulted in his first Busch Pole Award of the season. He became the 17th different pole winner of 1997, tying the modern-day record.

Behind Burton and Martin, Kenny Irwin made his extensive Martinsville testing pay off with the third-fastest lap, and Hut Stricklin continued to make strong progress with the fourth fastest. Ricky Rudd and Kenny Wallace claimed the third row, while Rusty Wallace and Joe Nemechek won the seventh and eighth spots. Ken Schrader and Jeff Burton beat Jeff Gordon and Jimmy Spencer for the fifth-row starting positions. Johnny Benson was the fastest second-round qualifier, and Jeremy Mayfield, Steve Grissom, Brett Bodine and Derrike Cope used provisionals to make the field. Those failing to qualify were Gary Bradberry, in his team's sponsor's race, Morgan Shepherd and Dave Marcis.

Daylong rain on Sunday made the race impossible to run as scheduled, so the teams assembled on Monday to contest the Hanes 500. Unlike many Martinsville races of the past, when a competitor establishes his dominance early and then runs to the flag, this 500-lapper on Clay Earles' superb little half-mile took more than half the race to begin to take shape. Rusty Wallace had charged to the front of the field, and, eventually, took the point on lap 210. For the remainder of the event, Wallace and Jeff Burton had the dominant cars, with Rusty seemingly having the edge when it counted. His brilliant run in the lead came to naught, however, when he was black-flagged and penalized with a stop-and-go on pit road after jumping the restart with 20 laps to go. He had been admonished twice before for his early starts ahead of the designated spot on the track, and the third time cost him the race. He made his stop, and Burton fought his way past Bobby Hamilton to claim the lead with 11 laps remaining, notching his third victory of the season. Dale Earnhardt found a way past Hamilton in the closing laps to score his second consecutive runner-up finish.

Hamilton finished ahead of Gordon, with Bill Elliott and Kenny Wallace fifth and sixth, ahead of Ward Burton, Ricky Craven and Ken Schrader. Ernie Irvan was 10th. Martin, who finished 11th, was involved in an accident on the track. He also had to come back to pit road after one of his crew members left a weight-jacking wrench in the car, costing Mark precious track position. After a fire erupted in his primary car during practice, Jarrett fought an ill-handling backup car throughout the day and had to take the 12th place. Both Martin and Jarrett lost points to Gordon.

Hanes 500

Fin. Pos.	Start Pos.	Car #	Driver	Team
1	10	99	Jeff Burton	Exide Batteries Ford
2	13	3	Dale Earnhardt	GM Goodwrench Service Plus Chevrolet
3	22	43	Bobby Hamilton	STP Pontiac
4	11	24	Jeff Gordon	DuPont Refinishes Chevrolet
5	16	94	Bill Elliott	McDonald's Ford
6	6	81	Kenny Wallace	Square D Ford
7	1	22	Ward Burton	MBNA America Pontiac
8	36	25	Ricky Craven	Budweiser Chevrolet
9	9	33	Ken Schrader	Skoal Bandit Chevrolet
10	30	28	Ernie Irvan	Texaco Havoline Ford
11	2	6	Mark Martin	Valvoline Ford
12	21	88	Dale Jarrett	Quality Care/Ford Credit Ford
13	5	10	Ricky Rudd	Tide Ford
14	24	9	Lake Speed	Melling Engine Parts Ford
15	7	2	Rusty Wallace	Miller Lite Ford
16	4	8	Hut Stricklin	Circuit City Ford
17	41	11	Brett Bodine	BDR Motorsports Ford
18	39	37	Jeremy Mayfield	Kmart/RC Cola Ford
19	26	30	Johnny Benson	Pennzoil Pontiac
20	32	96	David Green	Caterpillar Chevrolet
21	23	16	Ted Musgrave	Family Channel/PRIMESTAR Ford
22	25	5	Terry Labonte	Kellogg's Corn Flakes Chevrolet
23	38	75	Rick Mast	Remington Arms Ford
24	18	17	Darrell Waltrip	Parts America Chevrolet
25	8	42	Joe Nemechek	BellSouth Chevrolet
26	29	44	Kyle Petty	Hot Wheels Pontiac
27	20	18	Bobby Labonte	Interstate Batteries Pontiac
28	37	7	Geoff Bodine	QVC Ford
29	15	98	John Andretti	RCA Ford
30	33	29	Jeff Green	Cartoon Network Chevrolet
31	19	31	Mike Skinner	Lowe's Chevrolet
32	27	21	Michael Waltrip	CITGO Ford
33	12	23	Jimmy Spencer	Camel Cigarettes Ford
34	35	46	Wally Dallenbach	First Union Chevrolet
35	34	97	Chad Little	John Deere Pontiac
36	42	36	Derrike Cope	Skittles Pontiac
37	3	27	Kenny Irwin	Tonka/Winner's Circle Ford
38	17	77	Robert Pressley	Jasper Engines/Federal-Mogul Ford
39	14	4	Sterling Marlin	Kodak Film Chevrolet
40	40	41	Steve Grissom	Kodiak Chevrolet
41	28	40	Steve Park	Coors Light Chevrolet
42	31	90	Dick Trickle	Heilig-Meyers/Simmons Ford

NASCAR WINSTON CUP SERIES 1997

UAW-GM Quality 500

(Charlotte Motor Speedway • October 5, 1997)

The Martinsville victory, coming at the track just 60 miles from where he had grown up in South Boston, brought an extra helping of pride for Jeff Burton, fulfilling a dream he had for several years.

He clearly remembered his exit out of the fall race at Martinsville in 1994 and then watching Rusty Wallace roll to victory to clinch the NASCAR Manufacturer's Championship for Ford. He thought then, "How cool it would be to do that same thing," and with his Monday victory on the half-mile, he had done just that. His win locked up the 1997 manufacturer's title for the Blue Oval brass, and moved Ford onto the stage at the New York banquet to accept the trophy in front of a national television audience. It was Ford's third NASCAR Manufacturer's title in six years.

(Right) Geoff Bodine sets sail in the opening laps of the UAW-GM Quality 500 at Charlotte after becoming the surprise pole-winner during the Wednesday night qualifying session. Bodine's day reached the extremes when a multi-car accident sent him to the garage in last place.

(Left) It's high fives all around for Dale Jarrett and his Quality Care team in Charlotte's winner's circle after they had notched their sixth victory of the season.

190

Quality Care
QVC
7
Ford
THUNDERBIRD
Western Auto
MOOG
STP
Motorcraft
BATTERIES
plasti-kote
76
Edelbrock
COMP CAMS
JE
CRAFTSMAN

A crowd of more than 150,000 begins to fill the grandstands at Charlotte Motor Speedway with the starting field already lined up on pit road. Terry Labonte's specially painted Kellogg's Chevrolet sits last on the grid, with Terry using a former champion's provisional to make the race.

The October race weekend at Charlotte, which is always a hotbed of activity, brought the much-anticipated announcement that Sterling Marlin would drive the Coors SABCO Chevrolet next season. This would reunite Marlin with crew chief Tony Glover, who had moved to SABCO at the end of last year. SABCO owner Felix Sabates said he and driver Robby Gordon had parted company, and that the Coors car would be driven by Elliott Sadler at Charlotte. Other drivers would compete in the Chevrolets for the remainder of the season before Marlin moved into the team following Atlanta.

Burton's third victory of the season was aided by Wallace's late-race stop-and-go penalty for jumping the restart, and, following the race, Rusty had a few things to say about his opinion of the call. It cost him a $5,000 fine — which he paid at Charlotte by presenting NASCAR President Bill France with $5,000 worth of pennies.

Michael Waltrip and wife Buffy had welcomed their first child,

A very dejected Parts America crew loads Darrell Waltrip's Monte Carlo onto the transporter before pulling out of the garage area and making the short trip back to the shop. When Labonte elected to use the former champion's provisional, Waltrip was left out in the cold.

192

(Above) Outside pole-sitter Bobby Labonte sizes up Geoff Bodine just before bolting past the black Ford to lead lap five. Bobby then dropped the hammer and proceeded to trash the field, lapping all but six cars during the first 100 laps of the race. *(Left)* Todd Bodine debuts the Tabasco-sponsored Pontiac that he will drive in the 1998 NASCAR Winston Cup season.

daughter Margaret Carol to the world Sept. 29, and Michael had more reasons to smile at Charlotte. The Wood Brothers had painted the CITGO Ford in the famed pearl and candy-apple red reminiscent of the team's glory days of the '70s, and Michael was itching to take the new paint scheme to victory. Michael's wasn't the only new paint job at Charlotte — with Terry Labonte's car sporting Kellogg's Spooky Fruit Loops and the Frankenstein Monster in a special promotion.

Cale Yarborough revealed that sponsor RCA had dropped the bomb that it would not return as the "98" car's sponsor for the coming season. Rumors immediately began circulating that John Andretti could find himself the driver of Richard Petty's "43" next year, and that crew chief Tony Furr was being wooed by the Hendrick organization. Cale appeared confident that he would be able to find sponsorship for the team and keep it all together. While Cale was talking about his situation, Winston and Travis Carter's team were unveiling Jimmy Spencer's new colors for the coming season. The Camel brand, sponsor of the team since its inception in 1994, would be replaced by the familiar red and white of Winston. It would mark the first time since R.J. Reynolds became involved in NASCAR Winston Cup racing in 1971 that a team would be sponsored by the Winston brand.

As teams lined up to qualify, Ford-driving Dale Jarrett and Mark Martin were focused on their tasks. The problems the two had suffered at Martinsville had put them in a very difficult position with just five

behind Burton. Dale found himself 222 behind the Exide Ford driver, but hoped to continue his pace and displace Jeff for fourth place before the season was completed.

With qualifying held in the cool of the evening — and with the second round in the heat of the day — it was obvious to every team

(Left) Bobby Labonte grips the wheel and bears down on his Interstate Batteries Pontiac, with Dale Jarrett sneaking up behind him, ready to mount his challenge for the lead. Labonte had spent some 100 laps scratching and clawing his way back to the point after spinning in oil on lap 104. (Below) In the middle portion of the race, Dale Jarrett and Dale Earnhardt stage a stirring, side-by-side battle for the lead. Earnhardt had worked his way to the point over the first half of the event, and fought valiantly for his first win of the season before finally fading to a third-place finish.

races left in the season. Martin had fallen farther back in his battle for the title, dropping to 135 points behind leader Jeff Gordon. The margin could be erased, Mark knew, with just a single poor finish by Gordon and a strong one by the Valvoline Ford, but it would have to happen soon. The season was running out of opportunities for the Thunderbird driver to catch the DuPont Chevrolet. For Jarrett, the challenge was even greater. He was now 222 behind, and it was beginning to look as though he would be forced to wait until 1998 for another chance to win his initial NASCAR Winston Cup title.

Dale Earnhardt's fighting second places at Dover and Martinsville, coupled with three poor finishes by Terry Labonte, had moved the Goodwrench Chevrolet driver back into fifth place in the standings,

that the best opportunity for a fast lap was in the first round of qualifying. For the longest time, it appeared that Bobby Labonte would claim the pole — but then Geoff Bodine rolled out and ripped his way to the fastest lap of the first session. This served as vindication for him after being forced to watch the Coca-Cola 600 in May when a practice accident kept him from competing. It also turned out to be a great gift from Bodine and his crew to new owners Jim Mattei and John Porter, whose investment had salvaged the team in mid-season.

Martin, fastest in practice, held down the inside of the second row, with Jeff Gordon right alongside and Jarrett right behind him. The Chevrolet teams had received an additional 1/4 inch rear spoiler beginning with the Charlotte race, but the expected additional down-

Among the announcements made during race week at Charlotte was this rousing introduction of the Team Winston Taurus, to be fielded by car owner Travis Carter and driven by Jimmy Spencer in 1998.

force wasn't of great help to the teams in qualifying. Dick Trickle continued his outstanding recent performances, qualifying sixth fastest, while Ward Burton and Jeff Purvis made up the fourth row, ahead of Spencer and Morgan Shepherd.

The second round of qualifying brought some major surprises. Terry Labonte was forced to use a provisional to make the field, and he chose to use a former champion's. That left Darrell Waltrip out of the race — the first time Darrell had failed to qualify for an event since he made his NASCAR Winston Cup debut, and ended his streak of Charlotte starts at 50. Kenny Wallace was the fastest second-round qualifier, with Jeremy Mayfield, Kyle Petty, Bobby Hamilton and Ricky Craven forced to use provisionals. In addition to Waltrip, Rick Mast, Steve Park, Dave Marcis, Sadler and Mike Skinner failed to make the field. Also failing was Greg Sacks, who was driving Bud Moore's Daytona USA-sponsored Ford in its second attempt to make a field this year.

When the green flag dropped on the UAW-GM Quality 500, Bobby Labonte immediately threatened to make it a runaway victory. He streaked to the point, and led at will — but his hopes went away when he slipped in some oil on the track and nearly wrecked. Ultimately, he suffered a cracked cylinder head and didn't have the power at the end to challenge for victory. That left Jarrett and Martin to contend for the win, and, although Jarrett rolled to his sixth victory of the season, it took a couple of incidents to give him the impetus he needed. First, a spring rubber fell out of the car during a tire change, and improved the handling of the Quality Care Ford in the middle of the race. Then, in the final pit stop of the afternoon, the Todd Parrott-led crew turned him off pit road first, giving him the track position he needed to hold off a determined late-race bid by Labonte.

Dale Earnhardt continued his run back to the front, finishing third ahead of Martin, but Gordon was fifth and kept his grip on the point standings. Jeff Burton was sixth, Bill Elliott seventh, and Ward Burton finished eighth, ahead of Kyle Petty and Johnny Benson.

UAW-GM Quality 500

Fin. Pos.	Start Pos.	Car #	Driver	Team
1	5	88	Dale Jarrett	Quality Care/Ford Credit Ford
2	2	18	Bobby Labonte	Interstate Batteries Pontiac
3	19	3	Dale Earnhardt	GM Goodwrench Service Plus Chevrolet
4	3	6	Mark Martin	Valvoline Ford
5	4	24	Jeff Gordon	DuPont Refinishes Chevrolet
6	29	99	Jeff Burton	Exide Batteries Ford
7	33	94	Bill Elliott	McDonald's Ford
8	7	22	Ward Burton	MBNA America Pontiac
9	40	44	Kyle Petty	Hot Wheels Pontiac
10	15	30	Johnny Benson	Pennzoil Pontiac
11	43	5	Terry Labonte	Kellogg's Froot Loops Chevrolet
12	25	2	Rusty Wallace	Miller Lite Ford
13	17	41	Steve Grissom	Kodiak Chevrolet
14	6	90	Dick Trickle	Heilig-Meyers/Simmons Ford
15	11	33	Ken Schrader	Skoal Bandit Chevrolet
16	24	42	Joe Nemechek	BellSouth Chevrolet
17	14	16	Ted Musgrave	Family Channel/PRIMESTAR Ford
18	35	28	Ernie Irvan	Texaco Havoline Ford
19	34	27	Rick Wilson	David Blair Motorsports Ford
20	21	4	Sterling Marlin	Kodak Film Chevrolet
21	41	43	Bobby Hamilton	STP Pontiac
22	10	1	Morgan Shepherd	R&L Carriers Pontiac
23	31	97	Chad Little	John Deere Pontiac
24	30	21	Michael Waltrip	CITGO Ford
25	42	25	Ricky Craven	Budweiser Chevrolet
26	36	35	Todd Bodine	Tabasco Pontiac
27	39	37	Jeremy Mayfield	Kmart/RC Cola Ford
28	26	81	Kenny Wallace	Square D Ford
29	20	29	Jeff Green	Cartoon Network Chevrolet
30	18	11	Brett Bodine	Scandia/Bodine Ford
31	27	96	David Green	Caterpillar Chevrolet
32	23	98	John Andretti	RCA Ford
33	13	36	Derrike Cope	Skittles Pontiac
34	38	78	Gary Bradberry	Hanes Ford
35	37	8	Hut Stricklin	Circuit City Ford
36	28	77	Robert Pressley	Jasper Engines/Federal-Mogul Ford
37	16	46	Wally Dallenbach	First Union Chevrolet
38	32	9	Lake Speed	Melling Engine Parts Ford
39	8	12	Jeff Purvis	Opryland USA Chevrolet
40	12	91	Kevin Lepage	Pionite Chevrolet
41	22	10	Ricky Rudd	Tide Ford
42	9	23	Jimmy Spencer	Camel Cigarettes Ford
43	1	7	Geoff Bodine	QVC Ford

NASCAR WINSTON CUP SERIES 1997

DieHard 500

(Talladega Superspeedway • October 12, 1997)

There was not a single team in the garage area at Talladega Superspeedway that would not be delighted when the DieHard 500 weekend was completed. It was the end of the long 11-race, 11-week stretch run that had begun with the Brickyard 400, and, for the first time since early August, crew members would have a weekend off to spend with their families to rest and recoup.

For three teams, however, the Talladega weekend signaled the beginning of a new stretch — the four remaining events that would determine who sat at the head table at the Waldorf-Astoria in New York in December, to be honored as the NASCAR Winston Cup champion. Dale Jarrett's Charlotte victory had pulled him to within 197 points of leader Jeff Gordon, and Mark Martin came to Talladega 125 points behind. Both Ford drivers knew the sand in the hourglass was beginning to run out, and each needed to have solid runs at the mammoth superspeedway — and hope that Gordon had a problem.

In the days prior to the DieHard 500, which had moved from its usual late-July date to this one in October, series sponsor Winston made an announcement that could have great

(Right) Terry Labonte flashes a smile of satisfaction – and relief – after the defending NASCAR Winston Cup champion scored his first victory of the season.

(Below) Former NASCAR Winston Cup Champion Bobby Allison poses next to the Robert Yates Thunderbird, which is painted in the colors of 10 seasons ago when his son, Davey, drove to his first career victory and the first for the Yates-owned team. Fittingly, Ernie Ivan qualified the Texaco Ford on the pole at Allison's home track.

Kellogg's
FROSTED FLAKES
HAAS CNC
-800-MARROW-2
GMAC
Kellogg's Racing
GMAC
Hendrick Motorsports
Kellogg's
Starburst
ACDelco
Kellogg's
DieHard
WINNER
DieHard 500
TALLADEGA SUPERSPEEDWAY

win in the Winston 500, which would change dates with the DieHard 500 at Talladega in 1998. Taken in sum, an additional $5 million was up for grabs in the designated five races in 1998. Needless to say, the program was greeted with an enormous amount of enthusiasm by competitors.

McDonald's had made Bill Elliott's 42nd birthday one that The Redhead would remember by signing a multi-year extension of its sponsorship for his "94" team, and Melling Racing was delighted to have Advantage Camouflage on its cars for the remainder of the season. On a less happy side, Brett Bodine and Andy Evans, his partner in the "11" team, dropped sponsor Close Call from their Fords, choosing to run with bare quarter panels until a new sponsor could be found.

(Above) Dale Jarrett listens to the voice of experience — his dad, former two-time NASCAR Champion Ned Jarrett. In spite of six victories and three Busch Poles already this season, Dale sat third in the points, and was hoping to close the gap at Talladega. (Right) Pole-winner Ernie Irvan takes his turn at the point, leading the pack through the tri-oval. Irvan would stay among the leaders throughout the event and eventually finish fifth to become the last qualifier for the Winston No Bull 5, at the 1998 Daytona 500.

impact on the sport during the 1998 season. The Winston Million program would be put on hiatus for a year, and in its place, as a way of helping NASCAR celebrate its 50th anniversary season, Winston would initiate the Winston No Bull 5, a promotion tied to its current advertising theme.

The first five finishers in the DieHard 500 on Sunday would be eligible to win $1 million if one of those five were to win the 1998 Daytona 500. Further, the top-five finishers in the Daytona 500 would then be eligible for another $1 million if one of them could win the Coca-Cola 600. The top five in that race could win another $1 million at Indianapolis, and the top five at The Brickyard would be eligible to win another $1 million in the Mountain Dew Southern 500. Finally, the top-five drivers at Darlington would be eligible for yet another $1 million if one of them could take the

198

Inches apart at 190 miles per hour, Terry Labonte (5), John Andretti (98), Michael Waltrip (21) and Jeff Gordon (24) use up the width of Talladega's frontstretch with Rusty Wallace (2) and Ricky Craven (25) poised to choose their drafting partners when the four-way battle sorts out.

On the crew chief front, Terry Shirley signed on with Wally Dallenbach's First Union Chevrolet, with Brad Noffsinger deciding to return to his driving career, and the Kellogg's team was under the direction of Randy Dorton for the second week, after Gary DeHart resigned his position as Terry Labonte's crew chief prior to the Charlotte race.

International Speedway Corporation officials said they had come to an agreement with Kansas City to build a 75,000-seat, 1.5-mile superspeedway, with ISC owning 72 percent of the track, the state of Kansas owning 22 percent and the remaining six percent being owned by the city of Kansas City and the county. It was the first partnership of this type in stock car racing history.

Terry Labonte (5) uses the inside to slip past Ken Schrader (33) to take the point. Labonte led the most laps during the race, but would need help from his brother, Bobby, to take the lead for good with just two laps remaining in the race.

At the May Charlotte race, Robert Yates Racing had fielded its Texaco Havoline Ford in the same paint scheme used by Davey Allison a decade ago — a color combination that has been ingrained into the hearts of race fans. The same combination of white, black, gold and red graced the "28" car at Talladega, the sight of Allison's first win, and the first victory for Yates Racing after Robert bought the team from Harry Ranier a decade ago. As in Charlotte, the paint and decals on the car brought back fond memories for Yates, who announced he would donate all souvenir and apparel royalties based on the appearance of the car to the children of Davey and Clifford Allison.

It seemed only proper, then, at the site of some of Davey's greatest triumphs, that the Havoline Ford would end up on the pole for the running of the DieHard 500. Ernie Irvan, making his final appearance in the car at a restrictor-plate race, found something in his qualifying run that was just enough to nip John Andretti for the Busch Pole Award. Jimmy Spencer and Jeff Burton claimed the second row, and

199

The Goodwrench Chevrolet (above) and the Valvoline Ford (below) show the aftermath of the 23-car accident that took them from winning contention on lap 140. Drivers Dale Earnhardt and Mark Martin both were able to return to the track and finish the race, but were listed 29th and 30th, respectively, 21 laps down.

Earnhardt's qualifying run — much better than most he has posted this year — raised some eyebrows in the garage area. There was no denying that the Goodwrench team was on the way back, and Dale's recent string of three straight top-three finishes signaled that there was fire in the bellies of the black-clad team.

Billy Standridge, driving his own car, was the fastest second-round qualifier, and Ted Musgrave, Jeremy Mayfield, Ricky Rudd and Kyle Petty needed to use provisionals to make the field. Those who went home included Martinsville pole-winner Ward Burton, Hut Stricklin, ending his recent string of solid qualifying performances, Gary Bradberry, Jeff Green and the Cartoon Network Chevrolet and Ed Berrier.

There is no question that restrictor-plate racing is great for the fans, and the first 140 of the 188-lap DieHard 500 made it one of the most spine-tingling, nail-biting, teeth-gritting events of the season. Side by side, four and five abreast, the pack of some 38 cars rumbled and roared around the mammoth track, with just a pair of seconds separating the leader from the back of the field. Drivers were moving everywhere on the track, trying to find the tiniest advantage that would mean the difference between running in the top five and the final 10. It was hairy, wild, thrilling — and simply an awesome spectacle for the huge throng of more than 120,000 who were on hand. Some of the moves were brilliant, some were daring, and some were

Derrike Cope gave the Pontiac forces reason to cheer with his fifth-fastest lap. Terry and Bobby Labonte were sixth and seventh, while Gordon, Rusty Wallace and Elliott completed the top 10, barely beating Robert Pressley and Dale Earnhardt.

Ken Schrader (33) tries to close the gap on leader Terry Labonte (5) in a nose-to-tail draft that includes Bobby Labonte (18) and Ricky Craven (25). Running well of late, Schrader would pick up his first top-five finish of the season in the DieHard 500.

For the better part of the race, three- and, sometimes, four-abreast racing was the norm on Talladega's 33-degree-banked turns, with barely more than a heartbeat separating the leaders from the back of the pack, in a race that featured 32 official lead changes among 16 different drivers.

those that turned out right because another driver checked up just enough to give the other one room. Without question, it was the most competitive race of the year.

And then it happened.

Near the front of the pack, with everyone running full-tilt, Gordon cut a left-rear tire, banged Andretti, and then turned hard left — at full speed — triggering a 20-car melee. Nearly every driver who had been a contender for victory was involved, including Earnhardt, ending a brilliant run that had stamped him ready to end his long winless streak. Martin and Jarrett were also involved, and all of the cars spent time either on pit road or in the garage area for repairs.

The incident left Terry and Bobby Labonte, along with Ken Schrader and Andretti, who suffered minimal damage from the whack by Gordon, at the front of the field for the restart. With 41 laps to go, fuel was not an issue, and the race ran uninterrupted to the finish. And what a finish it was. Schrader found a way past the Labontes with seven laps left, but Bobby lined up behind Terry, and the two Texans pushed their way back to the front, with Bobby shoving Terry to the point with two laps to go. Bobby found his own way past Schrader, and then set out after his brother, both drivers searching for their first victory of the season. Coming out of the final turn, Bobby tried the inside, the outside and the inside again, but each time, Terry countered, and the Kellogg's car flashed to the line to win by just over a car-length.

Andretti came home third, ahead of Schrader and Irvan, with Ernie earning the final slot for the Winston No Bull 5 at Daytona by holding off Ricky Craven. Petty was seventh, with Geoff Bodine eighth and Rick Mast ninth, ahead of Rusty Wallace.

Martin, Jarrett and Gordon all returned to the track, running at reduced speed, but making laps and gaining points. When the race was over, Gordon was listed 35th, but had retained his point lead over Martin who was 30th, and Jarrett who finished 21st.

DieHard 500

Fin. Pos.	Start Pos.	Car #	Driver	Team
1	6	5	Terry Labonte	Kellogg's Corn Flakes Chevrolet
2	7	18	Bobby Labonte	Interstate Batteries Pontiac
3	2	98	John Andretti	RCA Ford
4	14	33	Ken Schrader	Skoal Bandit Chevrolet
5	1	28	Ernie Irvan	Texaco Havoline Ford
6	15	25	Ricky Craven	Budweiser Chevrolet
7	42	44	Kyle Petty	Hot Wheels Pontiac
8	25	7	Geoff Bodine	QVC Ford
9	23	75	Rick Mast	Remington Arms Ford
10	9	2	Rusty Wallace	Miller Lite Ford
11	39	16	Ted Musgrave	Family Channel/PRIMESTAR Ford
12	29	1	Morgan Shepherd	R&L Carriers Pontiac
13	10	94	Bill Elliott	McDonald's Ford
14	4	99	Jeff Burton	Exide Batteries Ford
15	35	81	Kenny Wallace	Square D Ford
16	37	96	David Green	Caterpillar Chevrolet
17	38	91	Kevin Lepage	Pionite Chevrolet
18	5	36	Derrike Cope	Skittles Pontiac
19	19	30	Johnny Benson	Pennzoil Pontiac
20	34	43	Bobby Hamilton	STP Pontiac
21	18	88	Dale Jarrett	Quality Care/Ford Credit Ford
22	17	11	Brett Bodine	Scandia/Bodine Ford
23	21	90	Dick Trickle	Heilig-Meyers/Simmons Ford
24	3	23	Jimmy Spencer	Camel Cigarettes Ford
25	32	71	Dave Marcis	Realtree Camouflage Chevrolet
26	40	37	Jeremy Mayfield	Kmart/RC Cola Ford
27	11	77	Robert Pressley	Jasper Engines/Federal-Mogul Ford
28	27	21	Michael Waltrip	CITGO Ford
29	12	3	Dale Earnhardt	GM Goodwrench Service Plus Chevrolet
30	31	6	Mark Martin	Valvoline Ford
31	13	42	Joe Nemechek	BellSouth Chevrolet
32	22	41	Steve Grissom	Kodiak Chevrolet
33	16	31	Mike Skinner	Lowe's Chevrolet
34	41	10	Ricky Rudd	Tide Ford
35	8	24	Jeff Gordon	DuPont Refinishes Chevrolet
36	20	9	Lake Speed	Advantage Camo Ford
37	33	17	Darrell Waltrip	Parts America Chevrolet
38	30	4	Sterling Marlin	Kodak Film Chevrolet
39	28	40	Greg Sacks	Coors Light Chevrolet
40	36	97	Chad Little	John Deere Pontiac
41	24	46	Wally Dallenbach	First Union Chevrolet
42	26	47	Billy Standridge	Jayski's Ford

NASCAR WINSTON CUP SERIES 1997

ACDelco 400

(North Carolina Motor Speedway • October 27, 1997)

After 11 consecutive races, the weekend off had given team members a chance to catch their collective breaths. For title contenders Jeff Gordon, Mark Martin and Dale Jarrett, it also offered a chance to lick their Talladega wounds and prepare for the upcoming three races that would determine who would be the 1997 NASCAR Winston Cup champion.

Gordon may have been the driver breathing the largest sigh of relief.

At first glance, the 20-car accident at Talladega appeared to end Gordon's chances of finishing the race. It was the long-awaited opportunity for Martin and Jarrett to close the gap and make the final three races of the season a real run to the title, forcing each of the drivers to race for the championship. But Martin also was involved, with serious damage to his Valvoline Thunderbird, and Jarrett failed to escape unscathed, as well. Jarrett had the least damage of the three, and continued immediately, while the DuPont and Valvoline crews staged their own race behind the wall to return their drivers to action. Martin's team won that battle, and all three cars were running at the finish.

Martin finished five positions ahead of Gordon in the final rundown, but it meant just 15 points in the overall scheme of things when the race was completed. Jarrett was 21st, gaining the most points, but it was not at all what the Quality Care driver needed.

Now, as the teams arrived at North Carolina Motor Speedway for the ACDelco 400, Gordon was still at the top of the standings with a 110-point margin over Martin, while

(Right) Joe Gibbs keeps a watchful eye on the track as his driver, Bobby Labonte, searches for his first win of the season. After two straight second-place finishes, Gibbs and the Interstate Batteries team were on the verge of victory, but it would not come at Rockingham.

(Below) Pole-winner Bobby Labonte (18) stalks Bobby Hamilton, looking to take the lead during the first third of the race. At Rockingham, Labonte had scored his third pole of the year, tying him with Dale Jarrett and Mark Martin for the year-end Busch Pole Award with just two events left in the season.

Gatorade
INTERSTA
BATTERI
PONTIAC
18
18
ARCTIC POWER
GENERATORS

(Above) Lake Speed and Joe Nemechek sport new paint schemes for the ACDelco 400. Speed and the Melling Racing team had received a needed lift from Advance Camouflage for the remainder of the year, while Nemechek, whose brightly-colored BellSouth Chevrolet turned black and blue for this race, drove to his second top-10 finish of the season. *(Right)* Crew chief Andy Graves slings the right-rear tire around the Budweiser Chevrolet, helping his team get driver Ricky Craven back on the track to keep him among the leaders. Craven led the most laps during the race, fighting at the head of the field with Gordon, Jarrett and Hamilton, before finally finishing third.

Jarrett had closed to 155 behind. One race, with Gordon on the sidelines early and good finishes by Martin and Jarrett, could still turn the point battle into a shootout, but it appeared that perhaps Gordon had weathered the challenge and was headed for his second career NASCAR Winston Cup.

Jeff Burton remained solidly in fourth place, while Terry Labonte's Talladega victory, coupled with Dale Earnhardt's finish after being involved in the wreck, had moved the defending champion back into fifth place, but it was by the merest whisker. Only two points separated the Kellogg's and Goodwrench cars when practice opened at The Rock. Bobby Labonte, Bill Elliott and Ted Musgrave held down the seventh, eighth and ninth places, respectively, and behind Musgrave was an enormous battle for the final position on the stage at the Waldorf-Astoria. Rusty Wallace was 10th, just two points ahead of Ken Schrader. Five points behind Schrader was Johnny Benson, while 18 points separated Benson from Jeremy Mayfield, who held a three-point margin over Ernie Irvan. A total of 28 points separated the five drivers in their battle for 10th place.

Musgrave, who has been in the battle for a spot in the top 10 throughout the year with his consistent performances, had reason to smile at Rockingham as sponsor PRIMESTAR had renewed for the 1998 season with the Jack Roush-owned team. Joe Nemechek found his BellSouth Chevrolet carrying a different paint scheme for the ACDelco 400, touting a new service from the telecommunications company. Lake Speed and the Melling team also carried different paint as part of their sponsorship from Advantage Camouflage that would remain for the rest of the season. At the Heilig-Meyers stall in the garage area, crew members and driver Dick Trickle were all smiles, with the unexpected but pleasant news that crew chief Tom Baldwin had taken himself out of the running for a crew chief's slot at Hendrick Motorsports and decided to remain with the team from Richmond, Va.

Over the past five races, Pontiac's hopes of ending a year-long absence from victory lane had been rising. With the help of some spoiler changes mandated by NASCAR, the teams were rounding into competitive form, and a top-three finish for the marque in each of the last five races pushed hopes even higher. Bobby Labonte had

(Right) Crew chief Ray Evernham wears a concerned look, knowing how close his team had come to losing significant points, and realizing that their second championship was anything but in the bag.
(Below) The Rainbow Warriors make repairs to the rear axle of Jeff Gordon's Chevrolet while under caution, keeping Jeff on the lead lap and in contention in the race.

finished second in the last two races — at Charlotte and Talladega — and the Tin Indian execs hoped that one of the Pontiac teams would figure out how to get to Rockingham's victory lane.

With the first round of qualifying complete, the Poncho hopes had risen even higher. Bobby had put the Interstate Batteries Grand Prix on the pole, and Ward Burton had claimed the outside of the second row with his MBNA Pontiac. Making it three Pontiacs in the first five starting spots was Kyle Petty, with a solid run in his Hot Wheels-sponsored car. The championship contenders weren't far from each other, either, with Jarrett starting on the outside of the front row, barely missing his fourth Busch Pole of the season,

(Right) Fifth-place starter Kyle Petty (44) positions his Pontiac on the inside of Kenny Wallace along the frontstretch. Petty had expected to be a contender at Rockingham, but missed the race setup and dropped two laps off the pace to a 22nd-place finish. (Below) Richard Petty jokes with his driver after Bobby Hamilton scored the win for the STP team. The victory would cost Petty more money than his car had won, but he was satisfied just to be a winner for the second straight season.

and Martin in third place. Gordon turned the sixth-fastest lap to grab the outside of the third row, ahead of Geoff Bodine and Bill Elliott. Ricky Craven and Mike Skinner rounded out the top-10 qualifiers.

For the second time in the last four races, crews stood around under ponchos and umbrellas, waiting to see if the race-day weather would clear in time for the event to take the green flag on Sunday. Like Martinsville, however, Mother Nature turned a disdainful face on the Sandhills region of North Carolina, forcing the race to run on Monday.

On the second lap after the green flag dropped over the field for the ACDelco 400, many Gordon fans in the crowd gasped when the DuPont Chevrolet slapped the wall exiting the second turn. Was this the race in which their hero would lose his point lead? But Gordon continued on with no significant damage to the Monte Carlo. Later, his team would discover an axle cap had come loose and made repairs under a yellow flag. He survived both dramas to finish fourth, negating strong finishes by Jarrett and Martin.

For the longest time, it appeared that either Jarrett would win his seventh race of the season, or Ricky Craven would win his first. Both drivers had strong cars and battled at the point in the second half of the race, but when the final yellow of the day waved when Greg Sacks slowed and

Dirty and battered, having survived 400 miles on Rockingham's high banks and an extensive post-race inspection, the famed "43" receives final preparations for the ride back home in a deserted garage area at Rockingham.

was unable to return to the pits, the caution played into the hands of Bobby Hamilton.

The STP Pontiac driver had been playing a waiting game. He fought his way from his 28th qualifying position to the front pack, led early, and then found a place in the top five to run for the bulk of the 400-miler. He had been shrewd, holding back a little for the end, and when the green dropped with 21 laps left in the race, he was third in line — and prepared to lay his aces on the table. On successive laps, he ripped past Craven, and then Jarrett, and eased away. Jarrett, finding his car better on old tires, had no chance to challenge Hamilton. He fought with Craven for second place, and emerged with the position, passing the Budweiser Chevrolet driver on the final lap.

Gordon came home fourth, losing a few points to Jarrett, but beating Martin by two positions. Between them was Trickle, with a brilliant run to fifth after fighting at the front of the pack throughout the day. Terry Labonte and Earnhardt were seventh and eighth, enabling Labonte to maintain his fifth place in the point standings, while Sterling Marlin and Nemechek claimed the final positions in the top 10.

Hamilton's victory came a year to the day after his Phoenix victory, and he could be excused for going "Ka-ching, ka-ching" over the radio to his crew and car owner during the final laps of the race. After making the decision to leave the Petty team and join the Kodak effort next season, Petty and Hamilton made a bet over dinner one evening. Petty told Hamilton that he felt Bobby would not win a race for him before 1997 was over, and challenged him to do so, saying he would bet $100,000 that Bobby wouldn't. Hamilton took the bet, shaking hands. The Rockingham victory won the bet for Hamilton, and he and Petty were both grinning from ear to ear when they stood in victory lane with the Pontiac folks at the end of the event.

An expensive proposition for Petty, to be sure — but one he gladly paid to prove his team was back as a serious challenger on a weekly basis.

ACDelco 400

Fin. Pos.	Start Pos.	Car #	Driver	Team
1	28	43	Bobby Hamilton	STP Pontiac
2	2	88	Dale Jarrett	Quality Care/Ford Credit Ford
3	9	25	Ricky Craven	Budweiser Chevrolet
4	6	24	Jeff Gordon	DuPont Refinishes Chevrolet
5	12	90	Dick Trickle	Heilig-Meyers/Simmons Ford
6	3	6	Mark Martin	Valvoline Ford
7	33	5	Terry Labonte	Kellogg's Corn Flakes Chevrolet
8	26	3	Dale Earnhardt	GM Goodwrench Service Plus Chevrolet
9	35	4	Sterling Marlin	Kodak Film Chevrolet
10	19	42	Joe Nemechek	BellSouth Chevrolet
11	1	18	Bobby Labonte	Interstate Batteries Pontiac
12	8	94	Bill Elliott	McDonald's Ford
13	27	77	Robert Pressley	Jasper Engines/Federal-Mogul Ford
14	17	21	Michael Waltrip	CITGO Ford
15	24	37	Jeremy Mayfield	Kmart/RC Cola Ford
16	16	97	Chad Little	John Deere Pontiac
17	30	9	Lake Speed	Advantage Camo Ford
18	18	2	Rusty Wallace	Miller Lite Ford
19	7	7	Geoff Bodine	QVC Ford
20	14	36	Derrike Cope	Skittles Pontiac
21	29	29	Jeff Green	Cartoon Network Chevrolet
22	5	44	Kyle Petty	Hot Wheels Pontiac
23	10	31	Mike Skinner	Lowe's Chevrolet
24	37	41	Steve Grissom	Kodiak Chevrolet
25	23	8	Hut Stricklin	Circuit City Ford
26	4	22	Ward Burton	MBNA America Pontiac
27	15	96	David Green	Caterpillar Chevrolet
28	39	28	Ernie Irvan	Texaco Havoline Ford
29	43	17	Darrell Waltrip	Parts America Chevrolet
30	38	33	Ken Schrader	Skoal Bandit Chevrolet
31	41	98	John Andretti	RCA Ford
32	34	16	Ted Musgrave	Family Channel/PRIMESTAR Ford
33	32	14	Steve Park	Burger King Chevrolet
34	31	1	Morgan Shepherd	R&L Carriers Pontiac
35	21	46	Wally Dallenbach	First Union Chevrolet
36	20	30	Johnny Benson	Pennzoil Pontiac
37	25	81	Kenny Wallace	Square D Ford
38	11	99	Jeff Burton	Exide Batteries Ford
39	42	40	Greg Sacks	Coors Light Chevrolet
40	13	10	Ricky Rudd	Tide Ford
41	36	78	Gary Bradberry	Hanes Ford
42	22	75	Rick Mast	Remington Arms/Stren Ford
43	40	23	Jimmy Spencer	Camel Cigarettes Ford

NASCAR WINSTON CUP SERIES 1997

Dura-Lube 500 Presented by Kmart

(Phoenix International Raceway • November 2, 1997)

If there is one thing that championship contenders Jeff Gordon, Mark Martin and Dale Jarrett have in common, it is that none of them are the type driver who gives up.

For Gordon, it wouldn't have mattered if he and his DuPont teammates were on the brink of title extinction as they headed for Phoenix. He and his crew would put forth their best efforts, emulating a terrier with its teeth locked in the denim of a pant leg, if needed.

Obviously, that wasn't the case as the teams headed for the Valley of the Sun and the annual late-season stop at Phoenix International Raceway. Gordon was 125 points clear of Martin following the finish of the rain-delayed Rockingham event, and he needed to merely put together solid finishes in the final two races of the season to lock up his second NASCAR Winston Cup championship.

Sure, he talked about the fact that he could see his point lead melt away in the heat of the desert, but, in reality, he and his team were in excellent shape to make their move to the stage of the Waldorf-Astoria Hotel in New York on December 5.

At the same time, he found himself unable to shake either Martin or Jarrett in the final run to the title. Martin, one of the most determined competitors in the garage area, had been unable to capitalize on Gordon's Talladega problems, and then was unable to beat Jeff

(Right) Kyle Petty could hardly believe he was about to start his 500th event in a career that began in 1979, 18 seasons ago. Kyle made a good showing in his milestone event, climbing from the 34th starting position to take his eighth top-10 finish of the year.

(Below) Rusty Wallace slings one of his favorite mounts, "Ronnie," through the turns on the inside of Steve Park's Burger King Chevrolet, with Dale Jarrett and Bobby Labonte in pursuit. Rusty, still winless in the Arizona desert despite running well there in the past, led 117 of the 312 laps, but had to settle for a second-place finish.

208

KYLE PETTY
'79
500
STARTS
'97
Hot Wheels
MATTEL
Racing
GOODYEAR
Winston Cup
PONTIAC
MAC TOOLS

(Right) Nestled in the valley at the foot of the mountains, Phoenix International Raceway, recently purchased by International Speedway Corporation, offers one of the most picturesque stops on the NASCAR Winston Cup tour. *(Below right)* NASCAR inspectors check their equipment prior to technical inspection at Phoenix. A recent rule change affecting the bodies of the Grand Prix had Pontiac teams hoping for a second straight win. *(Bottom)* In a preview of the 1998 NASCAR Winston Cup Rookie-of-the-Year battle, Steve Park (14) holds off Kenny Irwin (27) as the two drivers log valuable laps in a tune-up for next season.

head-to-head at The Rock and close the gap even more. He was within striking distance, something he had worked to maintain throughout the stretch run, but he still needed some help from the racing gods at Phoenix, or the title would be out of his reach when it came to the final event of the season at Atlanta.

Jarrett, doggedly determined as well, but perhaps more fatalistic in his approach to the point battle, said that if it was his time to win the championship, then he would win it. He knew his team would provide him with good cars and motors, but he also knew that everything that happened on the race track was not necessarily under his control. He could be collected in a wreck, have a mechanical problem or fall victim to some other strange situation that could intervene in his bid for the title. He would just do the best he could, he said, and see where things fell.

With Jeff Burton solidly in fourth place in the standings, the battle for fifth raged on between Terry Labonte and Dale Earnhardt. Labonte had held the

(Above) Robert Pressley drives the Jasper Ford into the back of Kenny Wallace's Square D Thunderbird as the two drivers joust for position. Pressley, making his seventh start for the Jasper team, was hoping to build on the momentum gained from his 13th-place finish the week before at Rockingham. *(Right)* Dale Jarrett narrowly escapes a potential problem in the form of a spinning Dale Earnhardt. Earnhardt was able to gather up the Goodwrench Chevrolet, maintain his lead-lap status and come home with a top-five finish by the end of the day.

position by two points going into The Rock and emerged 11 points ahead of Earnhardt. Bobby Labonte was solidly in seventh, while Bill Elliott had secured eighth place, with little chance of moving up or down in the standings before the season ended. Elliott's crew, under the direction of Mike Beam, had rounded into a solid effort behind The Redhead, and the crew members had underscored their emergence by winning the Unocal 76-Rockingham Pit Crew Race in the annual competition at North Carolina Motor Speedway.

Behind Elliott, however, there was total war for the final two positions in the top 10 — and the last two invitations to the stage at the Waldorf. Ted Musgrave held ninth place after Rockingham, 38 points ahead of Rusty Wallace, who, in turn, was 16 points ahead of Jeremy Mayfield. Ken Schrader had moved up to challenge Mayfield, and now trailed by 22 points, while Ernie Irvan was 20 points behind Schrader, but just three markers ahead of Johnny Benson. Less than 100 points separated positions 9-14, and the final two events of the season would determine who finished in the top 10 — and who did not.

As the teams pushed their cars to the line for the first qualifying session at Phoenix, Ford crews were discussing the latest change at the top of Ford's racing program, headquartered in Dearborn, Mich. The Blue Oval brass had shaken up the company's Special Vehicles Operations, Ford's racing arm, and had named Dan Davis as the new worldwide head of competition programs, replacing Bruce Cambern. The Ford teams hoped this would prompt the return of Preston Miller, Ford's NASCAR representative, who had resigned two races earlier. There was little question that the Ford forces would need every bit of experience Miller offered, with the teams facing the task of changing Thunderbirds to Tauruses during the coming months leading to the Daytona 500.

While the Ford teams were talking about their situation, there was an added spring in the steps of the Pontiac team members at Phoenix. Bobby Hamilton's brilliantly-measured victory at Rockingham had given all the teams reason to believe in their Grand Prix, and Hamilton

Ward Burton grinds to a halt in the MBNA Pontiac after clobbering the first-turn wall. The resulting caution caught Dale Jarrett in the pits, putting him nearly a full lap down for the ensuring restart.

had continued where he left off at The Rock from the moment the STP Pontiac rolled off the transporter in the Dick Beaty Garage at Phoenix. Hamilton had been at the top of the speed charts during practice, and was the odds-on favorite to win the pole.

He didn't disappoint, rolling to his second pole of the season and setting a new track record in the process, whipping Jimmy Spencer's second-best effort by nearly a full tenth of a second. Rusty Wallace and Bobby Labonte claimed the second row, ahead of Rick Mast and Ken Schrader, while Dale Earnhardt turned in a solid qualifying run to grab the seventh spot on the grid, with Johnny Benson alongside. Jarrett and Lake Speed made up the fifth row, ahead of Kenny Irwin and Jeff Gordon. Martin qualified 14th.

Following the second round of qualifying, Ricky Rudd, Jeff and David Green and Chad Little used provisionals to make the field, and Ricky Craven was added in the 43rd and final position. The entry blank had called for a NASCAR Winston West provisional, but no cars from that division were at the track, allowing the West provisional to revert back to the Cup side. Although Craven had no provisionals to use, he was added to the field when it was determined that none of the drivers who failed to make the race had provisionals to use, and NASCAR went to this year's car owner points to determine who would get the final provisional. Wally Dallenbach, Jack Sprague, Morgan Shepherd and Gary Bradberry all went home.

For the first two-thirds of the 312-lap race, it appeared that either Hamilton or Rusty Wallace would emerge as the victor in the battle under the hot desert sun. Hamilton had plenty of juice under the hood of his STP Pontiac, and was determined to make it two straight

Ted Musgrave (16) flies through the corner with Rick Mast looking for position on the inside with his Remington Ford. Mast was coming off a superb qualifying effort, having secured the fifth spot on the grid at Phoenix, but eventually fell three laps off the pace to finish 31st.

Dale Jarrett lets the champagne fly in victory lane. Jarrett took the lead for the first time with 73 laps remaining and never looked back to take his seventh win of the year, netting him 68 points on Jeff Gordon and moving him past Mark Martin into second place in the standings. Would it be enough to challenge for the championship at Atlanta?

victories at Phoenix. Wallace, looking for his second victory of the season, ripped and snorted his way through the field and put the Miller Lite Ford at the point, jousting with Hamilton for the victory. Gordon soldiered on, looking for a solid top-five finish, and Martin was having a handling nightmare, unable to tame the Valvoline Ford. Earnhardt, meanwhile, was on form and appeared ready to challenge for his first win of the season.

Jarrett's hopes for victory seemingly disappeared on lap 130 when, just one lap after Dale had made a green-flag stop, Ward Burton hit the wall to bring out the caution, trapping Jarrett nearly a full lap behind. He fought and drove his heart out, unleashing the combination of a chassis born in the Yates Racing shop and the fury of the Yates-built engine under the hood. He made up the entire lap under green, and took the lead from Wallace on lap 240.

As Jarrett began to pull away from the field, Gordon began having problems with a right-front tire. He slid backward in the field, hoping to last until a scheduled pit stop could remedy his problem, but, on lap 273, the tire shredded, forcing Gordon to head for pit road. He lost two laps in the process and returned to the track in 30th place, but fought his way back to finish 17th.

Jarrett, stretching his fuel to the limit, finished two seconds ahead of Wallace, with Hamilton third. Schrader had another fine run to finish fourth, while Earnhardt was fifth. Martin fought his way to sixth place, ahead of Benson and Steve Grissom. Kyle Petty, competing in his 500th career NASCAR Winston Cup race, took ninth, ahead of Geoff Bodine.

The Ford Quality Care driver's seventh victory of the season, combined with the finishes of Gordon and Martin, moved Jarrett into second place in the standings as the teams prepared to head for the newly configured Atlanta Motor Speedway. He now trailed Gordon by 77 points, with Martin still in the hunt, just 10 points behind Jarrett and 87 behind Gordon.

Dura-Lube 500 Presented by Kmart

Fin. Pos.	Start Pos.	Car #	Driver	Team
1	9	88	Dale Jarrett	Quality Care/Ford Credit Ford
2	3	2	Rusty Wallace	Miller Lite Ford
3	1	43	Bobby Hamilton	STP Pontiac
4	6	33	Ken Schrader	Skoal Bandit Chevrolet
5	7	3	Dale Earnhardt	GM Goodwrench Service Plus Chevrolet
6	14	6	Mark Martin	Valvoline Ford
7	8	30	Johnny Benson	Pennzoil Pontiac
8	20	41	Steve Grissom	Kodiak Chevrolet
9	34	44	Kyle Petty	Hot Wheels Pontiac
10	17	7	Geoff Bodine	QVC Ford
11	29	5	Terry Labonte	Kellogg's Corn Flakes Chevrolet
12	19	17	Darrell Waltrip	Parts America Chevrolet
13	37	99	Jeff Burton	Exide Batteries Ford
14	2	23	Jimmy Spencer	Camel Cigarettes Ford
15	36	94	Bill Elliott	McDonald's Ford
16	16	36	Derrike Cope	Skittles Pontiac
17	12	24	Jeff Gordon	DuPont Refinishes Chevrolet
18	25	28	Ernie Irvan	Texaco Havoline Ford
19	22	37	Jeremy Mayfield	Kmart/RC Cola Ford
20	11	27	Kenny Irwin	Action Performance Ford
21	28	40	Greg Sacks	Coors Light Chevrolet
22	23	16	Ted Musgrave	Family Channel/PRIMESTAR Ford
23	4	18	Bobby Labonte	Interstate Batteries Pontiac
24	18	42	Joe Nemechek	BellSouth Chevrolet
25	42	97	Chad Little	John Deere Pontiac
26	30	21	Michael Waltrip	CITGO Ford
27	26	4	Sterling Marlin	Kodak Film Chevrolet
28	32	31	Mike Skinner	Lowe's Chevrolet
29	41	96	David Green	Caterpillar Chevrolet
30	33	8	Hut Stricklin	Circuit City Ford
31	5	75	Rick Mast	Remington Arms Ford
32	40	29	Jeff Green	Cartoon Network Chevrolet
33	15	11	Brett Bodine	Scandia/Bodine Ford
34	38	71	Dave Marcis	Realtree Camouflage Chevrolet
35	21	81	Kenny Wallace	Square D Ford
36	39	10	Ricky Rudd	Tide Ford
37	10	9	Lake Speed	Advantage Camo Ford
38	24	77	Robert Pressley	Jasper Engines/Federal-Mogul Ford
39	35	98	John Andretti	RCA Ford
40	13	90	Dick Trickle	Heilig-Meyers/Simmons Ford
41	31	14	Steve Park	Burger King Chevrolet
42	27	22	Ward Burton	MBNA America Pontiac
43	43	25	Ricky Craven	Budweiser Chevrolet

NASCAR WINSTON CUP SERIES 1997

NAPA 500

(Atlanta Motor Speedway • November 16, 1997)

A season that began with a brilliant Speedweeks at Daytona, winning the Busch Clash and his first Daytona 500, had evolved into a year in which he and the DuPont Chevrolet had been at the top of the NASCAR Winston Cup point standings for the majority of the season, and included victories in The Winston and 10 point races. Now, it all came down to a single event in which Jeff Gordon would win or lose his quest for his second NASCAR Winston Cup.

The tire problem at Phoenix had cost him — but not as much as it initially appeared. He was able to regain 14 positions and finish 17th, and when the Hendrick Motorsports team left the Valley of the Sun, even Dale Jarrett's brilliant run to victory had not prevented Gordon from maintaining his point lead.

(Left) Saving the best for last for the second consecutive year, Bobby Labonte accepts the winner's trophy for his victory in the NAPA 500 at Atlanta. His season-ending win, a virtual repeat of one year ago, extended his string of consecutive winning seasons to three.

(Right) The starting field completes the first warm-up lap around the newly configured Atlanta Motor Speedway on a crisp, sunny Sunday to begin the final event of the 1997 NASCAR Winston Cup season.

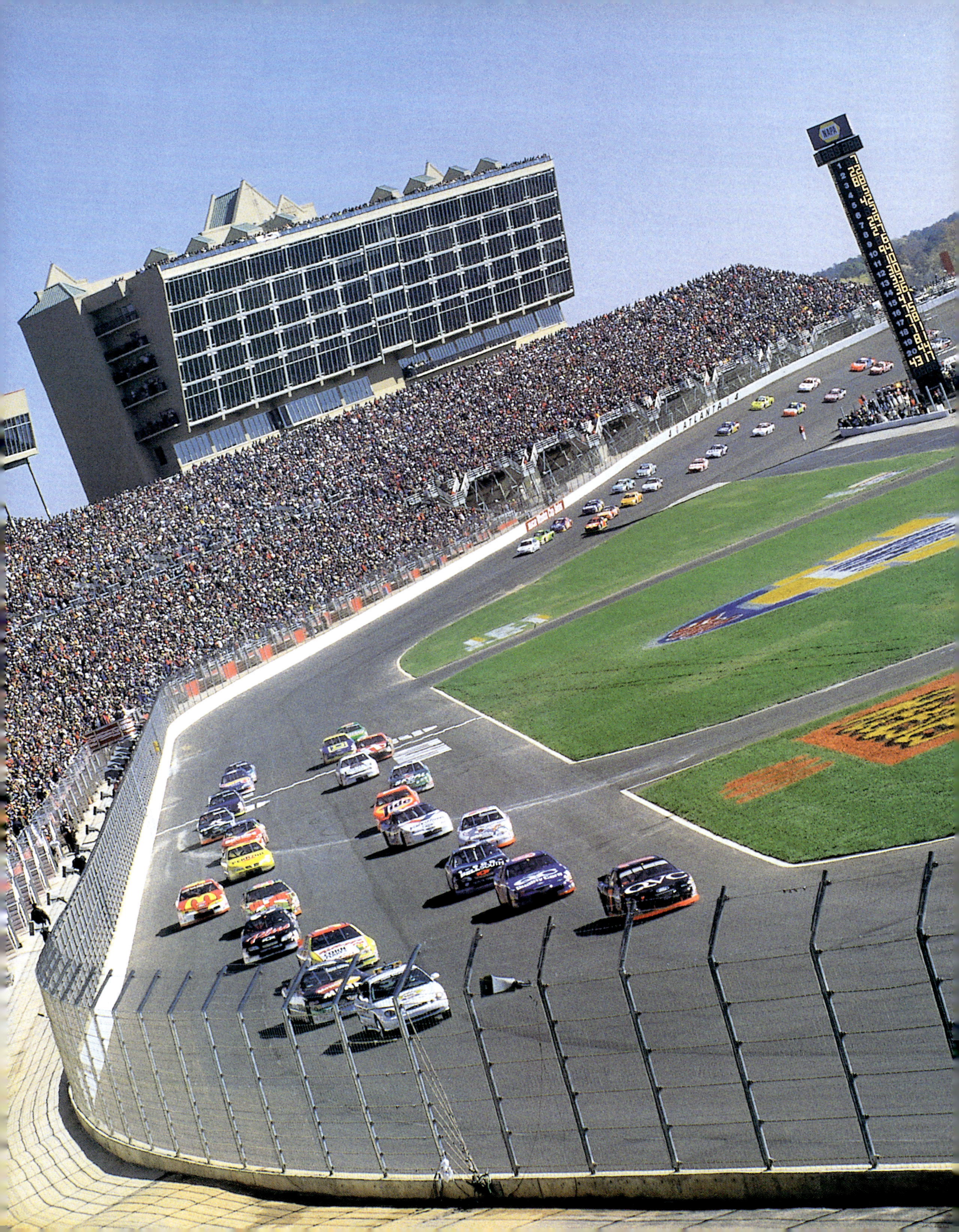
NAPA

Crew members prepare to load the primary DuPont Chevrolet onto the flat-bed for the ride back to the shop. In a freak accident on pit road during Saturday's practice round, Gordon lost control and hit the STP Pontiac, forcing both teams to use their backup cars for qualifying and the race.

The final event of the year would be at a facility very different than when the teams had competed there in March. During the months between the spring event and the opening of practice for the NAPA 500, Ed Clark and his horde of worker bees had demolished the old 1.522-mile oval and built a new 1.54-mile quad oval. New grandstands, suites, media facilities and supporting facilities had been built, and although the roads leading to the track looked the same, everything was different for fans and competitors upon their arrivals.

Teams spent time testing at the new facility prior to the event, and while the crews worked on shocks, springs and other chassis settings, Clark's contractors were installing miles of fence, acres of sod and thousands of flowers and plants to finish off the $30 million-plus construction effort. The Speedway, part of Bruton Smith's Speedway Motorsports, had basically been redone, with the March start/finish line now on the backstretch, the facility "flopped" similar to what had been done at Darlington between the spring and Labor Day weekend races.

Testing had shown that the new track was extremely fast, with some projecting the pole to come at 195 miles per hour — or more. It meant that the championship contenders — point leader Gordon, second-place Jarrett (-77) and Mark Martin, third and trailing by 87 points — would have to contend not only with each other, but also with a new track in the race that would determine the championship.

Gordon was in the driver's seat, and he knew that only once in the '90s had the driver leading the points into the final race of the season not come away with the championship. But that statistic also meant little, he knew, in terms of what could happen on Sunday.

Teams were hoping for every minute of practice time they could amass prior to qualifying, but, as she has done at several other junctures during the season, Mother Nature intervened. Rain alternated between mist and heavy storms for three days, and Friday's Busch Pole qualifying was eliminated. Teams had only a brief practice session to prepare for a single round of qualifying on Saturday morning that would set the field for the NAPA 500. With 50 entries competing for the maximum 43 slots in the field, it was clear that some good cars, teams and drivers would miss the final race of the season.

The battle for the final position on the stage at the Waldorf-Astoria would also be waged at Atlanta. Ted Musgrave held 10th place entering the weekend, just 45 points behind ninth-place Rusty Wallace. But Ken Schrader stood just 13 points behind Musgrave, while Jeremy Mayfield and Johnny Benson were tied for 12th place, 45 points behind the Roush driver. Ernie Irvan, who was 84 points behind Musgrave, also had a shot at claiming the final top-10 position.

Four drivers — Dale Earnhardt, Sterling Marlin, Geoff Bodine and Bobby Labonte — had won in 1996 and now faced going through the entire 1997 season without a win. It was the last chance for all four, and Earnhardt's proud 15-year string of at least one victory per season was in jeopardy.

Saturday's schedule consisted of a brief period for teams to scuff tires in preparation for Sunday's race, before the run for the Busch Pole captured fans' attention. And in the middle of the session, one of the strangest occurrences of an already bizarre season happened. Gordon,

heading onto the track, began weaving on pit road while scrubbing his sticker tires. He lost control and smacked into the rear of Bobby Hamilton's STP Pontiac, which was sitting still, waiting to enter the track. Both cars were damaged beyond immediate repair and crews from each team scrambled to their transporters and began pulling out the backup cars in time for qualifying.

(Right) The Rainbow Warriors perform another superb pit stop under green. They consistently turned Gordon in and out of the pits with sub-18-second stops to help keep their driver in a position to pick up the championship. (Below) Dale Jarrett finds the quarters rather tight as he positions his Quality Care Thunderbird behind Ken Schrader (33) and Jeff Burton (99), trying to keep a bead on Bobby Labonte's Interstate Pontiac. Labonte took the lead for the first time on lap 107 and had by far, the dominant car for the remainder of the afternoon.

Nemechek and Dale Earnhardt claimed the third row, with Jeff Green and Kenny Irwin turning laps faster than Mark Martin and Bill Elliott. With only one lap and a single round of qualifying, it was "get it done or go home." In addition to Hamilton, Jeff Burton, Ricky Craven and Jimmy Spencer used provisionals, with Darrell Waltrip taking the former champion's provisional. Those who failed to make the field were Todd Bodine, David Green, Robert Pressley, Hut Stricklin, Greg Sacks, Dave Marcis and Ed Berrier.

(Top) Brett Bodine (11) slides sideways through the second turn with Buckshot Jones' Pontiac bearing down on him. Moments later, the two cars got together and hit the retaining wall, bringing both of their days to an early end. *(Above)* Derrike Cope guides the Skittles Pontiac through the turns on the outside of Mark Martin (6), Mike Skinner (31) and Bobby Hamilton (43). Cope, in his final outing with the Skittle team, finished a season-best fifth in a very strong run, two spots behind Martin. Hamilton took seventh in his last ride in the STP Pontiac, while Skinner secured the 1997 Rookie-of-the-Year title.

During the session, Gordon's lap was only good for 37th place on Sunday's starting grid, while Hamilton had to use a provisional to make the field. DuPont crew chief Ray Evernham dialed the Hendrick shop in Charlotte, and five hours later, a third rainbow-hued Monte Carlo rolled into the track on the back of a truck, a backup for the backup, in case anything happened during the final "Happy Hour" practice.

At the front of the field, it was an issue of who could hold his breath the longest — and on this raw Saturday morning it was Geoff Bodine. He rocketed to a lap at nearly 197.5 miles per hour with his Ford, which was wearing the familiar black-white-and-orange QVC colors for the final time. More than two miles per hour behind Bodine was Ward Burton, with Jarrett third fastest, ahead of Terry Labonte. Joe

The strategies of the three contenders were immediately unveiled when the green flag flew over the field in front of a capacity crowd of heavily-bundled race fans on the sunny, cold Sunday afternoon. Gordon began fighting his way toward the front, hoping to put himself safely in position to win the championship. Martin and Jarrett had no choice but to try to lead the most laps and win the race, hoping that somehow Gordon faltered. Mark moved into contention early, and his Valvoline Ford was clearly one with a chance to win. Jarrett's battle was a longer one, with the Quality Care Ford finally leading just before the one-third mark of the race. Earnhardt thrilled his legions by leading handily in the early going, but eventually slid into the second-turn wall, ending his chance to win a race for the 16th straight season.

Ray Evernham watches stoically as his driver, four laps off the pace and fighting an ill-handling race car, tries to hold a position on the track that would be good enough to bring home the championship.

In the point battle, Jeff Burton finished fourth ahead of Earnhardt, with Terry Labonte sixth. Bobby Labonte was seventh, and Bill Elliott claimed eighth ahead of ninth-place Rusty Wallace. The final position on the stage at the Waldorf-Astoria went to Ken Schrader, who managed it by the merest whisker. After a year of competition that stretched from border to border and took 10 months to complete, he finished just a single point ahead of Benson.

Mike Skinner finished 23rd in the final race of the season to claim the NASCAR Winston Cup Rookie-of-the-Year title.

Gordon fought with tires and handling, and as the afternoon wound on, it was clear he had no chance to win the race. He found the right place in the pack, put in the laps he needed, protected his position with solid performances on pit road by his crew, and in the end, won the title by the fourth-closest margin in the modern era of NASCAR Winston Cup competition.

Bobby Labonte came to the front for the first time on lap 107 and dominated the final two-thirds of the race. With the last half of the event run under green, Labonte had one final challenge from Martin after Mark took two right-side tires on his final pit stop to emerge as the leader with 39 laps left in the event. The gamble paid off, putting Martin in command, but Labonte began closing the gap and moved past Mark with 11 laps left in the race. Bobby pulled away and, almost immediately, Martin lost a cylinder and fell victim to a hard-charging Jarrett with just over a lap remaining.

Labonte's victory made him the first driver to win back-to-back NAPA 500s since Richard Petty did it in 1970-71, while Jarrett finished second and Martin third. Their finishes, combined with Gordon's 17th place, gave Jeff his second title in three years by a 14-point margin over Jarrett. Martin claimed third, 29 points behind.

Jeff Green had a superb run to fourth place behind Martin, and ahead of an equally brilliant drive by Derrike Cope in his final ride in the Skittles Pontiac. Kyle Petty led the lap-down cars in sixth place, ahead of Hamilton and Nemechek. Ward Burton and Benson completed the top 10 in the final race rundown.

NAPA 500

Fin. Pos.	Start Pos.	Car #	Driver	Team
1.	21	18	Bobby Labonte	Interstate Batteries Pontiac
2.	3	88	Dale Jarrett	Quality Care/Ford Credit Ford
3.	9	6	Mark Martin	Valvoline Ford
4.	7	29	Jeff Green	Cartoon Network Chevrolet
5.	14	36	Derrike Cope	Skittles Pontiac
6.	20	44	Kyle Petty	Hot Wheels Pontiac
7.	40	43	Bobby Hamilton	STP Pontiac
8.	5	42	Joe Nemechek	BellSouth Chevrolet
9.	2	22	Ward Burton	MBNA America Pontiac
10.	12	30	Johnny Benson	Pennzoil Pontiac
11.	27	4	Sterling Marlin	Kodak Film Chevrolet
12.	23	28	Ernie Irvan	Texaco Havoline Ford
13.	35	21	Michael Waltrip	CITGO Ford
14.	22	90	Dick Trickle	Heilig-Meyers/Simmons Ford
15.	25	14	Steve Park	Burger King Chevrolet
16.	6	3	Dale Earnhardt	GM Goodwrench Service Plus Chevrolet
17.	37	24	Jeff Gordon	DuPont Refinishes Chevrolet
18.	24	97	Chad Little	John Deere Pontiac
19.	38	37	Jeremy Mayfield	Kmart/RC Cola Ford
20.	13	33	Ken Schrader	Skoal Bandit Chevrolet
21.	4	5	Terry Labonte	Kellogg's Corn Flakes Chevrolet
22.	31	98	John Andretti	RCA Ford
23.	28	31	Mike Skinner	Lowe's Chevrolet
24.	42	23	Jimmy Spencer	Winston No Bull Ford
25.	8	27	Kenny Irwin	Winners Circle Ford
26.	29	9	Lake Speed	Advantage Camo Ford
27.	36	1	Morgan Shepherd	R&L Carriers Pontiac
28.	15	41	Steve Grissom	Kodiak Chevrolet
29.	26	91	Kevin Lepage	Pionite Chevrolet
30.	19	81	Kenny Wallace	Square D Ford
31.	34	16	Ted Musgrave	Family Channel/PRIMESTAR Ford
32.	33	2	Rusty Wallace	Miller Lite Ford
33.	1	7	Geoff Bodine	QVC Ford
34.	39	99	Jeff Burton	Exide Batteries Ford
35.	16	75	Rick Mast	Remington Arms Ford
36.	10	94	Bill Elliott	McDonald's Ford
37.	11	10	Ricky Rudd	Tide Ford
38.	30	46	Wally Dallenbach	First Union Chevrolet
39.	41	25	Ricky Craven	Budweiser Chevrolet
40.	43	17	Darrell Waltrip	Parts America Chevrolet
41.	18	11	Brett Bodine	Scandia/Bodine Ford
42.	17	78	Gary Bradberry	Hanes Ford
43.	32	00	Buckshot Jones	Aquafresh Pontiac

NASCAR WINSTON CUP SERIES 1997

Reflections from 1997

On a less-glamorous side of the sport, Kyle Petty's crew prepares to install a Martinsville race engine in the Hot Wheels Pontiac. In their first season, the PE2 team made a solid showing and nearly collected a win, laying a firm foundation to build upon for the 1998 season.

(Above) Sharing a happy moment with wife Linda and son Landon, Ricky Rudd prepares to go to work at Dover in May. Ricky's day ended on an even happier note when he recorded his first win of the year, extending his string of winning seasons to 15. *(Right)* Three-time NASCAR Winston Cup Champion Darrell Waltrip celebrated his 25th season at stock car racing's highest level in 1997. As part of his Silver Anniversary Celebration, Darrell treated the fans with special paint schemes reminiscent of various stages of his stellar career. Included were the orange and white of his days with Hendrick Motorsports and sponsor Tide, the red and white used on the Budweiser Chevrolets fielded by owner Junior Johnson, and the green, white and orange signifying the Gatorade sponsorship from his early career with DiGard. *(Below)* The management of Texas Motor Speedway staged a gala welcome for the NASCAR Winston Cup Series in its return to the Lone Star State in April. TMS joined California Speedway as two new venues on the tour in 1997.

(Top Left) John Andretti gets a victory kiss form his daughter, Olivia Elizabeth, with son Jarrett and wife Nancy also on hand in Daytona's victory lane to help celebrate John's first career NASCAR Winston Cup victory in the Pepsi 400. *(Above)* Morgan Shepherd eases the pre-race tension by practicing one of his hobbies, ballroom dancing, with his wife, Cindy, at Daytona in July. *(Left)* Derrike and Renee Cope have some pre-race fun before Derrike climbs aboard the Skittles Pontiac for another day's work. Cope is slated to move to the Bahari team to drive the "30" Pontiacs in 1998. *(Below Left)* Jeff and Kim Burton share a very special moment at Texas early in the '97 season after Jeff scored his first career NASCAR Winston Cup victory. Burton had an outstanding year in the Jack Roush-owned Fords, stamping his team as a title contender for the coming season. *(Below)* With motors silent and grandstands empty, the sun's reflection graces the sky before fading behind Pennsylvania's Pocono Mountains.

NASCAR WINSTON CUP SERIES 1997

Autographs

UMI Publishes The Official NASCAR Preview and Press Guide. For subscription information call (704) 374-0420.